The Complete Idiot's Reference Card

Following the Accounting Cycle

Here are the basics of the accounting cycle for all financial activity in any business. Susan, the accountant, will help keep you from getting lost in the accounting process. You may want to use this card as a bookmark, to keep from getting lost in this guide.

1. Business transactions take place—sales, purchases, payments on account, credits, and so on.

2. Documentation of these transactions—such as sales receipts, purchase orders, invoices, canceled checks, check stubs, credit memos, deposit tickets, bank statements, and management memos—is passed along to Susan.

3. Every time Susan receives documentation of a transaction, she analyzes the transaction to determine which accounts are affected, and whether the transaction should be recorded as a debit or credit to that account.

4. Susan records each transaction in the journal (also known as the book of original entry). Journalizing generates a chronological record of all transactions. She records the date, describes the transaction, and indicates which accounts are to be debited and credited, as well as the amounts.

5. Susan then posts the journal entry to the appropriate subledger and records that subledger identification number in the posting reference (Post. Ref.) column in the journal.

6. Periodically Susan posts subledger entries in batches to the general ledger.

7. After posting to the general ledger, Susan runs a trial balance to make sure the entries agree and the two sides of the account equation balance.

8. Since Susan's company operates on an accrual basis, at the end of the accounting cycle she must make adjustments to match revenues and expenses within the proper period, making entries to the general ledger to bring the accounts up to date and ensure that both sides of the account balance.

9. At the end of each accounting period, Susan journalizes and records entries in the general ledger, to make sure the ledger will agree with financial statements.

continues

alpha
books

Following the Accounting Cycle (continued)

10. Susan then prepares a worksheet to summarize debit and credit amounts for each account and calculate the adjustments to be made. This process consists of six steps:

    ➤ Enter and total the account balances, in the Trial Balance columns.

    ➤ Enter and total the adjustments to be made, in the Adjustments columns.

    ➤ Enter and balance the balances as adjusted, in the Adjusted Trial Balance columns.

    ➤ Extend the Adjusted Trial Balance figures to the Income Statement or Balance Sheet columns, as appropriate.

    ➤ Total the Income Statement columns and the Balance Sheet columns.

    ➤ Enter the net income or net loss in both the Income Statement columns and the Balance Sheet columns, to balance the columns, then recalculate the column totals.

11. Susan uses the completed worksheet to prepare the company's financial statements.

12. After Susan processes, records, and posts activity to the proper account, she tallies and reports data in the revenue and expense accounts on the Income Summary.

13. Susan then closes the balance to the owner's equity (capital) account. (If her company were a corporation, she'd list the balance as retained earnings.) After she journalizes and posts the account balance, she checks the amount of the equity (retained earnings) and the amount reported in the statement of owner's equity (retained earnings) and the balance sheet: They should balance.

14. After closing any temporary accounts, Susan prepares a trial balance, to make sure the ledger is in balance and ready for the next accounting period. That step ends the company's accounting cycle.

That's it, more or less. You may want to keep this card handy and consult it as necessary. You should customize it for your company, indicating, for example, what documentation you need to provide for each transaction that goes through your department, to make your accountant's job easier, and what types of financial reports your accountant prepares, so you know what financial information is available to you.

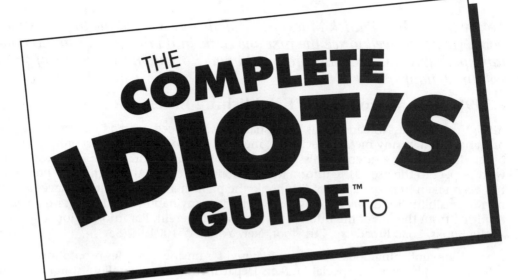

THE COMPLETE IDIOT'S GUIDE™ TO

Finance and Accounting

by Michael Muckian

alpha books

A Division of Macmillan General Reference
A Simon & Schuster Macmillan Company
1633 Broadway, New York, NY 10019

To my late father, Patrick Muckian, who always wanted me to publish a book. He never lived to see the first one come into print but, as an accountant, probably had the most profound impact of all on the success of this volume. Thanks, Dad.

©1998 John A. Woods, CWL Publishing Enterprises

Macmillan Publishing books may be purchased for business or sales promotional use. For information please write: Special Markets Department, Macmillan Publishing USA, 1633 Broadway, New York, NY 10019.

THE COMPLETE IDIOT'S GUIDE name and design are trademarks of Macmillan, Inc.

International Standard Book Number: 0-02-861752-5

Library of Congress Catalog Card Number: 97-071175

00   8 7 6 5 4

Interpretation of the printing code: the rightmost number of the first series of numbers is the year of the book's printing; the rightmost number of the second series of numbers is the number of the book's printing. For example, a printing code of 98-1 shows that the first printing occurred in 1998.

Printed in the United States of America

This is a CWL Publishing Enterprises Book, developed by John A. Woods for Macmillan General Reference/Alpha Books. For more information, contact CWL Publishing Enterprises at 3010 Irvington Way, Madison, WI 53713-3414, (608) 273-3710.

Alpha Development Team

Brand Manager
Kathy Nebenhaus

Executive Editor
Gary M. Krebs

Managing Editor
Bob Shuman

Senior Editor
Nancy Mikhail

Development Editor
Nancy Warner

Editorial Assistant
Maureen Horn

Production Team

Production Editor
Mark Enochs

Copy Editors
Susan Aufheimer
Lynn Northrup

Cover Designer
Michael Freeland

Cartoonist
Judd Winick

Designer
Glenn Larsen

Indexer
Joelynn Gifford

Production Team
Angela Calvert
Laure Robinson
Christy Wagner
Maureen West

Contents at a Glance

Contents

Foreword

I know what you're thinking: Why should I invest my valuable time and energy reading a dry book about finance and accounting? You probably imagine the author to be some boring bean counter who wears green eye shades and sits in a dusty back room writing soporific tomes filled with technical details and a host of complex mathematical formulas.

Fortunately for you, Michael Muckian is *not* that author. Since Michael is not an accountant, but a well-informed nonfinancial manager, he makes finance and accounting fun and easy to learn. He explains these subjects in a way that makes sense to you, even if you've had little or no exposure to them. Along the way, he demystifies all that puzzling jargon and he does so with interesting and humorous anecdotes. And the most complex math you'll find in this book is simple addition, subtraction, multiplication, and division. In an informal, friendly tone, Michael will also show you why it's important for nonfinancial managers, entrepreneurs, and anybody else to understand finance and accounting.

This book is really about increasing your value—whether that takes the form of a greater business value, a higher salary, or more money in your personal bank account (through better management of your own finances). I'm confident that you will find this book to be a valuable resource. After reading *The Complete Idiot's Guide to Finance and Accounting*, you'll never again catch yourself thinking, "Who was the complete idiot who invented finance and accounting just to keep the rest of us in the dark about money matters?!"

The bottom line is that *The Complete Idiot's Guide to Finance and Accounting* will help you get ahead in life. After all, everyone needs to have a practical, down-to-earth, basic understanding of accounting and finance to be successful. Here's your guide to that understanding.

Steve Pullara, CPA

Smith & Gesteland, LLP

Introduction

You've probably picked up this guide because you have a nagging feeling that you don't know as much about finance and accounting as you should. Maybe you've been running a business, but you feel like you may not be doing quite as well as you could—and you might be taking some major risks. Or you might be a manager in a company, doing your part to help that company succeed...and wondering if you could do your job better if you understood a little more about how the numbers all fit together. Then again, there's a good chance you might be like so many of us, dreaming about starting your own business. But where do you start?

Here! In this guide we provide a complete overview of the finance and accounting basics with special emphasis on the needs of small business nonfinancial managers. After all, if you're out there working away, you don't have the time to take business courses or even to read a pile of thick books. You want a single resource, a practical guide to understanding finance and accounting. Most of all, you want information you can apply immediately, whether you own a business, manage a department, or plan to open a place of your own.

And, because the topic is something that makes some people nervous and bores many others, we try to keep things from getting too painful or heavy. We know a book can mean business without being too serious.

How to Use This Book

We've broken down the basics of accounting and finance into six sections.

We begin, logically, with Part 1. In this part, we review reasons for knowing more about financial management. Then we plunge into business strategies and business plans. We close the first part with the shortest course you'll ever take—"Budgeting 101."

Part 2 brings you through the essential parts of an accounting system. After you finish the six chapters in this part, you'll be able to talk with anybody about the general ledger, the chart of accounts, accounts receivable, accounts payable, and that all-important cash flow—and know what you're talking about.

In Part 3, we go behind the scenes, to explore the ways in which every business should be taking care of its employees, keeping track of its inventory, cutting its costs, and guarding its assets. These four chapters provide information vital for managing a business or a department. That's why we call Part 3 "Managing with Accounting."

In Part 4, we talk about money—specifically, about how to get what you need when you need it, without sacrificing too much. We discuss commercial lending institutions, of course, and venture capitalists—a funding source of growing importance to businesses of all types. And what might those types be? That's the question we answer in our chapter on proprietorships, partnerships, and corporations.

Part 5 is devoted to taxes. In three chapters, we help you understand about business taxes, reduce your taxes, and appreciate the tax differences among the several types of business structures. The only thing we don't do in this section is pay your taxes. Sorry!

From the drudgery of taxes to the excitement of business growth—that's quite a leap. But that's where we go in the final part. We delve into the details of putting together your financial plan—a must for any business that intends to stay in business. Then, once you know where you are financially, the next step is figuring out where you're going and how to know when you get there. So, we present some tips on forecasting. Next, we discuss "The Bottom Line" and the importance of having a money manager dedicated to preserving and growing your assets.

Then, in Part 6, we get to the heart of it all, with the chapter on "Developing Growth Strategies." Because we all can benefit and profit from a little help here and there, we follow with a chapter about partnering with vendors. That strategy could give you that little edge that you need to survive and thrive in your business.

Finally, because Murphy may have been right—that if something can go wrong, it will—we end our guide with a chapter on recognizing problems in your business system and remedying them. It's a chapter we hope you never need—but suspect you might.

Extra Help

From time to time we'll call your attention to some useful terms, tips, notes of caution, or additional information. Unfortunately, we can't be at your side as you go about your business, but we'll be there in spirit.

Journal Entry

There are a lot of things that you should note. These boxes are how we call them to your attention.

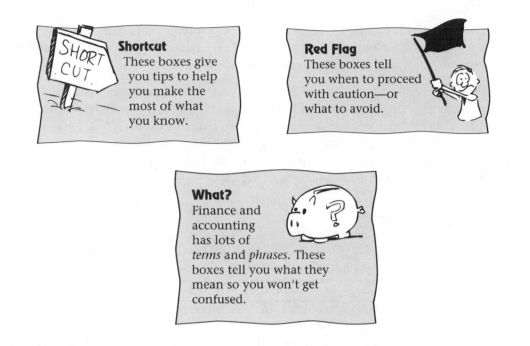

Shortcut
These boxes give you tips to help you make the most of what you know.

Red Flag
These boxes tell you when to proceed with caution—or what to avoid.

What?
Finance and accounting has lots of *terms* and *phrases*. These boxes tell you what they mean so you won't get confused.

Special Thanks from the Publisher to the Technical Reviewer

The Complete Idiot's Guide to Finance and Accounting was reviewed by experts who not only checked the technical accuracy of what you'll learn in this book, but also provided invaluable insight and suggestions. Our special thanks are extended to Allen Bachenheimer and Scott R. Haumersen.

Allen Bachenheimer is a CPA in New York and New Jersey with over 30 years of diversified experience in public accounting. Allen's professional background has involved working with closely held, family businesses including manufacturers, importers, and service organizations. He has extensive experience in dealing with start-ups and troubled companies. His work with such clients encompasses interacting with management and financial institutions, assisting with cashflow, developing business projections, and forecasting.

He currently serves as the Managing Director of TIBS, Total Involvement Business Services, a program in the New York metropolitan area, which focuses on a team approach to delivering total "hands-on" client service. Under Allen's tutelage, TIBS Group professionals offer clients close interaction; staff continuity; a greater sensitivity to company and individual needs; an enhanced workflow of information and communications; maximum efficiency; and overall consistent, reliable, and responsive service. The TIBS team gains in-depth knowledge of the client's operations, understands the client's goals, and works to fully satisfy those objectives. They act as liaisons to all professional service areas, thereby providing seamless, comprehensive services.

Scott R. Haumersen received his BBA in accounting, finance, and management from the University of Wisconsin-Madison in 1981. He has 16 years experience working on tax-exempt audits for Wegner & Associates and is a member of the AICPA and WICPA. Scott is the past President of the Madison Chapter of the National Association of Accountants, serves on numerous planning and organization committees, and presents training seminars on financial management of tax-exempts.

Acknowledgments

A book like this doesn't get written without a little or, in this case, a lot of help from our friends. In addition to saying thanks to everyone who encouraged me, I'd like to acknowledge a few special people.

My accounting education became complete with input from Steve Pullara, Smith & Gesteland LLP; Cathy Lippart, formerly of CUNA & Affiliates; and Eleanor Oppreicht, Edgewood College. And as for everyone who made me learn this stuff on my own over the years, well, you probably helped the most—much as I hate to admit it.

Thanks, too, go to John Woods of CWL Publishing Enterprises for recruiting me to write this book and for his guidance and support throughout its development. And thanks to Bob Magnan of CWL Publishing for his editorial grooming and suggestions on the final draft of the manuscript.

Finally, many thanks to my wife, Jean Muckian, for her help and support and, when the days were darkest, her calm assurances that no matter how bad things got, we still needed the money.

Part 1
Getting Started

As a manager, you know a lot about working with people and with processes—whatever goods you produce or services you provide. But no matter who is doing what to make your company successful, somebody there is taking care of business in terms of finance and accounting. Thank goodness!

However important your knowledge and skills may be, you will be a better manager if you understand the financial principles and practices that underlie every business, big or small. It's just that simple.

We're starting this guide the way that virtually every business starts. Whoever founded your company probably began with what you'll be learning in the first three chapters. We'll begin with the basics of finance and accounting. Then, we'll discuss business strategy and how plans get organized on paper. After that, we'll be ready to move into an area that you'll likely find at least somewhat familiar—budgets.

Mastering Financial Management

When you took your place among the executive hierarchy as vice president of marketing, director of sales, or head of product development (or maybe you're not there yet, but it's a goal), you had all the professional skills you needed at your fingertips, right? You graduated from a good school, fought in the workaday trenches of corporate warfare, climbed to the top of your respective discipline thanks to talent, drive, determination, and guts.

Did you remember to master financial management? Do you have at those same fingertips the same level of mastery for the accounting, financial planning, and forecasting side of your business? If not, you've still got some important lessons to learn, and you better start now.

Financial management, even for nonfinancial managers, is a crucial part of any job you have in your company. It's the glue that holds together the business side of your discipline, and its goals are the framework around which you must build your efforts.

Recognizing a Necessary Evil

Frank was the editor of a large finance industry weekly and filled with the vinegar he needed to savagely compete against his closest rival. He was a demanding manager filled with a journalistic flare. His reporters even went to jail…just so they could write about the experience. He expected no less of himself and worked long, hard hours to make the publication a success.

Frank knew a good story and spared no expense to go after it. He was acclaimed in the financial services industry, but often spent too much of his publication's own financial resources going after a story. Frank paid little attention to how much he and his staff were spending, waving off his publisher and accounting department on a regular basis when they called this to his attention. He felt his job was to get the story and spent whatever it took to pursue the higher purpose of newsgathering.

Frank could manage the news, but he couldn't manage the financial side of his editorial responsibilities. Frank soon was replaced by another manager who, while not as strong on the editorial side, knew the value of a dollar and the role it played on a balance sheet. He had mastered financial management for the sake of the newsgathering responsibilities. In the end, the publication and its readers were better off.

Journal Entry

Accounting properly performed is not a cost item or overhead expense (as some executives like to think). If your company's accountants prepare a monthly report and managers use the findings to adjust the operations of the business to a more profitable scenario, then the accounting operations directly contribute to help the company make money.

It doesn't matter what your professional responsibilities are. If you're in management at any level—and especially if you're running your own business—financial management is one of your most important responsibilities. In fact, some would say it is THE most important responsibility. Without it, you won't be able to practice the profession for which you've spent so many years preparing.

Frank's experience is typical of nonfinancial managers, but there's another group I hope will benefit from this book. That's the entrepreneurs and small business owners, professionals who at one time may have been nonfinancial managers, but who have decided to go off on their own. They have similar financial management needs, and we will be moving back and forth between the nonfinancial manager orientation and the entrepreneur orientation throughout this book.

Understanding the Financial Side of Business

Any company, large or small, has trained professionals whose task it is to manage the money-go-round that keeps their organization afloat. Whether the title is accounting manager, controller, or chief financial officer, the responsibilities center around the same concerns. The financial department is the hub around which all financial activity revolves. The larger the company, the more sophisticated and complex those revolutions may be.

These financial professionals will be the first to say that the financial side of any business is important to every employee. Whether it's good resource utilization that reduces expenses or the ability to present a positive public image for the company so people will buy more company products, thus increasing revenues, it's clear the company's financial success is influenced by everyone who works there.

If you're in a management position, however, that responsibility runs a little deeper. You have direct responsibility for managing key streams of resource expenditure or income generation. Take too careless or casual an attitude and your department may spring a financial leak that can begin to drain business finances dry.

In fact, no matter who you are or what you do, as a manager, you can't afford not to be on top of your financial position at all times. Eventually, you'll find you're not only capable of managing that function, but you also have begun to enjoy it. In time, you may recognize this as the single most important function for which you're responsible. But let's walk a little bit before we try to run.

Red Flag
Often managers leave finances to the accounting department and never think again about their company's financial position until the company declares Chapter 11—bankruptcy. As an executive or owner, your primary responsibility may not be accounting, but accounting for your specific functions in the company is a key component of your job. If you want to keep your job, that is.

Solid Reasons to Manage Finances

Somewhere inside you, a little voice is cringing at financial management and accounting. That voice is telling you it's right, good, and proper to understand finances as well as you understand the individuals who report to you and the products or services you manage. You don't want to believe it because finances can be complex, boring, even frightening. But you know it's true. Here's why:

➤ Your management responsibilities contribute directly to your company's profitability.

➤ Understanding how the company's finances work is simply good management practice.

➤ The rationale for understanding financial matters may be as simple as making the accounting department your ally.

➤ Understanding your department's finances puts you in a good position to understand other departments' finances, thus other departments.

➤ You'll be better able to manage your department if you understand the financial implications of your actions.

In some office in another state, another country, or perhaps just down the hall, the company president is nursing a grand vision for making your company a financial success for its stockholders, employees, and the customers it serves. In the vision, you and your fellow nonfinancial managers sit squarely in the middle, key components to helping or hindering progress. Are you a conduit or a roadblock? Your financial acumen can make a big difference in how you answer this question.

If you're in marketing, it helps your efforts to know how the products you sell are developed, assembled, packaged, and shipped. If you're in development, it helps to know what the marketing department is doing with your work. It will help you achieve the company's financial goals if you know the financial implications of what happens in your department and the other departments in the company.

If the folks in accounting have routinely stepped down hard when it comes to development expenditures, marketing plans, and other cash outlays you want or need to make, then maybe it would help to see it from their point of view. Knowing how to manage your finances makes you and the finance and accounting departments allies (rather than adversaries) in achieving the goals of your department and the company as a whole.

Nothing impresses financial professionals more than a manager who sees it from their point of view, who finally *gets* what they're nagging everyone about. And no matter how much you may dislike the discipline they stand for, they're powerful allies to have.

Red Flag

Too many nonfinancial managers are intimidated by the language of accounting—credit, debit, amortization, accrual, and the like. But the concepts behind accounting are basic. Pay attention to those, not the vocabulary. You'll be better off.

Top management will think more highly of you if you bring overall financial acumen to your position. Moreover, since financial principles are fairly standard for companies throughout North America, you may be the one they choose to take over other departments floundering in financial waters. ("She may not know anything about building widgets, but at least she has a clear grasp of the finances.") Consider your financial expertise a gateway to other opportunities. Remember: Most managers hire an applicant not only for the position currently open, but also with a view toward promotion and greater responsibilities later. Knowledge of financial matters transfers very well—and that makes the person who hired you look very smart!

That's the primary reason you picked up this book and the true reason to master business finance. Financial ebb and flow affect the growth and operation of your department, from product-development decisions all the way to hiring and firing. It's not only the right thing to do; it's also necessary, given that your department is interwoven with other aspects of the company. Financial decisions you make will affect other department's financial well-being. Make sure you're making the right decisions for all parties concerned.

Shortcut
Build up to financial management incrementally by mastering basic concepts and principles first and then moving up the ladder. Slowly but surely the pieces will fall into place.

Use What You've Got

You can never be too financially savvy for your business. For example, when a magazine decided to hire a new editor, they chose Mary, who had both a journalism degree and an accounting background. In addition to having better product knowledge about the financial industry on which the publication focused, she also had a much better sense of the procedures for managing the department's finances.

Knowing Mary's background, the accounting department managers never questioned Mary's judgment. In fact, they never even looked that closely at her accounts, as long as her bottom line was within budget. For anyone who's jousted regularly with an accounting department, that kind of freedom from scrutiny can be a little slice of business heaven.

The amount of financial knowledge you need to have will be relative to your responsibilities. In past decades, a background in finance and accounting was a quick avenue to a corner executive office. These days, however, more and different disciplines are leading the charge, with marketing moving to the head of the pack in many consumer sales-based industries. That's not to say that finances are becoming a less important consideration. Today, those who make it to the top have financial acumen to go with their marketing or other operational expertise.

Building a Foundation

What components of financial management do you need to know about? Here are some of the elements with brief explanations:

A basic knowledge of accounting practices and principles is worth the effort that it takes to learn them.

In addition to earning the unbridled respect of your company's accounting professionals—and that goes a lot further than you might think—understanding how things are done and why from an accounting perspective will broaden your understanding of financial management. You already know why you budget so many dollars per year for sales calls, but understanding how those figures affect the rest of the company will help you make better decisions for your department and for the company as a whole.

What?

Liquidity is a finance term that refers to cash or assets that can be readily converted to cash. It's a company's potential ability to meet obligations or to seize opportunities. Having access to a reasonable amount of cash is a good thing for a business. But too much liquidity may mean the company is missing out on investment possibilities.

Red Flag

Never underestimate the value of financial knowledge and management skills. It's no longer a matter of *if* you need the knowledge, only *how much* and *when*.

Learning how to work with the funds in your business will help you understand cash flow and how liquidity affects your ability to manage your department.

Simply put, that means that your company's revenues and expenses and their flow through the firm will affect your ability to do certain types of activities at certain times. We are all familiar with this financial flow in our personal lives. When we get a paycheck (revenue), our liquidity increases. When we pay a stack of bills (expenses) or put money into a certificate of deposit (investment), our liquidity decreases. Just like us, sometimes the company is more liquid and sometimes it's less. Knowing about that can help you adapt to its current circumstances better and take actions that will improve the financial situation.

Understanding the true cost of things and their true worth will ultimately bring greater value to your operation.

Such understanding is called cost accounting, and it measures the real cost of doing business. Those widgets you produce and sell cost more than merely the amount you pay for the material to produce them. You have to add staff costs for everybody who does anything else affecting those widgets—design, development, production, marketing, and distribution, not to mention overhead—all the costs of keeping the company running so you can continue to produce those widgets. We'll get into the details later. The point to remember here is that cost accounting offers broad-based principles useful for any business. These principles can also be applied with great success to individual departments to help measure the relative cost and worth of operations from a financial management point of view that you, as a nonfinancial manager, might not otherwise see.

Good financial controls flow from sound understanding.

All companies exercise some type of financial controls. Those controls should be based on financial management principles that can be applied to your department to measure, address, and troubleshoot operations from a perspective that's relevant to your profitability goals. You won't have the necessary orientation without learning more about financial management principles.

The fact is that once you get your feet wet, you'll want to move beyond the basics listed here into more sophisticated and comprehensive issues while still addressing them at a level germane to your goals and purpose. And this book is designed to help you do just that.

Getting Ahead with Finance

If you've picked up this book because you have your eye set on a promotion or your boss says you need to master the basics of finance quickly, then you're in good hands—relax. By the time you finish working through this guide, you will have not only a better understanding of financial management, but also a new respect for what financial management can do for you.

Understanding the financial side of your business and its application to your operation will give you more power over your own department and a new depth of influence within your company.

The Least You Need to Know

➤ Financial management and basic accounting, even for nonfinancial managers, is a crucial part of being an effective manager.

➤ As a manager, you can't afford not to be on top of your financial position at all times.

➤ Understanding your department's finances inside and out puts you in a good position to understand other department's finances, and thus other departments.

➤ You'll be better able to manage your department if you understand the financial implications of your actions.

➤ A basic knowledge of accounting principles and practices will help you work more effectively with the accounting department to your mutual benefit.

Chapter 2

From Strategy to Business Plan

In This Chapter

➤ Defining the best strategy for your business

➤ Understanding strategic characteristics

➤ Building a business plan, plan objectives, and plan components

Most enterprises have something called a *strategy*. Invading armies have one. Football teams have one. In most cases, just having a strategy may mean the difference between success and failure.

More than any other enterprise, a business needs a strategy. Why? Well, just consider what you're trying to do and what you're up against. You're trying to get a share of the dollars out there. You're competing with businesses that provide similar goods or services, yes, but also with *any business at all,* because the amount of dollars is limited. You're risking economic changes as well—not only downturns that could threaten your financial stability and growth, but also upturns that could favor competitors ready and able to capitalize on them, especially if you're not prepared. Then there are the other dangers, such as the potential loss of vital financial support, a key manager, or a valuable employee. Then, toss in the reaction of customers, which might mean a lawsuit that could sap your resources and damage your public image.

So, every company is facing tough challenges. That's why every company needs a strategy. That's often the key to a company's financial success. Without an overall strategy, you're less likely to meet your financial goals.

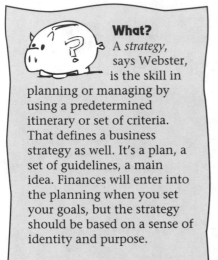

What?
A *strategy*, says Webster, is the skill in planning or managing by using a predetermined itinerary or set of criteria. That defines a business strategy as well. It's a plan, a set of guidelines, a main idea. Finances will enter into the planning when you set your goals, but the strategy should be based on a sense of identity and purpose.

Even if you're not responsible for running your company, you must first grasp the overall concept behind what the top managers are doing, just to be able to properly manage any part of that company. If you don't understand the strategy behind the company, how much can you help it succeed?

Everything starts with a sound business strategy.

Is this a departure from the focus of this book? Not at all. Developing a strategy and, subsequently, building a business plan based on that strategy are critical to developing the sound financial strategies appearing in later chapters.

Companies that take the time at the start to define a strategy and then build their business plan around it improve their chances for greater financial success. And department managers have an obligation to help build that success by understanding the strategy and their part in making it work—through the strategy each defines for his or her department.

Although you may not actually be involved (yet!) in forming your company's strategy, the following discussion will put you there among the movers and shakers who determine that strategy. Then you'll better understand the principles behind a business strategy.

Defining a Strategy

Here are some steps that should help you develop your business strategy:

➤ *Know your business.* This seems basic, but it's the most often forgotten step along the road to business success. Were railroads in the business of being railroads or part of the transportation industry? There's a distinct difference between the two and a distinct difference in the psychology and strategy that awareness will bring to the business. It's important, as we noted earlier, when you're defining your philosophy, identifying your competition, and finding your niche. But it's just as important when you're determining how you're going to achieve your goals.

➤ *Identify the philosophy behind your company's way of doing business.* If it's a service business, articulate how important that service is to the overall goal. If the company makes products, define the purpose and goal each product line has for the company. Is there a level of quality or production time important to success? If so, that must be part of the strategy.

➤ *Identify your competition.* This may seem obvious, but it's not necessarily a simple task. For example, if you decide to start a magazine for the local business community, who are your competitors? If your answer is there are no other business magazines around, then you don't understand the question. Maybe the local newspaper has a regular section devoted to business. That's competition for coverage. Do you intend to sell ads? If so, you're competing for advertising money with newspapers, radio, TV, and billboards. Do you intend to sell subscriptions? If so, then you're competing for customer money, time, and loyalty with national business publications, and to a great extent, with *any* subscription publication. This example should show that identifying your competition can be far from simple.

➤ *Pick out the two or three major advantages your company has that set it apart from your competitors.* An accounting firm, for example, might have experience with not-for-profit businesses. Such a market advantage becomes a cornerstone of the firm's business strategy.

Journal Entry

Some people call that particular segment of a specific economy a "niche." It's the slice of the dollar pie your business hopes to claim; that piece of the public consciousness you want to capture and hold. You need to understand what chunk of turf you want to stake out, or success in doing so will be primarily a matter of luck.

➤ *Articulate your goals as clearly as possible.* For example, the manufacturer who wants to develop three new product lines is more likely to do it than the manufacturer who simply wants to "grow." The more specific a company can be in setting its goals, researchers have found, the more likely it is it will reach that goal.

➤ *Identify the key steps toward the goal.* Knowing the steps the company needs to take to reach its goal is as important as identifying the goal itself. Sometimes entrepreneurs trust too much in their enthusiasm and spirit. That may be enough to motivate their *employees*, but *leaders* must plan their campaigns.

Shortcut

The quickest way to shortcut both a strategy and a goal is to specialize: Your company and your product or service are the same. Identify one core goal and go for it. Of course, this approach won't work for diversified companies, although it should apply within each division.

So, to sum it all up, you should know what you're doing (your business) and how you're doing it (your philosophy). You should recognize who else is out there in your way (your competitors) and decide what sets you ahead of them (your major advantages). Then, you determine where you want to go with your business (your goals) and how you intend to get there (your key steps). All of that forms your business strategy.

Strategic Characteristics

After you've followed the steps and defined your business strategy, you should test the elements of that strategy. There are many ways to do so, but there's one simple test that can be tried without fear or risk:

Say the company's goals aloud.

Red Flag

Strategies are important, but never mistake *strategizing* for *acting*. The best strategy in the world is no strategy if action isn't built into the plan. There are companies that spend a lot of time meeting and working out strategies, but not moving on to map out a plan of action. You're not likely to have heard of them, of course. Wonder why?

This can be done as part of a meeting of the board of directors, in the executive suite, or even in the privacy of the department manager's office. Identify the internal elements of the strategy and say them aloud. Some business people refer to this approach as "Run it up the flagpole and see who salutes." But at this point you don't want acceptance and allegiance—you want critical thinking and tough questions. It's time to test, not to salute.

Do the elements of your strategy make sense? Do they define the direction in which your company wants to go? Do they sound forced or contrived or simplistic? Or are these elements that can guide your company toward success?

If the strategy doesn't sound right spoken aloud, it's time to start over. If it makes sense and if it could make sense to any new employee, that means your business likely is on the right track in developing its business plan.

Attach a Financial Goal to Your Strategy

How are you going to measure your success as a company in financial terms? The most basic measurement is a profit goal. You might also want to set ancillary goals—growth goals, sales goals, or whatever you think would be the best ways to gauge your progress and help you achieve your primary financial goal.

Then, ask a few hard questions. Is your goal realistic? Is it achievable? Are there ways to leverage the overall goal to achieve the financial goal? If not, one or the other has to be reconsidered.

Some CEOs seem to set goals according to their sense of business ideals or to really push their workers to the limit. Goals of 15 percent profitability and 10 percent growth, for example, may sound great and look great on paper. But are they realistic for your company? Can you actually expect to achieve them? Also, if the overall economy is suffering, 15 percent and 10 percent might be improbable goals even for established companies.

It's possible to plan on the low side, of course, to set a financial goal that your company can reach easily. That may be a good idea for some new companies, allowing them to focus on building a solid foundation rather than stretching to meet a higher goal. But if the economy is generally good, easy goals can promote lax attitudes, keeping your company from becoming truly competitive. Then, if the economy starts to decline...

The bottom line here, as throughout this chapter: Know your company and then set an appropriate financial goal.

Identify the Steps to Reach the Financial Goal

Except in the movies, nobody has ever made the leap from start-up to success in one jump. The company needs a well-thought out plan built on steps, strategies, and benchmarks to reach its financial goal.

If your financial goal, for example, is a profit of $12 million, you might decide on the following steps:

➤ Increase sales

➤ Cut expenses

➤ Develop new products

➤ Innovate marketing

➤ Improve efficiency

That's good—as a beginning. Now, you need to get into details, by asking a few questions and coming up with solid answers:

➤ How are you going to increase sales?

➤ What expenses are you going to cut? How?

➤ What new products will you develop?

➤ How will you reach different markets in different ways?

➤ How can the company become more efficient? In what areas?

Of course, you may want to set ancillary goals in each of these areas. But beware of goals that set department against department, worker against worker. For example, goals for marketing, which are measured in terms of sales, might cause resentment if there are other factors that could affect sales—just as sales goals might not be met because an improvement in efficiency caused a drop in the quality of the products the sales reps are trying to sell.

Set a Timeline for the Steps to Help Achieve the Goal

Timelines provide the second dimension for a goal. When will you achieve your goal? This dimension is vital. Imagine two sisters each deciding to start a business. One sets a profit goal of $100,000 and the other sets a goal of only $50,000. All things being equal—which they never are—which sister is likely to be more successful? Does it make a difference if you know that the second sister set her goal on a timeline of the first quarter, while the second sister didn't set any timeline at all?

A goal without a timeline is like a graph with only a single coordinate. You've got your goal on the Y-axis, but without a time set on the Y-axis, where are you?

Go for It!

That's the final step. Plans that you don't execute are just pieces of paper. Period.

Building a Business Plan

Defining a sound strategy is vital preparation for success. But even the best strategy will fail without a good business plan to put it to work. The strategy is the idea behind the business, but the business plan is the first of many tools by which that idea will turn into actions.

The business plan is the *where*, *when*, *how*, and *why* of what a company must do to implement its strategy. It's just that simple—and that difficult.

What?
A *rolling* plan is a perpetual motion engine for your business vehicle. Once you finish the first year in your plan, you add another year to the end of the plan, so the company always is looking five years ahead. Not only does this ensure greater continuity of vision, but it also spares managers the enormous task of creating subsequent five-year plans.

The business plan offers general and specific guidance on reaching company goals. It outlines actions. It also separates the dreamers from the doers. It is often the great equalizer between the enthusiastic idea generators and the serious business people who will accomplish their dreams.

Business plans are usually annual, based on the fiscal year. But there also are multiple-year plans—the most common of which is the five-year plan.

An annual plan is operational and necessary to manage the company's economic needs for the coming year. A five-year plan is more strategic and designed to chart the firm's direction. In addition, five-year plans should be rolling plans.

The thinking behind a rolling five-year plan can be applied to other cyclical planning, such as the annual budget process or the marketing schedule. When May ends, for example, the managers can study the forecasts for that month and the results, determine the reasons behind the variances, then use their findings to shape a budget for the following May. Rolling plans allow managers to make the most of their budget analyses, provide greater continuity, and ease the burden of annual planning.

Another Reason to Have a Business Plan

A business plan helps you achieve your goals. It also helps discipline the way you think about what you're doing. But business plans have another important purpose.

Companies need business plans to apply for loans, grants, or other forms of funding to start or expand the business. Lenders and financial managers like to see something in writing that shows a firm is committed to its objectives and knows how it's going to accomplish those objectives. Without a plan, serious outside funding—or any funding, for that matter—might not be available. After all, if you were in the business of investing money, how would you select the companies that would be the best risks?

But that means you need to write your business plan in different ways for different financial participants:

> ➤ Plans used to attract *equity investors*—financial partners who will prosper as the business prospers—must be written to show how investors will gain from the company's success. Investors expect a high rate of return, so they will be looking at growth and profit projections. Plans that project a successful profile are what equity investors are seeking.

> ➤ Plans designed to appeal to *lenders* must demonstrate methodologies for repaying loans. At the risk of being simplistic, lenders have little financial stake in the success or failure of the company. They're interested in how the company plans to repay the principle and its interest. And lenders are more likely than equity investors to be concerned about cash flow. Your business plan should provide a timetable with repayment amounts the lenders believe your company will be able to make.

Red Flag
The best business plans tend to look like a truck ran them over. They are well-thumbed, heavily annotated, and popping their staples or bursting their bindings. That means they're being used. The worst plans are clean, pristine documents that went straight from the printer into the file cabinet. That means they're not being used. That may mean that nobody needs them, which might suggest that the company is continuing to follow the same old routes to get to the same destinations. Or it might mean the business plan isn't worth the paper it's printed on for those who should be following it. Either way, the company may be in serious trouble.

Business Plan Objectives

The first step in developing a business plan is to define its key objective. Is it an annual plan used to drive business operations? Or is it a financial plan designed to attract investors and/or lenders? Is it both? It often is—and that's not at all bad…if the plan meets everyone's needs and if the language and goals don't conflict.

Business plans can take as many forms as necessary and include as many financial addenda as required. Balance sheets and financial reports are usually critical components in a business plan. Some companies seem to attach virtually every financial document available.

Assuming the numbers support the text, however, the real area of interest for most executives, financiers, and even staff will be the assumptions behind the plan. Why is the company expected to sell 150,000 units this year after selling only 50,000 last year? The assumption will make or break the success of the business plan. Show the thinking behind your figures.

Business Plan Shortfalls

Every good business plan consists of certain elements. But there's also a list of things that should be avoided when creating a plan:

➤ *Inaccuracies will kill any plan.* People won't give money to companies that can't count. It should go without saying that you need to be absolutely accurate in everything from addition to spelling. (Yes, even spelling, because some people may believe that inattention to accuracy in spelling might be symptomatic of inattention to accuracy elsewhere.)

➤ *More is not always better!* Plans must be complete but succinct. Plans that run on for pages, with attachments from every financial document generated, generally turn off people who don't have the time to read them—and today that's most of us. Answer the questions that likely will be asked, clearly and succinctly. Good move!

➤ *Don't underplay management team skills.* The number one reason investors walk away from companies is concern over management. Plans should showcase the strengths of your managers and tie their skills directly to both the needs and solutions for the company. After all, the success of a company cannot be predicted from figures alone. Who is behind those figures? Who will be leading the company toward its goals?

Shortcut
Many business plans are created with a circular approach that offers a summary at both the beginning and the end, using the points in between to enhance the introductory summary so the concluding summary is more complete and comprehensive. For investors, it answers the question, "Why should we invest in this company?" It can save the reader time and give a company a greater opportunity to attract the type of financing it seeks.

➤ *Don't editorialize.* Or, as a colleague liked to put it, "Tell, don't sell." Keep the tone of the plan factual and professional. As soon as the plan becomes familiar or promotional in its flavor, investors are likely to smell a sales pitch and walk.

➤ *Don't just write your plan and shelve it.* Use your annual plan to improve company performance and involve as many of the appropriate staff as possible in developing it.

These words of advice are intended to help you avoid problems with lenders and investors. But they are also sound guidelines for your business plan even if you don't expect it to be read by a single outsider. All the employees of a company—from top managers down to the mail room—are lenders and investors: they lend their abilities and invest their energy in your company. If your business plan fails to support their hopes and inspire them, you risk turning those employees—no matter what their level of responsibility or pay—into wage slaves.

Business Plan Components

So what's in a business plan? Variations range all over the map. Here's a list of 13 key components on which any business plan can build a strong foundation. In this case, the example of a start-up company provides an illustration of the basic concepts of a business plan:

1. Executive Summary and Current Situation

No matter how concise your business plan, it helps to summarize the following information in an overview of one page or less. The situation describes both where the company is now and the purpose of the business plan. Include the following:

a) Strategic Logic and Overview

➤ Identify the business by service, product, or some other tangible feature.

➤ Describe the direction the company plans to go.

➤ Summarize the market briefly—fast-moving or slow growth—and why plan components will help the strategy succeed.

School Colors is a firm that manufactures and markets golf umbrellas emblazoned with prep school and college colors and logos. The product will capitalize on two fast-growing trends: increased participation in the game of golf and increased support and nostalgia of alumni for their schools.

b) Business Growth and Development

➤ Describe the current status of the business's current stage.

➤ Outline, in summary, the steps planned for continued development.

The umbrella's first prototypes already have been developed and a limited number marketed successfully to Purdue University alumni by mail order. Sales have shown the market is viable, but to produce other umbrellas for 10 targeted schools throughout the next year will require a stronger capital position and greater marketing and distribution channels.

Our goal is to expand capacity and establish a beachhead for this new licensed merchandise among high-income alumni from 10 major schools: Harvard University, Yale University, Cornell University, Northwestern University, Duke University, UCLA, Stanford University, Texas A&M University, Tulane University, and Princeton University.

Red Flag

What aspect do financiers say is the weakest spot of most business plans? The management team. Either the group appears to lack the finesse they will need to carry out the plan, or not enough is known about them from the pages of the plan. Emphasize management team strength in ways that will show how they can contribute to the end result. Since managers come and go, you don't want to make it seem that the success or failure of your plan depends on management alone. But if your top people matter to your business, they should matter to your potential business partners.

c) Business Organization and Personnel

➤ Outline the structure of the business and key personnel.

➤ Explain how each will help promote achievement of your goal.

The business will be headquartered in Indianapolis, IN, a central location that will capitalize on the equal distance in shipping costs and travel time throughout the country. The Midwestern location also means reliable and cost-effective manufacturing and administrative staffs and reasonable office expenses. Key administrative staff include business school graduates from Northwestern and Harvard universities familiar with the product, licensing agents, and strategies. The head of manufacturing was formerly with a major Midwestern premium company.

d) Financial Goals

➤ Explain the financial goals of the enterprise and the purpose of the plan.

Based on the success of the prototypes at one school, we anticipate sales of 16 percent of total alumni, a figure that would double if we market only to alumni whom we pre-qualify based on typical customer criteria we develop and test in advance. Following this plan, first year sales should net $164,300.

Current capital sits at $48,400, with an additional $21,000 that can be leveraged from sales of advance orders. We need to raise an additional $31,500 to cover costs prior to sales.

Shortcut

Any business plan will get a better response from the people who must follow it if they're involved in the planning process. In addition, their involvement, if competently guided by management, will save time and energy and contribute to a better, more comprehensive result.

2. The Concept

This differs from the summary in that it explains the concept, only, behind product and strategy. This should include a clear and complete description of the product and what makes it stand apart from the competition. Include any other impact factors relevant to the concept.

School Colors, started on a shoestring by two Ivy League alumni who enjoyed golfing more than they did working, is the world's only exclusive distributor of golf umbrellas emblazoned with prep school and Ivy League college logos. Other premium firms may distribute similar umbrellas as part of a wider line of licensed merchandise. However, School Colors is the only firm devoted completely to umbrella manufacture and marketing.

Product designs were adapted from a major English umbrella manufacturing firm and streamlined to include the highest-quality fabric and ribbing. The stainless steel mechanism comes with a lifetime guarantee. The education of our customers, for which they paid dearly, was meant to last a lifetime. So are School Colors umbrellas.

3. The Market and Market Segmentation

This section includes a description of the potential market, along with an analysis of potential usage. Include a more in-depth description of the particular market segment the plan will address and why the company is uniquely qualified to claim that market.

Over the past 20 years, Ivy League colleges have graduated an average of 15,000 students per year, most of whom went on to secure highly paid executive-level jobs in the business sector. Using the average playing span of the serious golfer in the U.S., 42.5 years, we arrive at a figure of 637,500 individuals who graduated from these schools during the last two decades. If 16 percent of that group are now playing golf, then the qualified universe for this high-end premium product is 102,000. As more graduating classes matriculate, the base market continues to replenish itself.

4. Customer Analysis

Even within a sharply defined market, different aspects make those customers more or less likely to buy your product. The purpose of customer analysis is to determine which characteristics will make a product most appealing to the largest or most profitable segment.

Of the universe of 102,000 likely potential customers, the average income is $78,760. This is a market that appreciates and can afford quality. School Colors' umbrellas are different in that they offer the finest product on the market available with fully licensed logos and imagery. The allegiance to the school guarantees an interest. The lifetime guarantee supports the image of strength, quality, and durability. These are hallmark consumer purchasing characteristics for this particular group.

5. Competitive Analysis

The plan also must analyze the impact your competitors will have on projected sales. In what areas do competitors meet or beat your company? What are your company's inherent strengths or competitive advantages that will give it an edge over the competition? You need to clearly understand the competitive threat, not only to better meet and defeat your competitors but also to prove to financial backers that you know the challenges and are ready to turn these challenges into opportunities.

School Colors is the only firm devoted exclusively to producing golf umbrellas emblazoned with the school logo. Quality is our watchword, so we see our greatest competition from low-end multiple-premium providers who use pricing as an advantage. Not all golf umbrella customers are quality-conscious, because of the product's limited or seasonal use. In addition, the current throw-away society promotes low-end goods that are easily replaced. If the economy turns or tastes change, School Colors might find itself in a difficult position.

On the other hand, high quality is something our customers can easily afford. Their ties to their various alma maters give the umbrella greater permanence in their lives. Their continuing interest in golf also will create greater need and give the product greater exposure. This becomes an important advertising function. The permanence that raises the cost also gives the product greater life span. For the majority of our prospective customers, we believe this is a distinct competitive advantage.

Our high quality is also an advantage in the gift market. Even people who might settle for a cheaper umbrella if buying for themselves are likely to buy a high-quality umbrella as a gift.

6. Product and Positioning Statement

Products often are defined by their positioning. Positioning creates a product's identity in the marketplace. By extension, that includes defining the product's audience, its niche, and its marketing approach. How a company wants its customers to feel once they've bought the product is its positioning statement.

Customers for School Colors' umbrellas are upscale, well-to-do, highly educated professionals who enjoy golf and have deep regard for the schools that educated them. To that end, we will promote purchase as a show of loyalty backed by the practical nature of a utilitarian product that will help them better appreciate an activity they presumably already enjoy. We market our product subtly and entertainingly, like upscale outdoor clothiers market their products, and look for appropriate outlets to advertise and distribute our umbrella. Not available in mass-market shops or other low-end distribution channels, the umbrellas will be positioned as lasting mementos of an important earlier time that have practical and fun applications as well.

Journal Entry

Companies that choose to include a marketing component in their business plans should remember that marketing goes far beyond mere advertising and promotion. Marketing is literally any thought or activity involved with getting a product out to the market. Some marketers say the very creation of a business plan is a marketing exercise because it describes how the company will face the marketplace. Marketing enters into determining the price and positioning of the product, as well as defining the very product itself. Never underestimate marketing's importance in any business plan. Make sure your business plan reflects the company's marketing savvy.

7. Advertising and Promotion

A company's product positioning often will determine its promotional strategies. The more succinct and distinct the company can be in its business plan, the better guide that plan will be. Include the media mix, if known, and key components of the marketing strategy.

School Colors will rely on an extensive yet inexpensive series of black-and-white and color ads placed in high-level general interest publications such as *The New Yorker, Atlantic Monthly,* and *The Wall Street Journal* and various school alumni magazines—publications read by the target market. In addition, fliers will be mailed to select mailing lists of high-end products and golf paraphernalia. Limited test marketing will go on through ads in golfing publications.

In addition, we also will seek secondary distribution through high-end specialty and sporting goods catalogs in an attempt to build a broader market for the product among non-alumni interested only in the umbrella's cachet.

8. Sales Strategy

In addition to marketing, how will your company deliver the product to distributors and, ultimately, end users? A clear strategy reflects an understanding of the product and process.

We've defined several key retail outlets as well as some national opportunities for distribution. By placing two national sales representatives in strategic locations, we'll be able to make site visits as necessary to retail outlets on campuses and at country club golf courses catering to school alumni, primarily in the Northeast and in southern California. Telephone-based sales reps will be headquartered at our Indianapolis office. A percentage will be assigned to handle incoming calls from responses to our various ads. Others will be assigned to negotiate space for those ads. During certain seasons—August to December and February to July—squads of telemarketers will be hired to solicit sales to names chosen from among alumni lists, country club memberships, and other likely upscale candidates.

Red Flag
Plans that are too long or overwritten tell less, not more, to those trying to wade through them. Plans must be complete, but also succinct. That aspect can't be emphasized enough.

9. Product and/or Market Development

No business, no matter how good, can rest on its laurels. The business plan should reflect future goals and strategies for continuing to grow and stay competitive. Targets should be aggressive, but goals must be sensible. In addition, they must relate to the core business and key strategies.

Once School Colors has established itself in the marketplace as the purveyor of premium golf umbrellas, the firm will look to providing other golf products with Ivy League school logos and colors. Possible products include golf balls and towels, caps, polo shirts, and golf bags. Long-term strategies include sponsorship of a major golf tournament.

In addition, School Colors will explore other upscale sporting equipment premiums, including sailboat sails, trout fishing vests, and downhill skis emblazoned with school logos.

10. Operations

This component of your business plan can cover a wide range, from the actual manufacture of products to start-up considerations for a new business—any of a host of issues not covered under other categories.

School Colors' manufacturing operation, located in a small plant outside of Indianapolis, consists of a 16-person staff that can produce 300 umbrellas per day. The materials are purchased from sources throughout Indiana, Ohio, and Pennsylvania. The plant also owns a small fleet of trucks, augmented by personal vehicles, for local delivery. Commercial carriers are used during peak seasons. Distribution is managed from several offices within the plant. Seasonal telemarketing drives are handled by a commercial telemarketing firm located in downtown Indianapolis.

11. Staff

Detail any key personnel who exhibit the type of expertise necessary to run a firm of this kind. Emphasize prior experience and qualifications that will lead to success. Identify any internal or external boards that will provide increased expertise and contribute to a positive outcome.

School Colors' administrative staff includes Melanie Haverford, president, and Ronald Bolling, vice president. Ms. Haverford received her MBA in business from Harvard Business School. She still serves as president of the Harvard Business School Alumni Association. Mr. Bolling has an MBA from the Kellogg School of Business at Northwestern University. He also is active in the Endowment and Scholarship Fund for the school. Keith Susteen is director of manufacturing. A Purdue University graduate, Mr. Susteen formerly was manufacturing head of Universal Promotions, a major premiums firm located in Chicago.

Shortcut
A good business plan summarizes company financials as its last section so they are available but not overbearing. Readers need such detail, but will first be more interested in the suppositions that helped the company arrive at its conclusion than in the numbers.

12. Financials

Basic financial statements should form this very important section of your plan. The numbers back up the assumptions, the more important component of the plan, but financiers likely will review financials carefully, looking for accuracy and consistency. Later in this book, when we focus on venture capitalists and lending institutions, we'll discuss the various types of financial statements that you might want to include in your business plan.

13. Payback and Exit Plan

Private investors and venture capitalists usually want to exercise exit options within five years, ideally after the company has gone public and their investments have turned into highly liquid shares for trading. Lenders, too, want to know payback plans and when they can expect a full return on equity and interest. A good plan provides this information for them.

> School Colors anticipates that the beachhead established by its umbrella sales will open the door for more high-quality premiums as described earlier in this plan. The growing market in both licensed goods and sports equipment should make this company ripe for sales to a major premium or sporting goods firm within five years of capital infusion.

A good business plan benefits the company that develops it, regardless of whether it's successfully used to solicit additional funding or not. A good plan carefully drafted and firmly executed will result in a healthier, stronger business.

The Least You Need to Know

➤ A good strategy is critical to a company's financial success. Define your strategy as specifically as possible. Your success depends on it.

➤ Commit to the strategy, attach a financial goal, plot a timeline—then go for it!

➤ Know your business, its customers, and its competition better than anyone else.

➤ A good business plan is a good measure of the discipline necessary to succeed. Developing a business plan is necessary to developing a sound financial strategy.

➤ A business plan must be written so it appeals to the type of financial support the company wants to attract, whether lender or investor.

➤ Understand and incorporate the 13 components of an average business plan fully and succinctly. If you miss any of them, the financiers are likely to wonder what your company may be trying to hide.

Budgeting 101

In This Chapter

➤ Defining the budget and budget type

➤ Stepping into the budgeting process

➤ Understanding budget components

➤ Seeing fixed and variable costs in action

➤ Drafting a budget

The next section of this book focuses on the accounting techniques that will help nonfinancial managers understand the detailed financial management of their business. Most department heads won't be practicing these skills on a daily or even weekly basis. But understanding the rationale and methodology of how and why the accounting department operates the way it does will put these professionals in a better position to manage their own departmental finances. For managers of all kinds, such a knowledge base is a good thing to have.

But prior to that we're going to talk about building a budget, because the budget will serve as the link between the theoretical and the real. And, plainly put, it's also the way most managers are introduced to the finance and accounting function for their company.

The Budget: A Definition

Chances are when you were growing up, your family had a budget. It may have included expense categories such as groceries and clothing, a little cash kept in the sugar bowl or a desk drawer, and an envelope of coupons clipped from the newspaper. That was the first experience most of us had with budgets and, in its simplest form, it's the quintessential definition of budgeting for business.

Like any other strategic direction and business plan, every company requires a financial plan to face the future. The company and departmental budgets are manifestations of that plan, a year-long look at the peaks and valleys of sales and expenses, the projection of cash flow (or lack of same) and the financial direction a company will take over the next 12 months.

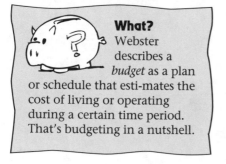

What?
Webster describes a *budget* as a plan or schedule that esti-mates the cost of living or operating during a certain time period. That's budgeting in a nutshell.

Although time periods vary, 12 months is the most common cycle and the most practical time frame for budgeting. It correlates with the tax cycle and covers all four operating quarters. Anything longer than a year may be wishful thinking at best. Anything shorter, while useful, may not anticipate all the bumps in the road a business will face.

The budget your family kept when you were young revolved around savings and expenditures, charting the ebb and flow of resources and supplies. When it comes to a company's budget, things grow a little more complicated, but the principles are the same. Budgets predict sales and other revenue (income) and production and operating costs (expenses), and the difference between the two (the company's profit or loss). The budget is the tool for estimating those numbers, and hopefully help managers prevent losses. And, working in tandem or as part of the business plan, it sets goals for either or both.

Budgeting is that simple. And it's that important.

Defining Budget Type

Budgets, like business plans, come in different makes and models depending on the purpose for which a company wants to use them. If its purpose is to plan strategies for the future, the company uses a long-term budget to set general goals for the next five or ten years. If its purpose is to plan the details of its operations, the company prepares a short-term budget, generally for a single year, to translate its goals into financial terms. Whether a budget is long-range or short-range, smart managers will revise them periodically, as conditions change.

> ➤ The one-year budget is most commonly known as an operational budget, designed to help a company or the departments within that company get through one more year of sales and production cycles with some semblance of financial success. The

12-month time frame does make the budget somewhat strategic in nature, but by and large its purpose is to anticipate and plan for coming issues and trends within the business year.

➤ Longer business cycles require longer-lived budgets. Even though they may be subject to review and revisions, some items or operations unfold more fully over a longer time period. This results in a longer-term or strategic budget. While the operational budget anticipates financial flow for a year or less, the strategic budget reacts more intrinsically with a company's long-term business plan. The net effect may be a less precise, but more comprehensive approach to financial management.

Not all companies need to create a strategic budget. Your company may be one of those happy to project from year to year, knowing that retained earnings and reserves may be all you need to set the stage for the subsequent year's financial growth. On the other hand, if the company is involved in major capital acquisition that will depreciate over time, includes extensive research and development that runs up expenses for years before any revenue might be realized from the project, or involves extensive investment plans that will take several years to bear fruit, then a strategic budget may be more appropriate.

Journal Entry

One of the major facets of budgeting is cost control, and that's also one of the major responsibilities of company managers. Budgets are the key to cost control, but only when managers have had a hand in developing those budgets. If management doesn't understand and use the budget, it will do a company no good. Involve all pertinent staff in the budgeting process. That allows them greater ownership of the process and enables them to better stay with the budget they've helped develop.

Strategic budgets help a company decide whether to invest in a business venture that may take several years to become profitable. A management consulting firm, for example, might be considering whether to develop a software division. A strategic budget would help it figure out (1) whether over the long haul this made good sense, and (2) how long it will take before the venture pays off.

Stepping into the Budgeting Process

Like any plan, a budget requires more than sitting down, crunching out some numbers that add up to a positive bottom line, and handing it over to the accounting department to plug in. Effective budgeting requires thought, careful planning, and a look at issues beyond the numbers. Consider the following components when you budget:

Red Flag

Be careful how the budget is created. Department managers who are strictly concerned with the bottom line may, just to look good, cut out expenses that are vital for the department to operate effectively. That's not an effective way to do a budget.

➤ *What company goals does the budget embrace?* These goals usually include profitability, but they also include investing in the company's ability to develop new product and service offerings to customers to help assure the company will be around tomorrow. Nearly all budgets help managers develop a balance between making money today and making money tomorrow.

➤ *What objectives can be identified in the budget?* Goals are important, but only clearly identified performance objectives will make them happen. Objectives clearly spelled out are crucial so that all parts of the company understand and pursue the same goals.

If your company's business is manufacturing and marketing luxury powerboats, its objective might be to increase sales 15 percent or establish a new outlet in a neighboring city. Increased sales of related paraphernalia as a financial objective might be a secondary objective. All such initiatives need to be reflected in the budget because all are strategic goals that will have either a positive or a negative impact on the bottom line.

➤ *Define the tactics that will help a department or company achieve its objectives.* Goals and objectives can be achieved only if the company sets out a tactical game plan. There are different ways to get from Point A to Point B and a company's success will depend on choosing effective tactics to reach those goals. The cost of pursuing those tactics also will be part of the overall budget, reflected as part of the cost of doing business.

The best tactics usually yield the highest reward, whether that's in terms of annual earnings, market share gain, or growth potential. But tactics vary with each situation, each company, and each strategy. The important thing is that those tactics are reflected in the budget in terms of their effect on both the revenue and expense side.

➤ *Identify procedures to help achieve that goal.* Procedures are to tactics what objectives are to goals. They are more specific, more operationally oriented—almost mechanical.

Journal Entry

A budget has many uses beyond charting the company's financial goals. It can assist in measuring the feasibility of technology development—both its likelihood and its application—and can help provide marketplace forecasts. It also may help measure the impact of new legislation affecting the market and may reflect new regulations—both internal and external—that touch the company. It's all there if you know where to look.

If your company makes ball bearings, the tactics for creating better bearings may be to define consistent settings on the milling equipment and monitor those settings as a way to reduce inconsistencies, thus reduce costs due to production problems. The procedure for doing so might involve a worker performing an inspection every half hour, noting the settings in a log, and reporting to the supervisor any variations beyond allowable limits. Or if your concern is with sales, the tactics may be to identify territory penetration for a sales force right down to the number of new contacts made per week with revenue computed on the number of sales per call made each week. The procedure would likely involve logging all new contacts and tracking the results. These are budget concerns and can be measured by the financial impact on your company of both revenues and costs generated.

Budget Components

Each budget will have two main sections, and a good manager will come to know each of these sections as intimately as his or her own family.

The first section measures company revenues, or income from sales, investments, and any other sources. You need to match up your expected revenues with your expected expenses, the other main part of the budget.

Say you work for a luxury boat manufacturer. Your company itemizes revenue from the sales of a certain type of speedboat. On the expense side, it then has to make sure the costs involved in building this boat will be less than the revenues it will generate. You don't want to build speedboats that cost more than people pay for them.

The revenue section's real job is to measure revenue projections—what the company thinks its going to earn through all its sources throughout the cycle of the budget—so that it may balance expenses against them. Unless there is a sound strategic reason for it, a business without a positive bottom line won't likely be a business very long. Expenses may be higher than revenues in certain months, but the goal is always to make sure revenues exceed expenses by the end of the year.

When it comes to the expense side of a budget, the more detail that can be included *within reason*, the more accurate a view the budget will provide of the firm's financial condition. More important, managers will be able to control cash flow better when they have a deeper level of information at their fingertips.

> **What?**
> A *capital budget* sets aside funds for capital expenditures. These are primarily new pieces of equipment or facilities, to be used over a period of years. Strategic in nature, a capital budget involves looking at the long-term profit that's likely to come from investing in that equipment or building.

> **Journal Entry**
>
> Many companies allow for flexible budgeting, a process by which budgets are adjusted to match output and/or marketplace factors that influence the company's revenues and expenses. Companies with a sudden short-term, unbudgeted income opportunity may create a flexible budget that adds to the expense side of the equation, but also adds corresponding revenues from product sales.

A Word About Costs

An example budget lies ahead. But before we get to that, let's look at the three types of costs that make up the expenses part of a budget.

What?
When budgeting for labor costs, the distinction to keep in mind is between *direct* and *indirect*. Direct labor costs are those incurred in any work on products or services that can be tracked readily, such as wages for assembly line workers. Indirect labor costs are for activities related to products or services that are not readily tracked, such as salaries for supervisors and support personnel. Both direct and indirect labor costs can be either fixed or variable.

➤ *Fixed costs* are perhaps the most important costs to manage. They are the costs that remain constant throughout and are impervious to the cycle of business. The rent you pay from month to month is a fixed cost because it doesn't vary no matter what your sales pattern might be. To a large degree, salaries also are fixed costs, although they may have variable components in terms of performance bonuses. Utility costs are the same way. Any expense that remains constant no matter what the cycle of business is a fixed cost.

➤ *Variable costs* are a little different and allow you some budgeting flexibility. These are costs that fluctuate directly with the amount of business you support. Variable costs—costs that are business-dependent—include supply of goods and materials and, to some degree, part-time labor necessary to keep the business operating apace with demand.

➤ *Semi-variable costs* are expenses with components that are fixed and components that are variable. For example, telephone expenses are semi-variable costs in that the monthly service charge is fixed and the charges for long-distance calls and the 800 number are variable.

Fixed and Variable Costs in Action

How are these costs used? Fixed costs must be spread over the total run of production throughout the budget cycle.

Consider a scenario involving a company that produces a specific item that sells for $9. If the fixed operations cost for producing a certain line of products is $10,000 per year plus materials cost, and the company produces 5,000 units in this product line, then fixed costs per unit are $2 each plus materials cost. If production doubles to 10,000 units, fixed costs do not increase; the cost per unit simply drops to $1 in fixed costs plus materials cost. Therefore, the more efficient and productive you are, the more economical and supportable your fixed costs can be.

But now let's say each one of these units requires $3 worth of raw materials and another $2 in assembly charges to create, or $5 per unit. Since those costs are based on the number of units being produced, those costs are variable with the production flow. If you produce 5,000 units, that's a variable cost of $25,000. Add to that your $10,000 per year in fixed costs, and you have overall production costs of $35,000, or $7 per unit. At a sales price of $9, the profit margin is $2 per unit.

But let's increase production to 10,000 at $5 per unit in materials and assembly charges. That's $50,000 in variable costs, plus $10,000 in fixed costs, for a total of $60,000 for 10,000 units. The price per unit is now $6, which yields a profit margin of $3 per unit.

Decisions over semi-variable costs, such as marketing expenses, may be made based on the number of units you need to sell, but they likely are not unit-specific—unless, for example, the marketers decide to give away something free with each purchase. However, if we were to add an additional $5,000 in marketing expense to our 5,000-unit run, we add an additional dollar in semi-variable cost to each item. The same $5,000, spent on the 10,000-unit run, would add an additional 50 cents per piece.

The net cost, then, on the 5,000 unit run jumps to $8 per unit. Costs for the 10,000 unit run jump to $6.50. The net profit margins are $1 and $2.50 per unit, respectively.

Even with these costs applied, it should be evident that the higher this particular production run, the wider the profit margin. That's all part of the sales income, to be sure. But the profitability per unit is determined primarily by the fixed and semi-variable costs. And that's influenced by the budgeting procedure.

What?
The term *overhead costs* is often used but rarely defined. It may include salaries and benefits, cost of physical plant, equipment depreciation, or any of a number of items. It's imprecise at best, but usually refers to the indirect cost of doing business or keeping the doors open so your product can be produced.

Drafting a Budget

So what does a budget look like? There are numerous variations, but the goal of any budget is to clearly communicate revenue and cost centers so that profit statements can be drafted and management of resources, including income, can be better accomplished. To that degree, all budgets tend to look the same.

For the sake of this lesson, let's assume our unit maker described earlier has been in business several years and is charged with budgeting for next year. That means he will have budgets from previous years from which to draft future business plans. The operational budget, then, likely will break revenue and expense components down to three columns:

1. The current year's budget, or what he originally projected his income and expenses to be.

2. The current year's projected year-end actual expenses and revenues. Even if it's a guess, which it tends to be, it must be as accurate a guess as possible.

3. The next year's budget, which tends to be a hybrid between the actual budget, the year-end projected actuals, and a best guess for what the new year will bring.

On the revenue side, it will tend to look something like this:

		REVENUE	
Item	**Current Budget**	**Projected Actual**	**Next Year's Budget**
UNIT A	$128,150	$120,800	$126,500
UNIT B	$136,450	$138,000	$143,000
UNIT C	$360,500	$288,550	$310,500
TOTAL	$625,100	$547,350	$580,000

As you can see, year-end projected actuals fell short of the budget in terms of revenue. Subsequently, next year's budget was modified to more realistic expectations.

Now let's look at the corresponding expenses:

		EXPENSES	
Item	**Current Budget**	**Projected Actual**	**Next Year's Budget**
Unit A			
–Materials	$13,500	$11,649	$12,280
–Assembly	9,600	7,333	10,100
Unit B			
–Materials	42,600	40,611	42,000
–Assembly	6,600	5,499	7,500

Item	Current Budget	EXPENSES Projected Actual	Next Year's Budget
Unit C			
–Materials	35,600	29,090	30,500
–Assembly	17,600	14,041	16,360
Rent	16,000	16,095	17,160
Utilities	5,660	7,939	9,000
Salaries/Benefits	109,900	117,656	119,500
Shipping/Delivery	27,700	36,079	38,650
Miscellaneous	15,000	9,010	10,000
TOTAL	$299,760	$295,002	$313,050

Let's compare revenues and expenses to calculate our net income before taxes:

Item	Current Budget	Projected Actual	Next Year's Budget
REVENUE	$625,100	$547,350	$580,000
EXPENSES	$299,760	$295,002	$313,050
NET INCOME	$325,340	$252,348	$266,950

Clearly the current budget was too optimistic, but having it in place provides a baseline to compare actual performance, which then helps provide guidelines for creating the next budget.

The Management Function

A budget is not a budget until it has been carefully scrutinized by management. Even if the numbers add up correctly, they may not have been estimated properly. It's middle-management's job to assemble the budget, but it's upper-management's job to question the budget. They do this because the budget is the financial tool that will guide the organization in the coming year. Not only does it need to be accurate, it needs to be well-considered and realistic.

In our example, the company missed the mark rather dramatically, showing a profit margin 22 percent less than the one projected in the budget. What questions should management ask?

1. *Why is the projected actual so far off from the budgeted amount?* Perhaps it was the fault of the budgeting process being too optimistic or of a budget based on considerations unrealistic to the current situation. Perhaps there was a significant change in market

conditions or materials costs. In any of these scenarios, management needs to understand why before it can accurately assess the new year's budget.

2. *Production costs for Units A, B, and C do not match their profit scenario. What gives?* It may be that the unit production varies and standardization needs to be applied. If a more costly unit is not earning more exponentially, it may mean that (a) the unit is improperly priced, or (b) demand has slacked off and there's too much inventory left in the warehouse. In either case, management must look at production standards and market demand before budgeting unit-production figures for the new year.

3. *Shipping/Delivery seems to have climbed precipitously in the last year. Why?* Clearly, this is a case where vendor price had exceeded market value. It may be a case of a long-term supplier who has gotten used to raising its prices a certain percentage each year with little incentive to remain competitive. Management should review any contracted relationship with the vendor and check the last three years' delivery and shipping charges to note the percentage increase. Chances are it's time to put the service out for competitive bid.

There are dozens of questions that can and should be raised, but the preceding three make the point: Setting up the budget is only half the task. The document must then be put through management scrutiny, not only to check the accuracy of its numbers and suppositions, but also to raise those issues that will enable the company to be more efficient and cost-effective.

If these questions aren't part of the budget creation, then management is doing only half its job.

The Least You Need to Know

➤ A budget is a plan by which a company operates the financial side of its business.

➤ Budgets can be operational or strategic in nature.

➤ A company's goals must be identified before creating a budget.

➤ Budgets vary, but all consist of revenue and expense items.

➤ Costs may be fixed, variable, or semi-variable.

➤ The budgeting process is incomplete if management doesn't scrutinize and question the budget.

Part 2
Accounting for Your Success

Staying on top of departmental operations and identifying your goals is one thing, but taking care of business from an accounting standpoint is quite another. All accountants are not department managers, but all department managers—both financial and nonfinancial managers—must account for their daily business. That's it in a nutshell.

The days of the green eyeshades and sleeve guards may have passed, but companies still need to have an accountant and probably a CPA in place to monitor the income and outflow of funds. But nonfinancial managers also must know how accounting procedures operate if they're going to make the most of business advantages and contribute fully to management of their company.

That's what this section is designed to do. With any luck, you may even begin to like accounting. Stranger things have happened!

Chapter 4

HIYA...

The Accountant in You

In This Chapter

➤ Accounting as business communication

➤ Understanding debits and credits

➤ Accrual vs. cash basis accounting

If you're a department manager used to flying by the seat of your pants, accounting often seems like the roadblock in the race for success. Accountants have rules and procedures that take time and sap resources. The very nature of their function—*accounting*—means they place more importance on the record-keeping associated with earnings and expenditures than on the efforts involved in generating those earnings in the first place.

Sometimes the accounting function seems like part of another world. Given the fact that accountants, like lots of other professionals, speak their own language and have their own icons that guide their behavior, that may well be the case.

So, if you're not a bookkeeper or an accountant, what does it matter? It should matter a lot, whether you're a manager responsible for the financial growth and development of a department, or the owner of a small business whose very success may depend on your financial acumen. You should have a clear idea of what the accounting function is about. In fact, it's critical.

What's So Important About Accounting?

Good salespeople know all about the items they're selling. Really good salespeople know the engineering calibrations, size, velocity coefficients, or other technical data about their product.

Why do salespeople need to know these things? Here are some reasons:

➤ Extensive product knowledge impresses the customer.

➤ Product knowledge gives customers faith in the salesperson's claims that the product is exactly what they're looking for.

➤ It gives the salesperson better insight into the product and its uses, which makes him or her better able to help customers believe this product is the solution to their problems.

➤ It makes the salesperson more successful. That means higher income, greater job security, and better opportunities for promotion, besides the obvious benefits for the company.

Red Flag
For accountants, the proof is in the paperwork. Accurate, well-organized records are a must. Sloppy bookkeeping is the road to financial failure—or at least to slowing down success, perhaps a lot. As a first step in becoming "accounting literate," take the time to write down all business activities, and make sure your records are accurate.

The same argument holds true when it comes to accounting knowledge for nonfinancial managers. The more a manager knows about how the people who deal in numbers handle department finances and the methodologies they use, the more that manager will be able to intelligently work with them, making everyone's job a little easier. So, let's take a few steps into that world of accounting.

Accounting IS Communication

In the dark recesses of their numerical souls, even some accountants may worry that their function is only a necessary evil, an overhead expense that in some organizations is no more than a glorified bookkeeping function. Not so. Sales, manufacturing, research and development, and management all generate raw financial data through their various activities. It's up to accountants to turn that data into useful information.

A good accounting function—whether in a large company headed by a highly trained chief financial officer (CFO) or a small company with a bookkeeper—produces and communicates information. This information shows department heads how they're spending the company's money and whether they're getting the results they want. Sure, accountants are still number-crunchers and bean-counters, but the true value of what they do is in how they interpret and present the results of all that crunching and counting.

Plain and simple, a company's accountants, whoever they may be, are guides to its finances. The way this group or this individual organizes figures and turns it into meaningful information provides the measures that help determine the success or failure of the company. Understanding those measures may make all the difference between the manager who's a well-rounded professional and the manager who's just another specialist with little sense of the larger financial implications of his or her decisions.

Shortcut
Think of accountants as scorekeepers and the documents they provide as scorecards that rate how well certain activities help the company make money.

Great Expectations

Given the important role of accounting, it only stands to reason that managers have certain expectations of the accounting function, including the following basic principles:

➤ The accounting system must accurately reflect the company's current financial condition. And it must do so in a timely fashion.

➤ The system must be clear, logical, and easy to use. Information should be understandable to all company officers and executive staff without the need for complex interpretation by the accountant.

➤ The system must provide useful information that officers and staff can use in making decisions and achieving the company's goals.

But even if the company's accountants are the best in the world, it won't matter much if the nonfinancial managers around them basically take the information in their reports and file it away—either horizontally or vertically—because they don't have much idea how the numbers were generated or what they mean.

What?
The essence of managerial expectations is found in what's called basic accounting *ARTS*—meaning that in reporting financial data, the accounting function should be Accurate, Relevant, Timely, and Simple.

Understanding Debits and Credits

You'll find in subsequent chapters that the accounting function has many steps and components. Although they may vary in complexity, all bookkeeping and accounting systems are essentially the same.

The concept behind accounting, what makes it more than merely adding and subtracting, revolves around a basic core consisting of debits and credits. This is an accounting system's soul, and understanding it will help managers better handle their share of responsibility for the firm's finances.

In some ways, debits and credits are more complex in theory than in practice. Debits and credits form the basis of all accounting functions, including the company's balance sheet. They are the two types of activity that can affect any financial account of any type—assets, liabilities, equity, income, or expenses.

The balance sheet is one of the primary accounting statements for any company. It's a list of assets, liabilities, and owners' equity—ownership value, if you will—in the business as of a specific date, usually the end of the financial month or fiscal year. Its ultimate goal is to keep all accounts in balance.

Company financial operations also generate two other accounting statements:

➤ *Income statement*—a summary of business revenue and expenses for a specific period of time.

➤ *Statement of owners' equity*—a record of the value or percentage of ownership held by individuals or firms with a stake in the business.

The primary purpose of all such statements is to help keep the company finances in balance. To that end, all debits must equal credits and all credits must equal debits when reflected on the balance sheet and income statement. If they don't, the balance sheet won't balance.

Your accountants may also generate another statement, for cash flow. We'll discuss cash flow in Chapter 9; for now, all you need to know is that while the income statement and the statement of owners' equity show the state of finances, the cash flow statement tells how the company reached that state. In essence, it accounts for how cash came in and how it went out.

T for Two

Credits and debits come into play in double-entry or dual-entry accounting, a method by which each transaction is entered twice—once as a credit and once as a debit—on the balance sheet and/or the income statement. That's how the financial statement stays in balance.

What?
Credits always appear on the right-hand side of T accounts. They represent an increase in items such as business liability, owners' equity, and revenue accounts, or a decrease in assets.

Why do accountants use the double-entry system? Well, we could explain how the system is based logically on the principle of duality, because all activities with any economic significance have two aspects—resources and uses, work and reward, loss and gain. Or we could simply point out that recording every transaction twice dramatically reduces the chance of error. The bottom line is that the system works, although it occasionally seems to defy common sense. Don't expect to understand it all completely now. Our discussion of the general ledger and subledgers should help make more sense of debits and credits.

The most common structure for financial documents, based on the need to distinguish between debits and credits, is the T account diagram. The left side of the T represents debits and the right side of the T represents credits. In the accounting process, a figure is recorded as a debit (left side) or as a credit (right side) depending on how the transaction affects that particular account.

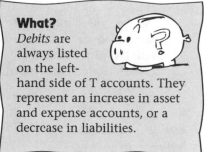

What?
Debits are always listed on the left-hand side of T accounts. They represent an increase in asset and expense accounts, or a decrease in liabilities.

It's Not Just Algebra

Sometimes, the accounting process appears to be a mirror image of what logical thought says it should be. But there's a root of logic to it that makes it more than just an algebraic equation. Remembering the following formula may help:

Assets = Liabilities + Owners' Equity

Assets are goods owned by the company—real estate, inventory, and other items of value. *Liabilities* are obligations, generally owed to suppliers. *Owners' Equity* is what belongs to the owners.

If the owners decided to sell all the assets and pay all the liabilities, what would remain belongs to them—their equity. The formula would then work as follows:

Assets – Liabilities = Owners' Equity

From this simple equation we derive the basic method for recording all business transactions in terms of their effect on the various accounts.

It's clear that owners' equity is increased by amounts invested by the owners, and decreased by what they withdraw from the company. It's also clear that if we order some materials, we're increasing our assets and increasing our liabilities. Unfortunately, it's not all that easy.

At this point, however, you should understand the basic concept of T account diagrams and how they reflect business activity in terms of debits and credits while maintaining the balance of the assets = liabilities + equity equation.

Opposites Balance

As you now know, asset and liability accounts go together, as opposite sides of a balanced equation—with owners' equity, of course. That's why they make up the balance sheet, which shows the financial position of the company. In a similar way, income and expense accounts go together and make up the income statement, which shows what's coming in and going out.

It's really two simple systems that become a little complicated when they're put together, because the double-entry system sometimes requires entries that may at first seem strange, because of the need to balance. It's usually easy enough to understand how assets and liabilities are affected by a transaction, but it may be harder with the effect of a transaction on income and expense accounts.

So, we'll provide a few examples to show it all makes sense, with a little effort.

Debits and credits balance according to the types of accounts affected by a transaction.

Account	Debit	Credit
Assets	Increases	Decreases
Liabilities	Decreases	Increases
Income	Decreases	Increases
Expenses	Increases	Decreases

The next figure shows the same kind of relationship between the assets and liabilities accounts. If we add $100 to assets, the debits go up $100, and the credits go down $100. At the same time, in the liabilities account, debits go down $100 and credits go up $100.

The figure shows how an accountant would record four common transactions in terms of debits and credits:

➤ The company borrows $8,000. Cash (an asset) is debited and Notes Payable (a liability) is credited.

➤ The company sells $5,000 in merchandise on credit. Sales Income (an income account) is credited and Accounts Receivable (an asset) is debited.

➤ The company pays its electricity bill of $200 immediately. Utilities Expense (an expense account) is debited and Cash (an asset) is credited.

➤ The company sells some of its older computers for $1,500. Office Equipment (an asset) is credited and Cash (an asset) is debited.

Simple as it should be, the concept of debits and credits is a little like a Zen koan (a paradox). Terms are easily defined, but how they integrate into your balance sheet and income statement and the effect they have on your accounts… Well, that's not so clearly understood without first understanding how liabilities and owners' equity are treated in relation to assets. That may take a little getting used to.

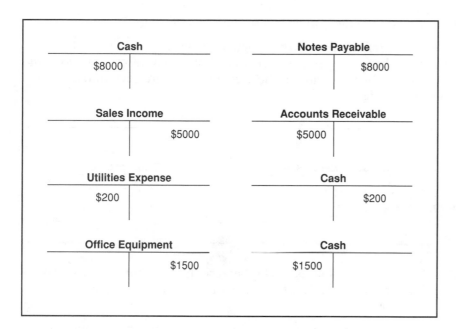

How an accountant would record four common transactions in terms of debits and credits.

Law of Opposites

The most important thing to remember about credits and debits is that when it comes to the balance sheet and the income statement, they always go together. It's like a law of physics: For every credit there is a equal (and opposite) debit and for every debit there is an equal (and opposite) credit.

Journal Entry

In any discipline, balance of all elements is crucial to success. The balance sheet operates in much the same way. Keep the accounts balanced by the proper entries, and there won't be problems. Throw it out of whack and the accounts won't function properly. Automated systems won't close out a document unless all columns are in balance. Companies that still do it manually, however, are on their own. But if the debits do not equal credits, the trial balance will not be in balance.

Let's try a small business example here, since it best illustrates the point.

Carl works for a health club, selling memberships. When he signs up a new member, the contract allows for a choice between cash payment and 30 days same as cash. Since most of his clients choose to delay the financial hit, the accountant records each of those sales as shown in the following figure.

How an accountant would record a credit sale for $200.

Accounts Receivable	Sales Income
$200	$200

The sale is posted to Accounts Receivable as a debit because that account is an asset and debits increase assets. The amount is also posted to Sales Income as a credit, because credits increase income accounts.

Things change where the actual funds are involved—and accounting's great irony is that money itself is almost irrelevant to the process. It simply allows a medium for accountants to practice their magic, much like white bread provides the necessary palette for peanut butter and jelly.

When the business office receives payment for any of the memberships, it accounts for the transaction as in the following figure.

How an accountant would record a $200 payment on a credit sale.

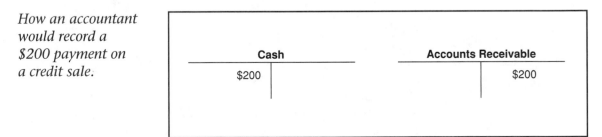

The accountant records the payment like this because Cash and Accounts Receivable are both assets: A debit increases the former and a credit decreases the latter (again, debit and credit balance).

However, from time to time a client chooses to pay Carl the membership fee up front. When that happens, we have a single transaction instead of the two depicted in the previous two figures. This cash transaction is shown in the following figure.

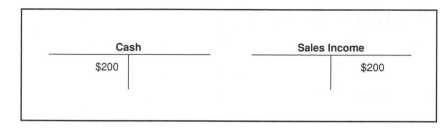

How an accountant would record a $200 cash sale.

Apply the principles of debits and credits, and what seems at first like a simple action—selling something, paying a bill, or borrowing money—suddenly becomes more complicated. But those complications of the double-entry system of accounting provide a basic mechanism of checks and balances and allow a more accurate understanding on how any financial activity affects company performance.

Those apparent complications, in fact, help define the difference between accounting and mere bookkeeping:

➤ Bookkeepers record financial data in a predetermined manner. It's a clerical position that revolves around accurate record keeping and little else.

➤ Accountants use the information in a conceptual way, interpreting the data, preparing the necessary reports based on that data, and drawing conclusions from the implications of that data on the financial side of their company's business.

It's at that point that the complexities of dual-entry accounting begin to make a lot more sense.

Journal Entry

Accounting itself is a process, not an end product. Thus it is subject to many of the laws of financial mutability. This impact isn't easily grasped unless you've learned the algebraic principles behind the accounting process. The rest of us are better off simply memorizing the following truths:

➤ On your balance sheet, assets increase debits and decrease credits, while liabilities decrease debits and increase credits.

➤ On your income statement, income decreases debits and increases credits, while expenses increase debits and decrease credits.

Accrual vs. Cash Basis Accounting

In applying the ARTS formula identified earlier—Accurate, Relevant, Timely, and Simple—the accounting function can be a major source of information vital to the success of a business. The discipline of the balance sheet, although it may seem foreign to some, gives it the strength and application to help you master all accounting steps within your business cycle.

One more distinction to understand is the difference between cash basis and accrual basis. The choice depends on the type of business, and we don't need to enter into the reasons here. What you do need to know is how the basis used by your company affects how financial transactions are handled.

The difference focuses to some degree on the question of cash flow. Accrual accounting, popular with large businesses, records transactions when they are made—regardless of whether any money has changed hands. The company is accruing sales revenue that will be deposited at a future date. The difference is that it is immediately posted to the general ledger. The actual cash is incidental to the accounting procedure under accrual accounting.

Shortcut
Henry David Thoreau wasn't an accountant when he said, "Simplify! Simplify!" but he captured the essence of balance sheet management. Keep it simple at first. Your accounting system will grow as your business grows.

Accrual accounting is used by all businesses of any size because it allows for better cash management, providing a better match between expenses and revenues, whether transactions are for cash or on credit. Without an accrual system, in fact, there's no need for more complex accounting functions. It's a way to better match revenues with the means for producing those revenues and gives a clearer picture of the actual profits your company makes.

In cash-based accounting, on the other hand, you record nothing until actual cash has traded hands. Whether you're purchasing raw materials for manufacture from a vendor or selling finished goods to a distributor, nothing is entered in the ledger without a money transaction attached to it.

The Least You Need to Know

➤ Proper accounting systems are critical to business success. Good accounting is communications among various parts of a company.

➤ Accounting ARTS—Accuracy, Relevance, Timeliness, and Simplicity—are the secret to successful financial management.

➤ Although it may appear illogical, debit and credit activity helps keep financial statements in balance.

➤ Credits increase liabilities and capital on the balance sheet and increase revenue on the income statement.

➤ Debits increase assets on the balance sheet and increase expenses on the income statement.

➤ Debits and credits always function together to keep the balance sheet in balance. That's called double-entry or dual-entry accounting.

Your Company's General Ledger

If a company's accounting system is its financial body, think of the general ledger as its heart. Everything emanates from and travels back to the general ledger, or G/L, and no financial transactions occur without passing through its pages. For many companies, losing the G/L amounts to losing the financial history of the business. It's that important.

The Purposes of a General Ledger

As the heart of the company's financial body, the G/L records all transactions that occur within the company's business activities. It also functions as the center of the firm's books of original entry. When individual transactions are recorded anywhere within the subsidiary ledgers (subledgers), such as accounts payable or accounts receivable, they feed up to the G/L. (If a business is relatively small, there may not be any subledgers. However, even if you work in a company with such a simplified accounting system, it's good to know how a more sophisticated system works.)

What?
The *general ledger* exists for three main purposes: It serves as a summary of every transaction as recorded in the books of original entry; it's the source document for all financial reports; and it offers an audit trail for tracking individual transactions, should that become necessary.

But the G/L is not a single document. Its content is augmented by receipts, journal entries, invoices—paperwork known as "source documents" that support the transactions recorded within. They all roll together, in fact, to form the company's accounting system, with the G/L at its heart.

Why is it important for any manager not responsible for financial matters to understand general ledger processing? Well, why is it important for a salesperson to understand the nature, properties, and construction of the item he or she is selling? Financial management is a crucial part of your position. The more you know about what takes place on the accounting side of the fence, the better off you'll be.

The General Ledger Does Not Stand Alone

Important as it is, the general ledger doesn't exist in a vacuum, but interacts rather cleverly with other parts of a company's accounting system. This occurs through a process called posting.

What?
Transactions posted directly to the general ledger include returns of merchandise, allowances from a supplier for credit, asset acquisitions, asset sales, investor capital contributions, loan drawdowns, and loans. These are called *journal entries*.

Posting is simply entering into the G/L a summary of transactions recorded in the subledgers or journals, with a reference number. We'll get further into the entire process later.

Some transactions are posted only to the general ledger and not to the subledgers. These transactions tend to be unusual. But proceed with caution. Items that should be entered in subledgers but are simply posted to the general ledger for the sake of convenience can throw the bookkeeping out of whack and unbalance your balance. That's an error no accounting system can afford.

Setting Up the General Ledger

There's no trick to setting up a general ledger, whether it's a manual or an automated system. The G/L setup usually mirrors a company's financial statement presentation. Generally speaking, the order is:

1. Balance sheet
2. Income statement

Consistency is the key to successful documentation in accounting. The layout of the chart of accounts—the list of all usual sources of revenue and expenses—should reflect the layout in your G/L. And vice versa.

Journal Entry

New businesses setting up their general ledger for the first time have to record the financial contributions made by owners, partners, and investors. In true accounting fashion, these entries credit the equity side of the balance sheet (as investments in the business) and debit the cash column (as an increase in assets).

Personal Business Options

Executives who run a personal business on the side—a consulting practice, for instance—may be tempted to center their personal G/L on their checking account, since the check register allows places for ending balance, income, and disbursement. But the check register does not allow for other entries, such as recording sales (so he or she knows who owes what amount) and other non-cash–related transactions, such as depreciation. A check register is appropriate for recording receipts and disbursements for the business, but it cannot handle all the other business transactions.

Automated Systems

Automated systems minimize the drudgery of accounting—and reduce the chances of error. Most systems automatically post the subledger balance to the G/L.

Executives not interested in computerizing their personal business with their own G/L may want to purchase one of several manual G/L kits available at many business supply stores. The kit often centers on a long, columnar sheet of paper with account types listed along the top and measured against the days of the month listed along the left. The layout allows accountants to balance their books both vertically and horizontally. Most kits also allow for the setup of subledgers and journals to make these true accounting systems.

What happens if you want to switch systems to automate your accounting function? Companies converting from one system to another should first run a set of trial balances on the news system and compare them with the old system's financial statements. If they don't match exactly, there's a problem with your system.

Making Journal Entries

Whether the accounting system is manual or automated, a company's G/L and its subledgers need to be fed information. The data added through activities at the department level should be supported by source documentation describing the reason for the entry and the reasoning behind each transaction. If a source document can't be provided—even if it's just a explanatory notation into the G/L itself—then a journal entry can't be made. That may mean that payments can't be made to suppliers or payments can't be credited to customer accounts—in short, a particular financial transaction won't appear on the books, thus affecting the departmental budget that department managers are working so hard to support.

To report transactions, use whatever standard journal entry forms the accounting department provides. In addition to asking all the right questions, the forms offer a familiar format that will enable more efficiency and accuracy. Finally, the accountants should keep all source documents so they can check them against the journal entries, if the need arises. It's easier for them if you document your transactions clearly, not just scribble a few words on a scrap of paper.

Red Flag
The single most important thing to remember about subledgers and the general ledger is that the two components must maintain balance. They must agree. If they don't, that means something was posted to one system and not to the other. A good accounting function can easily ferret out the offending entry, but you may be called upon to review your documentation and/or balances against departmental records.

Batching General Ledger Entries

One way accounting departments streamline the G/L process is to allow for entries in a subledger or a journal to be posted to the G/L in batches. Since some of the subledgers record a lot of similar transactions, batching can make the accounting process a lot easier.

Accountants prefer to batch similar transactions, such as a day's worth of payments received from customers or a week's worth of payments made to suppliers. This procedure may affect how invoices and deposits are submitted. Bigger batches can make accounting easier, but smaller batches allow easier verification of figures when a batch doesn't balance. (Some will, and balancing is a key component to an effective accounting system.)

In an automated system, the number-crunchers have easy access to the record of a batch. Make sure there are hard-copy proofs or safe electronic files that can be easily checked if necessary. That accessibility, too, is the value of the subledgers' batching capabilities. In addition, online systems often allow for easy entry of individual items, making the batching process obsolete. The process a company uses also may affect how accounts are managed.

Balancing Out

Periodically (usually every month), accountants should compare the amounts in the G/L against the amounts in the subledgers. They may do so in order to prepare financial reports, but they certainly should do it just to ensure accuracy.

Despite what some accountants say, they too are only human and sometimes find their subledger and G/L out of balance. It can happen on either side of the equation, and each requires its own remedies.

Since you won't be responsible for finding the source of the problem and making the necessary corrections, we won't go into the details of the procedures followed. Just remember that accountants are human and occasionally make mistakes. Be patient and understanding—as you'd expect them to be when you neglect to provide a source document or fill out the proper forms!

Once the company hits year-end, it's time to close the revenue and expense accounts and transfer the difference between the two accounts as net income to the statement of owners' equity. The bottom-line figure from that statement is then entered under "Owners' Equity" on the balance sheet. The accounting for the year is transferred, in effect zeroing out the accounts. You are then ready to start the next fiscal year.

On the Audit Trail

One of the purposes for the accounting function is to provide a history of transactions to anyone who cares or needs to know the financial inner workings of the company. That's generally someone within the company. But sometimes, situations brought on by outsiders require department managers to be able to follow a transaction through bookwork and come out the other side with positive proof that the right accounts were credited or debited. That's called building an audit trail. Done correctly and with the aid of the G/L, the system should provide the proof necessary to answer both internal and external questions.

Consider the example of the head of manufacturing who orders raw materials on a regular basis, with a constant flow of both deliveries and bills coming in. It wouldn't be hard for a careless supplier to send two bills, several months apart, for a single shipment. If the tracking system is equally careless, then you might be paying for that double-billing without realizing it.

Such problems are much harder to rectify once they've passed through the various channels. Here's how the G/L can help you perform a self-audit:

➤ Check the general ledger entry for the purchase. Chances are it's there, but may be part of the batch brought over from the subledger. If payments are categorized by date, tracing the purchase back to the due date should be relatively easy.

➤ In the accounts payable subledger, trace the invoice by company. The batch information should yield the date paid, the check number that paid the bill, the amount paid, and even the invoice number. Then you can find the invoice.

➤ From there, the canceled check and payment documentation listing the manufacturer's invoice on the canceled check stub should be easy to locate. A copy of the check and the original invoice should satisfy the vendor—at least until the next time.

Journal Entry

It's a good idea to set up individual vendor files against which to cross-check discrepancies with considerably fewer steps. The vendor files list all the various transactions being done with individual companies, including the very information necessary to counter double-billing claims. The best vendor files are linked directly to accounts payable so there is no chance of maintaining a duplicate data base and miskeying the information.

That interactivity of files between the G/L and subledgers is critical to keeping company accounts clean and in balance.

The Least You Need to Know

➤ The general ledger is the heart of the business. All transactions are summarized in it.

➤ The general ledger is more than a single document and summarizes receipts, invoices, and anything else necessary to support its entries.

➤ Posting to the general ledger helps it interact with its subledgers and other source documents.

➤ Source documents and journal entries are critical in supporting the general ledger.

The Chart of Accounts

Like the ancient mariner, no accountant would ever set sail on his or her financial journey without a map—in this case, the aid of a reliable chart of accounts. As a nonfinancial manager, you need to know that the chart of accounts is the primary tool used to help the accounting department keep the business's and your department's debits and credits straight.

By application, the chart of accounts becomes a map of the components of a business's finances. So, how does that affect a manager? It defines the categories into which you're expected to fit all your transactions. If you order a gross of pens, for example, you need to indicate the expense as "Office Supplies" or "Art Supplies" or "Promotional Supplies"—depending on the intended use and on the specific categories in the chart of accounts used by your company.

We indicated earlier that good accounting means good communications. If you're familiar with your company's chart of accounts, you can help make life easier for the accountants and make financial operations more efficient.

A Reliable Guide

The chart of accounts is a way to help systematize what the company spends money on. By having such information in a highly organized fashion, a manager can understand better how money is being allocated to run the business. A manager can decide to follow this allocation or try to revise it.

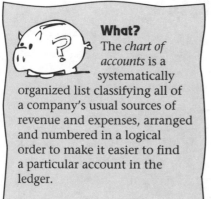

What?
The *chart of accounts* is a systematically organized list classifying all of a company's usual sources of revenue and expenses, arranged and numbered in a logical order to make it easier to find a particular account in the ledger.

Whether a business is big or small, it should have a chart of accounts. The complexity of that chart will depend on the size of the business, to some extent, but more on the nature of the business—whether it produces a single product or provides only one service, for example, or offers a wide assortment of products and services.

This is another instance where a small business example illustrates clearly the same type of situation your department might find itself in if you don't understand and follow the chart of accounts.

Creating the Chart of Accounts

The chart of accounts is a basic component to any accounting system and one that can't be misused or ignored. Also, as business needs change, the company should update its chart of accounts.

Red Flag
Accounting systems keep track of assets, liabilities, equity, income, and expenses. That's the same in any business. But to ensure consistency in the way in which employees in a particular company report business transactions into their accounting system, the company relies on its chart of accounts.

The typical chart of accounts has two parts for each entry: the account number and a brief description of the account. The account number is important because it shows how a particular account is categorized. The descriptions allow everyone to understand how any given transaction should be handled. It may be something like "Office Supplies," or it may be a bit more detailed.

Think of the chart of accounts as a checklist of items and areas the company has chosen to keep an eye on. A company that sells widgets might have an account called "Computer Equipment and Supplies," to adequately keep track of its several computers and printers, as well as diskettes, paper, and so forth. But a high-tech graphic design company might have three accounts for computers and printers alone (depending on the use) and separate accounts for diskettes and paper stocks.

Each chart of accounts differs, but one consistent rule exists: Set up the chart of accounts to list individually all those accounts for which detail is needed or management and control desired. A sales-oriented company probably won't need a account for "Rubber Bands," which are best listed under "Office Supplies." But telephone costs will be separate from gas, light, and heat (which might be classified together under "Utilities"). Because of the number of calls your sales reps make, that expense needs to be tracked as a separate item.

What's in a Name?

How does an accountant choose which accounts are listed separately in the chart of accounts? That depends on the business, as we have noted, and on two types of need: what the managers need to make informed decisions in running the company and what the business office needs to take care of taxes. So, setting up or revising a chart of accounts takes planning and cooperation.

The accountant starts by listing those accounts that are also on the balance sheet and income statement. Accounting systems consist of interactive components. By listing items on the chart of accounts that reflect those on the balance sheet and income statement, accountants have a better chance of coordinating all this information in a systematic set of cross-references among various documents that track and record the business's financial transactions.

How Many Accounts?

Red Flag

If you have an accountant who's unfamiliar with your business, he or she might want to establish an entry in the chart of accounts for every sort of expense or income source, or perhaps go to the other extreme and have only a few entries. If a new accountant is establishing or revising a company's chart of accounts, the managers should first help the accountant determine how much detail is appropriate.

Red Flag

A cardinal sin in setting up a chart of accounts is the failure to exercise discretion in identifying the accounts to track. The accountant should plan carefully and consult with managers in setting up the chart of accounts. Still, it's better to have too many than too few, since it's easier to combine several accounts than to split an account into two or more.

The number of individual accounts depends on what's important in the business, but it's also limited by two things: the number of accounts an automated system will hold and the number of accounts the company actually needs. The first limitation is a function of technology. The second is a matter of personal commitment. The more accounts the company has, the more complicated it will be to bring them all together for reconciliation at the end of every month. So a good rule is for the company to judiciously list all the accounts it needs, but no more.

Red Flag
Remember to list those items for which individual details are important or amounts are large. Less important items and smaller cash outlays require less attention, thus less detail.

Red Flag
Companies that do accounting by hand and plan on switching to an automated system soon should make sure their chart-of-accounts numbering methodology is basically compatible with that system's software requirements. That way, any renumbering of accounts can be kept to a minimum.

There is a systematic way to decide which accounts to list. The first step is to categorize all items by the nature of their accounts. The second is to list them according to the following categories:

➤ Assets, including Current Assets and Fixed Assets

➤ Liabilities, including Current Liabilities and Long-Term Liabilities

➤ Owners' Equity, including Retained Earnings

➤ Income

➤ Expenses

How should each of those categories be split into accounts? Decide that, and the company has taken a giant leap toward completing the chart of accounts. In addition to deciding how many accounts the chart will include, the company must also designate which accounts bear enough weight in the business to warrant a separate entry.

What's in a Number?

The theory behind numbering the chart of accounts is to keep it as simple as possible. But the numbering system must contain enough flexibility so that accounts can be added within the context of the sections of the chart in which they make sense.

Account Prefixes

There are several methods by which most chart of accounts are numbered: The three-digit numbering system is probably the simplest for small business, but it limits the amounts of actual accounts that can be included. An example is shown in Table 6.1.

Table 6.1 Three-Digit Account Numbering System

Account Description	Account Number
Assets	100
Current	110–149
Fixed	150–199
Liabilities	200
Current	210–249
Long-term	250–299

Account Description	Account Number
Equity	300
Retained earnings	400
Income	500
Expenses	600

The four-digit numbering system runs very much the same way, but with four digits rather than three digits identifying the account. The advantage simply is that the four-digit system allows for more detail, as well as greater latitude to insert additional accounts within the individual sections. The layout looks very much the same as the three-digit system. An example four-digit system is shown in Table 6.2.

Table 6.2 Four-Digit Account Numbering System

Account Description	Account Number
Assets	1000
Current	1100–1499
Fixed	1500–1999
Liabilities	2000
Current	2100–2499
Long-term	2500–2999
Equity	300
Retained earnings	400
Income	500
Expenses	600

Prefix systems help manage subsidiary accounts within specific sections of the chart of accounts and can be as long and contain as many prefixes as you and the accountant feel the need to have. However, simplicity is always best. Remember, the more accounts there are, the more accounts that must be reconciled each month.

Let's apply the prefix system to a hypothetical business, limiting our focus to a very specific area of assets, just to keep things simple here. The business: a restaurant. The assets: wines. This system shows how the wines are divided by type (red or white), country of origin, name of importer, and name of wine. Table 6.3 shows the prefix system.

Table 6.3 Subaccounts Are Prefixed with the Parent Account Number

Account Number	Account Description
100	RED WINES
100-25	Italian Reds
100-25-116	Ruffino Chianti Classico
100-25-117	Ruffino Valpolicella
100-25-218	Villa Banfi Bardolino
100-25-319	Zonin Lambrusco
100-27	California Reds
100-27-116	Gundlach Bundschu Cabernet Sauvignon
100-27-117	Gundlach Bundschu Pinot Noir
100-27-218	Jordan Cabernet Sauvignon
100-27-319	Sterling Merlot

The three-digit prefix 100 indicates red wine. The second two numbers indicate the importer or the winery. The third number indicates the name of the wine from the importer or winery. For white wines, the same numbering system is used, but the three-digit prefix is 200 instead of 100; sparkling wines have a prefix of 300; and dessert wines are 400.

The restaurant would use a similar system to track any other assets as well as its liabilities, revenues, expenses, and owners' equity. The detail here goes above and beyond what most businesses would need.

Account Suffixes

By itemizing the chart of accounts to such a specific degree, the restaurateur can use it as the basis for inventory control. He can also tell his suppliers and their competition at any given time how much he has spent on what wine to better leverage prices and consumption trends.

This wine cellar chart of accounts is an example of more than just a prefix-type numbering system. The fact that we've indicated the type of wine by changing the last three numbers in the string means we've also created a suffix system that uses the end number to indicate specifics. Let's add one more element to indicate vintages of some of the wines. This is shown in Table 6.4.

Table 6.4 Account Suffixes Are Used to Itemize Subaccounts

Account Number	Account Description
100	RED WINES
100-25	Italian Reds
100-25-116-01	Ruffino Chianti Classico '93
100-25-116-02	Ruffino Chianti Classico '94
100-25-117-00	Ruffino Valpolicella non-vintage
100-25-218-00	Villa Banfi Bardolino non-vintage
100-25-319-00	Zonin Lambrusco non-vintage
100-27	California Reds
100-27-116-02	Gundlach Bundschu Cabernet Sauvignon '94
100-27-117-02	Gundlach Bundschu Pinot Noir '94
100-27-218-05	Jordan Cabernet Sauvignon '92
100-27-319-05	Sterling Merlot '92

If you know your Italian wines, you know that the Banfi Bardolino and Zonin Lambrusco are non-vintage wines the same as the Ruffino Valpolicella. If you don't know your wines but know your chart of accounts numbering system, you quickly realize that the suffix -00 means non-vintage wines, something you should be able to tell from the numbering system itself.

Based on the same logic, you know that the suffix -02 means a 1994 vintage, which means both the Gundlach Bundschu Cabernet Sauvignon and Pinot Noir are vintage '94 by virtue of their suffix. The suffix -05 applies to the Jordan Cabernet Sauvignon 1992 vintage. Its use again for the Sterling Merlot should indicate to you that that wine is also a 1992 vintage.

Even if your chart of accounts is not as elaborate as in this example, it should help keep your company's business organized as well as helping the managers and accountants keep track of finances. And if you can follow the system used by this restaurant for the "wine assets" section of its chart of accounts, you can likely understand whatever chart of accounts your company uses.

Journal Entry

Accounting entries are part of the company's financial history. As such, deleting an account from the chart of accounts—even if it's inactive or maybe even obsolete and no longer of use in tracking financial activity—is generally considered bad form in accounting circles. At the end of a fiscal period or the fiscal year, the accounting department can simply transfer any amount remaining in such an account to an active account and then indicate that the old account is not to be used.

Linking Up

The last step in chart of accounts development (or the first step, some accountants might say) is linking that chart to other components of the financial record-keeping system. Many automated systems will automatically do that, and that's the easiest way. But if the company is small and hasn't automated its bookkeeping system, linkage is still a very good idea to help keep the accounts straight. The company just has to make sure all the right amounts are added to all the right lines in the financial statement and everything will work out all right.

The Least You Need to Know

➤ The chart of accounts is a map that shows how a company's assets, liabilities, expenses, income, and owners' equity are divided for accounting purposes.

➤ Each entry in the chart of accounts has an account number and a description.

➤ The company should choose the chart of accounts numbering system that best meets its business needs.

➤ Subaccounts will help the company better utilize its chart of accounts and make the system more manageable.

➤ The company should link the chart of accounts to other aspects of the record-keeping system.

Chapter 7

Accounts Receivable

In This Chapter

➤ Defining accounts receivable

➤ Setting up and tracking accounts receivable

➤ Using control points to succeed

➤ Making accounts receivable entries

Let's begin by defining accounts receivable, or A/R. Simply put, it's a subledger of the general ledger that lists money owed to the company by customers and other sources. (We should add here that a company with a very small group of customers might be able to keep all of those accounts in the general ledger. But this method would be unwieldy for most businesses, so accounts receivable are generally kept in subledger.)

That's a fairly straightforward way to describe what lies at the heart of the A/R subledger. The good news is that there's more, much more to A/R than that. But take time to master A/R's applications and opportunities—or it could turn into bad news.

Listing Items of Value

One of the most important realizations is that A/R is like cash in the bank...almost. The ledger lists items of value to the company, monies owed in the future by clients and customers against which the value of the company is measured, and other financial activities that can be leveraged, such as loans. A/R shows up as an asset on the balance sheet. A/R means value to the business.

One of the more important purposes of A/R is to organize the detail of these accounts, because the general ledger lacks the space and capability to handle great amounts of account detail. The information is then posted from A/R to the G/L.

Adding Up the Info

The A/R system can be manual or automated. Either way, it must contain the necessary information to support the G/L and be useful to anyone reviewing or using the information on the individual accounts it reflects. Each A/R subledger summary should include the following information:

➤ *Name of the Customer*—Enough information to sufficiently identify the customer.

➤ *Purchase Description*—All the information necessary to distinguish the item(s) purchased from other items in the inventory.

➤ *Date*—When the transaction took place.

➤ *Amount*—How much the transaction was for.

➤ *Sales Account*—The G/L account to which the transaction is to be posted.

➤ *Cash*—Whether or not the customer paid cash.

This information serves as the basis for regular posting to the G/L—whether entries are posted daily, weekly, or monthly.

Some businesses still use customer cards—individual cards for recording activity in each customer account—as the source of their A/R. Such a system requires several checks and balances to ensure that account information won't be lost. For any receivable transaction, do the following:

➤ Record the transaction on the customer's card.

➤ Show the new balance on each card after the day's entries have been completed.

➤ Record the transaction on the A/R subledger summary sheet at the end of each day, making sure that all debits equal all credits.

➤ Make sure daily cash entries balance against the bank deposit ticket. If they don't, there's a problem.

➤ Post the A/R subledger total to the general ledger.

Automating Receivables

Using a computerized system to manage A/R offers several advantages, not the least of which is a neat and orderly entry that can be easily adjusted for error. More important, perhaps, an automated system automatically links A/R to the general ledger and sales. That eliminates errors and decreases the accounting work. If the system also links A/R to inventory, items can be more quickly restocked as well.

Customer activity and transaction information is the start of any automated A/R system. When a sale is made, record the date, amount, item purchased, and invoice number (if any). After that data is entered into the system, the automated A/R will summarize the transaction to the customer file and create a batch detailing all receivable transactions by customer. The batch is then balanced according to the general ledger account to which the batch is posted.

Red Flag
Make sure the accounts receivable information begins at the customer level with transaction information that shows a record of all the necessary information—invoice number, date, items purchased, and amount paid. Leave anything out, and you risk not having the necessary data when it's needed.

The nice thing about automated systems is that they tend to be simple and foolproof. The single-entry database minimizes mistakes. Any errors that occur are generally flagged by the system immediately. That saves a lot of time and headaches down the road.

Using Control Points

Both manual and automated A/R systems have six control points that will help keep A/R accounting on track:

➤ Verification of all A/R balances

➤ Invoicing

➤ A/R posting

➤ Report on receivables

➤ Credit entries

➤ Ledger agreement

Use the following information wisely and well.

Verify All A/R Balances

No matter what your system, transaction accounting must include enough information to allow verification of the transaction. That may mean including some or all of the following documentation, all of which must be verifiable through the customer account records:

➤ For a *sale,* the *invoice* is required.

➤ For a *payment, cash* receipt batches, deposit tickets, or bank statements are sufficient.

➤ For a *credit*, a *credit memo* and *documentation to support that memo* are required.

Invoice Promptly

Nothing can bring greater joy or sorrow to a business than good or bad invoicing habits. Immediate invoicing exhibits good records management and fiscal reliability. Late invoicing does little more than delay payment, hurt the company's financial position, and perhaps even create difficulties for customers who no longer can or want to pay.

Shortcut
The best accounts receivable functions are automatically linked with other aspects of the accounting system. That linkage can reduce both effort and errors in bookkeeping.

A/R Posting

Any good receivables system will provide proof that all invoices have been correctly posted to the customer accounts. This is usually accomplished daily by comparing invoices with the A/R postings. If the company is large enough to have different facets to its accounting system, then it's a good idea for posting to be done by a department other than the one normally responsible for A/R. That area also should be responsible for verifying the postings, maybe not daily, but certainly regularly.

Report on Receivables

A good automated system provides regular reports on the state of the accounts, identifying delinquent customers and those that have purchased over their credit line. The system will indicate how many accounts have aged and how much.

This also is the basis from which we build collection efforts. It's inevitable that some customers must be prodded to pay. A system that doesn't assist in this effort really has little value to overall A/R management efforts.

Credit Entries

There are only three ways accounts may be credited—payment, credit memo, and journal entry. Payment is the most common, of course. But any system must have a method to address amounts in dispute, returned items, and errors—that's the job of credit memos— and to write off accounts that are considered uncollectible.

Ledger Agreement

An A/R system isn't a system unless there's agreement among subledger balances, the general ledger accounts receivable balance, and detailed customer transaction records.

Balancing these accounts should be among your system's routine maintenance procedures.

A Case Study

Consider the following example of a company that got into real estate management as a way to diversify usage of some of its funds. This example shows how that new source of income became additional A/R and how those new accounts were handled.

The company purchased a commercial real estate block that housed several stores and small offices. Two of the company's tenants, The Shade Shop and Hull & Hull Attorneys at Law, paid their rent in a timely manner. Titan Press was a little lax about its rent, while Creative Lens Photography was seriously in arrears. This posed challenges not only in terms of collections but also for the company accountants.

The landlord's A/R subledger needed to indicate how the various accounts aged, careful to show the current total amount due at the same time. Each aging category is called an "aging bucket," an unattractive but adequately descriptive term. The customer accounts are added horizontally to show what each debtor owes, which is a comment on the quality and reliability of the customer. The aging buckets are each totaled vertically to show how much is due, which is a comment on credit policy, collection procedures, or both. Balancing the aging categories vertically and the accounts horizontally will ensure an accurate A/R—even if it doesn't help the company collect the rent.

The company's A/R for its commercial rentals looked like this:

Red Flag
When posting to the general ledger, be sure that the sum of customer balances equals the subledger balance. An automated system will catch any mathematical description. A manual system may not.

What?
An *aging bucket* is the total of receivables aging in a certain category. The 30-day aging bucket is a the sum of all accounts past due by 30 days—so too with the 60-day aging bucket, the 90-day aging bucket, and so on.

Acct #	Customer	Current	30 Days	60 Days	90 Days	120 Days	Over 120 Days	Balance
150	Shade Shop	$1,000	$500	$0	$0	$0	$0	$1,500
175	Creative Lens	$1,000	$1,000	$1,000	$500	$500	$0	$4,000
200	Titan Press	$1,000	$1,000	$500	$0	$0	$0	$2,500
225	Hull & Hull	$1,000	$0	$0	$0	$0	$0	$1,000
	Total balance	$4,000	$2,500	$1,500	$500	$500	$0	$9,000
	Subledger balance	$4,000	$2,500	$1,500	$500	$500	$0	$9,000
	Difference	$0	$0	$0	$0	$0	$0	$0

The accounting function charged with managing the A/R above did a fine job footing and cross-footing the customers' accounts. Unfortunately, it wasn't very effective at collections. The company hired a collections firm, which quickly cleaned up the past due accounts. As you might imagine, Creative Lens Photography is no longer one of the company's tenants.

Journal Entry

An accurate and orderly A/R won't matter if the totals don't match those on the general ledger. Even automated systems sometimes develop kinks in the chain of data transmission, meaning care must be taken to cross-balance and verify entries in one against entries in the other. This is especially critical because the general ledger offers no details on account aging, just total amounts. Be accurate and be consistent...and make sure your system does the same thing. Match those credits and debits and make sure all totals total.

Making Entries to the Accounts Receivable

Making entries to the A/R is as easy as one, two, three:

1. Post each transaction to the customer's individual account.
2. Summarize those transactions and create an A/R subledger entry.
3. Post those entries to the A/R section of the general ledger and any additional accounts designed to offset receivables.

Automated systems often do this as part of their function, thus avoiding the error of additional or incomplete entry information. If entries are posted by hand, remember to follow each of the three steps to avoid tripping over the system or its components.

And, as entries are made, note that different types of entries require some different considerations.

Recording Sales

Customer sales usually originate from the sales journal. However, depending on the relative sophistication of the accounting system, the information may not come to A/R until the order entry system has processed the order and issued the invoice.

Regardless of the method, invoice records are often the best way to document sales, if the invoices have been designed to include the necessary information: date of transaction, customer name and account number, item purchased, amount, and payment terms.

Credit sales are summarized to the appropriate sales accounts. Aggregate sales for the designated period are then entered into the customer transaction subledger account. Finally, the subledger and sales accounts are posted in batch form to the appropriate general ledger account. And the original invoices? Those are filed for future use as necessary.

Recording Payments

When it comes to recording payments, usually made by check, it's important that all amounts match: the subledger listing, any receipt given to the customer, and the bank deposit. Sometimes customers help by sending along the invoice stub that's been issued, making matching to the subledger easier. But often they don't, which means careful matching is important.

Control totals often are preferable in recording payments; the most important control total is the bank deposit form. Since that signals the transfer of cash outside the company—to the bank—the total must be matched by the corresponding subledger amounts. And when recording a payment, list the total amount of cash at the same time. This becomes another control total to help keep the system balanced.

Journal Entry

If the financial institution returns a check for insufficient funds after the amount has been entered into the general ledger, the accountant makes a manual entry to debit that amount in the customer's account (to reinstate the proper balance) and to credit the cash account. Most automated systems allow this. Remember: Keeping the books balanced is vital to the success of the system.

Recording Credit Memos

Recording credit memos is a lot like recording payments. They reduce the customer's balance in the subledger and general ledger summary entry. The entry credits A/R and debits the original sales account. In addition, the origin of the debit will help determine where the proper entry will be. For example, memos from returned merchandise debit sales and sales returns.

Since credit memos operate much the same as cash, it's important to exercise tight control over their distribution and use. Require the appropriate paperwork and authorization before credit memos can be entered into the system. Consider batching credit memos separately when entering them into the A/R system. Proper controls dictate that credits need to be approved before they can be issued. Make credit memos work within the system, but make those who process credit memos work through the system checkpoints before giving the credit.

Recording Returned Merchandise

In most cases, merchandise returns involve four steps. First, the merchandise is checked against the invoice, inspected, and marked to be put back on the shelves. Second, the amount to be credited is verified. Third, credit is given to the customer returning the merchandise. Fourth, the amount of the credit is posted to the customer's account. Smaller companies have the advantage here. The larger the firm, the more challenging it is to keep track of every returned box, bag, and barrel.

Think about the last time you returned merchandise that you'd bought on your store credit card. How did that transaction go through the system?

You probably watched as the sales clerk took your sales receipt, inspected the merchandise, verified the amount, then made a note on the receipt and set it aside. But you didn't see the following steps in the accounting process, as the accountant:

➤ Reduced the balance in the A/R subledger with a credit

➤ Reduced the general ledger accounts receivable with a credit and sales returns and allowances account with a debit

➤ Increased the inventory account with a debit

All that work just to keep you a happy customer!

Handling Bad-Debt Write-Offs

No matter how well companies plan, how vigilant they are in verifying credit, and how efficient they are in collecting debts, it's inevitable some companies will have to write off an occasional bad debt. Some old accounts are worth pursuing, while others are never going to pay. Accounts that are past 120 days may need to be turned over to a collection agency. But if the customer has skipped town or gone out of business, it may be necessary to bite the bullet and write off the debt. A bad debt flows through the receivable system like a credit memo. In the end, you debit the bad debt expenses account and get on with life.

What?
Bad debts can result from many things, but they all boil down to one simple definition from an accounting point of view: bad debts are uncollectible amounts. In the end they are written off the books to keep the accounts in balance.

Smart companies and some that are regulated know they will have a certain percentage of bad debts and they reserve funds against the inevitable occurrence. Depending on the nature of the business, it may be worth doing just that, by estimating the projected level of bad debt and establishing a separate account of funds to offset those losses.

In the early stages, the bad debt accrual does not appear on the books, since we don't know which accounts will go bad. To accommodate this need, some companies, especially those that are audited, set up accounts based on aging categories or on a certain rate multiplied by sales. To set up such an account in the amount of $5,000, for example, the accountant debits Bad Debt Expense for $5,000, credits Reserve for Bad Debt Expense for $5,000, and notes this transaction as "Records accrual for bad debts."

When a receivable—such as back rent from Creative Lens Photography in the example used earlier—fails to materialize, you reduce your reserve for bad debts and A/R, thus lowering both accounts. The transaction looks like this:

➤ Debit reserve for bad debts $4,000

➤ Credit accounts receivable $4,000

➤ Note "Write-off of Creative Lens back rent"

The landlord company had to make sure its subledger also reflected the write-off by removing the balance owed by Creative Lens from the subledger file. The process flowed up to and through the general ledger just like any other A/R transaction. Both the G/L and the A/R remained in balance throughout the entire procedure—exactly as it should be.

Reinstating Write-Offs

If a miracle happened and Creative Lens suddenly made good on its back rent to the landlord company, the accounting department should follow this procedure:

Reverse the write-off entry to reinstate the receivable:

➤ Debit accounts receivable $4,000

➤ Credit reserve for bad debts $4,000

➤ Note "Reinstate Creative Lens amount written off (date)"

Reverse the bad debt expense:

➤ Debit reserve for bad debts $4,000

➤ Credit bad debt expense $4,000

➤ Note "Reverse bad debt account on Creative Lens bad debt receivable (date)"

Record the payment receipt:

➤ Debit cash $4,000

➤ Accounts receivable $4,000

➤ Note "Record payment from Creative Lens"

Tracking Receivables

The A/R system can be used to generate a lot of reports. All have value, some more than others, but all take time and resources to complete. The following reports help maximize the company's financial potential:

➤ *Receivables turnover.* The faster receivables turn over and amounts owed are converted into cash, the better. A/R turnover rate is calculated by dividing net credit sales by the average of accounts receivables. If the turnover rates of both accounts receivable and accounts payable match, so much the better. If the A/R turnover rate exceeds that of payables, fantastic! That means money is coming in faster than it's going out. And it doesn't get any better than that.

➤ *Liquidity.* The relative liquidity of an A/R portfolio determines the quality of that portfolio as collateral for loans. The higher the liquidity, the greater the value of that portfolio. Measure liquidity by the number of sales days tied up in A/R:

days of sales in A/R = 365 / A/R turnover rate

(The A/R turnover rate is the net credit sales divided by the average of accounts receivable, as calculated above.)

This can also be calculated as follows:

$$\frac{\text{Ending A/R}}{\text{Credit Sales}} \times 365$$

➤ *Receivables aging.* This sort of report has two basic purposes. First, it allows managers to understand how old the receivables are; the older a receivable, the less likely it will be collected. Second, the report helps accountants calculate the amount of money to allow for uncollectible accounts.

➤ *Customer balance tracking.* In preserving the asset value of the A/R, keep a close eye on customer-related accounts. Pay special attention to accounts that have aged excessively, accounts for which the balance exceeds the credit limit, accounts with the longest-running balance, and accounts with the highest balance.

The three indicators based on balance—balance in excess of the credit limit, longest-running balance, and highest balance—represent elective risk based on sales decisions the company has made regarding specific customers. If the risk grows too great, a change in policy and procedure may be in order. The credit manager may be too lax in his or her standards. (It may be good to stretch a little to meet new account needs, but too much stretch and the relationship will break.) The people responsible for collections may need to be more diligent in their efforts. Regular tracking in these four areas will help better control extremes in A/R.

Journal Entry

Receivables tracking reports provide a system to determine which customers need to be reminded to pay, a process called *dunning*. It's tough to nag customers for payment, but it may be necessary. The first approach is generally by letters—polite at first, then threatening if polite doesn't work. These efforts are usually automated. The letters may be supplemented by phone calls or visits. In the worst cases, plan on collections efforts and/or legal action. Then take a look at the reserve for bad debts.

Maximizing Your Collections Efforts

The first thing to realize is probably the most important rule of bad debt collection: the collection effort begins before the sale is made.

If you wait until a debt goes bad and the debtor goes south, the likelihood of collection is low. But if the sales person takes time to qualify the account, check bank references, and otherwise ensure this person or firm is a quality company with a good record, then fear of bad debt down the road is greatly reduced.

Managers can help the effort by making sure that the sales person is financially responsible for that account, by limiting his or her ability to earn commission on any sale that goes bad. That type of incentive will make all the difference in the world.

The accounting function can help, too, by sending timely accurate statements to customers to remind them of the debt they owe the company. The old phrase, "Out of sight, out of mind," was never truer than when it comes to debts.

Here are some basic guidelines your collection staff should follow:

Red Flag
For companies that simply must launch a collections action, a collections professional is always the preferred route. Whether it's a staff person specially trained at collecting past due amounts or a firm hired for this specific purpose, the money recovered should be worth the time and effort they spend. But make sure not to leave a bad impression with customers you may eventually want back.

➤ *Reach an agreement with the debtor on the amount owed.* One of the key things the collections person can do is help the debtor overcome his or her internal resistance. With the exception of a disputed amount, most debtors know they must pay and, more often than not, most want to pay. Getting them to verbally acknowledge their debt—recording what they said and when—may put the company ahead of another of that customer's creditors. The more a company can work with a debtor, the more likely it is that the company will see its money.

➤ *Help the debtor solve problems associated with the delinquency.* If the company alters its expectations a little, a debtor inconvenienced by a minor setback in personal fortunes may be able to pay more quickly and easily. Sometimes a debtor can feel overwhelmed, like it's impossible to pay off the debts. Companies that work with the debtor help make the dunning effort a service of sorts that may help resolve matters for the company and the debtor.

➤ *Elicit a promise to pay by a certain date.* Debtors, like everyone everywhere, work better with a deadline. If it's a due date mutually agreed to by the company and the debtor, the joint ownership often will elicit greater allegiance toward the company than it will for others waiting for payment. If the debtor's resources are limited, this becomes a very important strategy.

➤ *Follow up when payments aren't made.* All of this will be for naught if there's no follow-up. No matter how cooperative the company may be, the debtor must understand that the bottom line is to recover the debt. Despite preliminary work, a few reminder calls may be necessary. They can be very effective.

➤ *At all times, maintain a professional, unemotional demeanor.* If the collection efforts turn personal, your collector loses his or her professional leverage, destroys any spirit of cooperation, and may frighten the debtor away. Keep it professional, have a plan, and know the options.

And, if all else fails, sue the debtor for the amount owed. Good attorneys will counsel against spending more on legal fees than the company stands to collect. But even a small claims action will signal to the marketplace that the company means business.

However, winning a judgment is one thing. Collecting from a debtor who has no money… well, you've heard the story about getting blood from a stone? Learn from that.

The Least You Need to Know

➤ Accounts receivable is money owed the company by customers and other sources.

➤ Accounts receivable systems, automated or manual, must support the general ledger.

➤ Accounts receivable entries must be made in a consistent fashion.

➤ Bad debts should be reserved for in the accounting practices.

➤ Track your receivable results to better manage the accounts.

➤ Collection efforts must begin before the sale is made.

Chapter 8

Accounts Payable

In This Chapter

➤ Defining accounts payable

➤ Setting up the accounts payable

➤ Making entries and tracking payables

➤ Managing disbursements, trade discounts, and funds outflow

Just as there are accounts receivable (A/R), or money that is owed to you, there are accounts payable (A/P), or money that you owe to others. A/P isn't nearly as much fun as the former, but it's a part of business life. Taking care of the A/P is important, because your company's credit rating and reliability as a business could be at stake. As a manager, you will need to understand how this all comes into play.

Let's start with a definition. Similar in structure but opposite in purpose to accounts receivable, accounts payable is a list of monies owed by the company to creditors, usually from the purchase of merchandise, materials, supplies, equipment, or services.

Structured similarly to A/R, A/P is another subledger that feeds the general ledger with summaries of more detailed information. Information about disbursements flows through the A/P system from sources both within and outside the company and travels up to the general ledger to become part of your company's overall financial picture.

> ### Journal Entry
>
> A well-designed and well-managed accounts payable system will reliably track the amount owed each vendor and when to pay based on agreements with that vendor. The system keeps a running tally of amounts paid so it can be checked against budget. It also is the system that provides the necessary information for generating your company's 1099 statements (for reporting amounts paid to suppliers).

Going Manual

Despite the advantages of automation, there's nothing wrong with a manual A/P system. As long as the system performs the necessary tasks, such as assigning the right amount to the right account, tracking payments, and performing other basic accounting tasks, a manual system can be as effective as an automated one. But no matter how basic, each system must contain two primary components:

➤ Vendor ledgers

➤ A/P subledger summary

Each A/P system must contain a comprehensive set of vendor ledgers—whether they are recorded on index cards, in a ledger book, or on the back of candy wrappers stuffed in used envelopes—that track purchases and other financial obligations. Each record must be kept up to date with current purchases and total amounts, and they must all be sorted or categorized for easy access. After that, the format is up to your company's accounting department.

> ### Shortcut
> A/P reviews are usually done once or twice monthly, although they can be done more frequently for special items such as postage, petty cash, or freight deliveries. The important thing, from a cash management standpoint, is to pay bills exactly on time and not early, to better maximize cash flow.

No matter how subledger files are arranged, the A/P subledger summary must neatly organize, categorize, and summarize all accounts for posting to the A/P line of the general ledger. The most common method in manual systems is a column-ruled sheet of paper that lists the following information for summarization:

➤ *Date.* When the purchase was made or the debt incurred.

➤ *Vendor.* To whom the money is owed.

➤ *Purchase description.* What was purchased or how the debt was incurred.

➤ *Amount.* How much money is owed.

➤ *Expense or assets accounts.* The general ledger accounts to which the purchase or debt is posted.

> ➤ *Cash.* Whether or not this was a cash transaction.

> ➤ *Accounts payable.* Whether or not this was a credit transaction to be posted to this account.

In addition to serving as a transaction summary, this A/P subledger summary page also is a source document for posting to the general ledger, which is generally done monthly.

Embracing Automation

Many companies have added automated A/P files to their general ledger systems for all the reasons mentioned in earlier chapters. Most systems automatically track and report payables and provide summaries of amounts owed each vendor.

All in all, life becomes much easier with an automated system—providing the accounting department:

> ➤ Sets up vendor files properly.

> ➤ Sets up the A/P subledger to default to the general ledger.

> ➤ Establishes default files that categorize and track specific types of amounts owed and payments due.

The automated system includes the same types of information listed in the manual file, such as date of transaction, name of vendor, description of purchase, amount owed, and terms of payment. Using that data, the automated system will send the necessary information to the A/P subledger, which then batches all payables by entry date and balances the batch to the general ledger account.

Shortcut
Most accounts payable systems link with inventory control. That way, when a shipment of materials arrives and is logged in, the warehouse entry appears immediately on the A/P subledger and general ledger from which payment to that particular vendor is to be made. Again, double entries—and the occasional resulting errors—are avoided.

Accruable Accounts Payable

If your company operates strictly on a cash basis, you likely have no reason to even think about an accounts payable system. Put this book down and go back to petting the cat, talking on the phone, or watching TV.

But if your company operates like most businesses—with billable invoices, lines of credit, and net due plus 30 days—it probably could benefit from an accruable A/P system. Simply put, accruals are adjustment entries posted to the trial balance by the accounting department to provide for expenses that have not been invoiced to the company in the current period. The purpose, of course, is to better match income and expense. For many businesses, this is a good accounting practice and it makes good sense.

Entries to Your Accounts Payable

Making entries to the A/P system is as easy as one, two, three:

1. Post purchases or other transactions to the appropriate vendor account.
2. Post vendor purchases to the A/P subledger.
3. Post summary of A/P in the general ledger and any other offsetting accounts.

Shortcut
Automated accounts payable systems generally post to the vendor account, summarize those accounts, and post to the general ledger at the same time. Accountants working with manual systems will have to remember to complete all three steps with each and every entry.

Red Flag
Accounts payable may be affected by adjustments—decreased by vendor credits, for example, or increased by interest charges on delinquent accounts. The danger isn't great from inappropriate crediting, but be cautious nonetheless. These adjustments should be treated with as much care as adjustments to accounts receivable. Supporting documentation for any vendor adjustment should be required.

As part of the process, the A/P will be recording purchases. Most of that information comes from the vendor invoices, including vendor name, amount, and payment terms. If the invoice doesn't arrive before close of business at the end of the month, the amount is accrued through adjusting entries to the current period. (That's where accrual accounting comes in.) The transaction process, whether automated or manual, follows the three steps outlined earlier.

When companies are recording payments, it might make the most sense to run A/P reviews more frequently than once or twice monthly, to keep better control of invoice due dates and to pay those invoices when they're due and not before. The smaller the business, however, the more difficult this may be. At the very least, vendors should be paid on a timely basis and as regularly as possible.

No matter what the payment plan, the steps to follow usually will be the same from an accounting standpoint:

➤ Identify the invoices needing payment.
➤ Print the checks.
➤ Assemble the checks and invoices for review and signing.
➤ Sign and mail the checks.
➤ File supporting invoices and documentation in the appropriate batch.
➤ Post the amount paid to individual vendor accounts.
➤ Post the transaction to the A/P subledger.
➤ Summarize the subledger to the general ledger.

When all of that is done, match the total amount of the checks against at least one control total to make sure everything balances. Those control totals may include the total amount paid for all checks, the amount subtracted from the checking account, and the total from the A/P subledger summary posted to the general ledger. If these amounts all balance, then the process has been successfully completed.

At some point your company will also likely find itself having to record vendor credits and adjustments. That system works the same in your A/P system as it does in accounts receivable (see Chapter 6). Credits may occur for such things as returned merchandise, disputed accounts, and error correction.

Keeping Payables on Track

One of the keys to effective A/P management is keeping track of disbursements to make sure they are in line with the company's payment policy. Consider it the flip side of collections and remember that better tracking of payables results in better management of cash flow and reserves, even if only on a minor basis.

Earlier we suggested timely and regular payments. Let's amend that recommendation slightly to say that payables should turn over as quickly as they need to in terms of the vendor agreement, company policy, or both. If cash is released too quickly, the company may not be taking full advantage of the trade credits offered by vendors. Also, that money, if invested, could be earning interest a little longer.

Need a benchmark? Your accounting department may want to try and match payables turnover with receivables turnover whenever possible. If the average collection time on receivables is 30 days (you wish!), then the average payables turnover time also should be 30 days. Under that scenario, the firm is using its suppliers to underwrite inventory. That means it can keep less cash on reserve, freeing it up for other, more important things.

Carry That Weight

Many companies have their own policy about invoice aging, and payment terms make little difference. That's called "weighted average invoice aging," and the system dictates how old the invoice must be before it will be paid. In some industries, that time is regulated, or at least there are certain accepted standards. In others, it's whatever you can get away with.

That means there's a need to apply this policy as consistently as possible. There always are exceptions and your company may want to make some, especially if prompt payment will mean a discount on the bill. But otherwise stick to a formula, which probably looks something like this:

> weighted average age = weighted average percent × number of days in each aging bucket

Consider the fictional weighted A/P example in the following table.

Invoice Age	Amount Owed	Weight Percent	Weight Days
Current	$13,656	8%	0 days
30 days	$29,774	22%	7 days
60 days	$66,066	41%	20 days
90 days	$41,123	25%	15 days
120 days	$164	4%	3 days
A/P total	$150,783	100%	45 days

In this example, the company averages 45 days in its payments, which is good by the standards accepted in its particular industry.

Managing Disbursement: Where the Accounts Payable System Earns Its Keep

The purpose of A/P is to keep track of your company's payables in an orderly fashion. But the advantage is that it enables a company to manage cash disbursement, allowing better control of cash flow and maximizing the value of funds to the organization.

As a rule of thumb, vendors meeting a company's most critical needs—whether it's raw materials or the retail items that are most popular or allow the highest markup—are paid first. Others follow as funds become available.

Red Flag

Vendors unhappy with your company's payment policies won't be vendors very long. Give preferred suppliers priority status and reward them with more prompt payment. They will likely return the favor with better service and more understanding if your company really gets into a bind.

Sometimes cash flow is controlled out of necessity. There may be a snag in production or a liquidity problem that will require withholding or reducing some payments until the crisis is over. If that happens, the situation should be explained calmly and honestly to vendors. Chances are they've all been there and understand.

They will most probably want an estimated payment date. That's where the A/P system comes in handy.

A good A/P system can be used to forecast a payment schedule based on cash availability, anticipated income, and past policy practices. Then line up vendors in payment order, according to preference. Some will grumble, but the smart ones know they have little choice. If they don't play along, it will take that much longer to be paid.

Trade Discounts Can Add Up!

One of the untapped income sources for many companies is the trade discount offered for prompt payments. Many suppliers offer anywhere from a one percent to three percent discount if the invoice is paid within 10 days, as opposed the usual net 30 days and beyond. Use the following equation to predict your trade discount:

discount income = discount percent / (due date – discount date) × 360

Let's assume our example company from earlier in the chapter receives a two percent discount on payments made within 10 days, rather than by the 45-day average established through weighted average invoice aging. That discount equation would be as follows:

2% / (45 – 10) × 360 = 20.5%

Unless the company's cost of funds or interest earnings match or exceed 20.5 percent, the company gains more financial value if it pays within the trade discount period.

> ### Journal Entry
>
> Many companies curry favor with suppliers by paying either prior to the due date or as an exception to their own weighted average. A company that does this should make sure the vendors know the company is making a policy exception and, if appropriate, why it's doing so. If the company chooses to reward vendors with cash for some reason, the vendors should know why.

Other Opportunities Courtesy of Accounts Payable

As you've seen, the A/P system is more than just accurate accounting. It's also a cash management tool that helps the company manage cash flow better and protect funds for a longer time. There are two other techniques to try with this system:

➤ Playing the floats

➤ Disbursement options

Also known as predicting cash outflow, the technique of playing the floats allows companies to predict the time it takes vendors to receive and process payments as a way to capitalize on company cash. As long as the company operates ethically, it won't break any laws or get into any financial hot water.

Most businesses have three float options to consider: the mail float (between the time the accounting department posts payment and the time the vendor receives it), the vendor's internal processing float, and the bank system float.

What?
Have you ever been in a situation when the rent was due but your bank account was just a little low, so you sent out a check to pay your rent, figuring that you could get to the bank and deposit your paycheck a day or two later, before the bank processed the check? If so, then you were *playing the float*. What you might have done out of desperation, businesses do as a strategy for managing cash flow.

Red Flag
Playing the float can maximize cash disbursement, but those making that decision must be aware of possible changes that can affect that float, including a change in financial institutions or electronic payment patterns. The float could disappear overnight and your company may not realize it until it's too late.

The mail float is no longer as important as it once was, now that the U.S. Postal System has become more efficient in an attempt to become more competitive. The vendor's internal float, unless your company knows that particular vendor *very* well, is probably impossible to predict.

That leaves the banking system float. By having the accounting department track check-release dates against the time they clear the bank, your company may be able to predict with some accuracy the number of extra days at its disposal. Compute the weighted average clearing time, the book balance (what shows in your records), and the actual bank balance. If your company's payment capacity is sufficient, it's found the right float.

It's a risky strategy at best. When it doesn't work, the consequences can be serious. Your accountant should be an expert in cash management and be committed to making the float work.

If your company's greatest concern is excess funds, not excess time, the A/P system can signal the availability of excess and investable funds that won't hurt cash flow or threaten financial security. These are called disbursement options and can be managed in three ways: presentment reporting, balance reporting, and sweep accounts. We'll describe them here, although you don't need to understand them completely. But you certainly should better appreciate what your accounting department does!

Presentment reporting refers to the amount of checks presented to the bank for payment each day, an amount impossible to predict due the various floats applied by each individual vendor. Your firm establishes a separate disbursement account at the bank for the payment of those checks. The bank then reports to your company before noon the number of checks and amounts presented for payment. Funds are then applied to that account to satisfy those checks. No extra funds are required on deposit for that day, allowing more for investment.

Balance reporting simply refers to checking company accounts via direct online access to the bank's records using a personal computer. Similar in technique to presentment accounts, automated balance reporting allows direct access to information and gives your accountant the ability to deposit just as much money into the payment account as necessary and no more.

Sweep accounts are perhaps the simplest to understand and yet the most profitable of the three techniques. The bank simply reviews all active company accounts at the end of each business day and sweeps excess funds not used to satisfy payment needs into interest-bearing accounts in an overnight deposit. The next day those funds can be redeposited to satisfy more payments, if need be, or additional funds can be deposited. That night, the bank again sweeps the account and the interest grows.

The key point for you to remember is that A/P can be a key financial management tool for your company. Understanding how that works and why will help you contribute more effectively to your company's overall financial growth and prosperity.

The Least You Need to Know

➤ Accounts payable are the monies your company owes.

➤ Automated A/P systems link to other parts of the accounting system, reducing entry errors that might occur in a manual system.

➤ A/P files must organize and categorize all pertinent information.

➤ A/P transactions first post to the vendor account, then summarize vendor data and post to the general ledger.

➤ A/P turnovers must match accounts receivables turnover whenever possible to preserve cash flow.

➤ A/P's real value is in managing cash disbursements.

➤ Trade discounts should be used whenever possible. Use float or disbursement options to manage cash flow.

Chapter 9

Watching Your Cash Flow

In This Chapter

➤ Understanding cash flow

➤ Avoiding cash crunches

➤ Looking for ways to save

➤ Knowing the maxims of modern business—cash flow division

➤ Avoiding bankruptcy

➤ Respecting special creditors

Managing the finances of a business is not as easy as simply making sure your department or company always has more money than it spends. As you've seen in earlier chapters, business assets—of which cash is just one small part—are as prone to change as any other aspect of business. Planning for all business contingencies is part of the management equation. It's critical to your role as a nonfinancial manager and the success of your department.

As long as there are businesses, cash availability will continue to be a problem for all of the people some of the time and some of the people all of the time. (Although the latter group does not stay in business very long.)

At one point product sales may be brisk and revenues over cost of goods sizable. There is no problem there. Then suddenly demand will pick up and costs will escalate—a by-product of needing more of everything to increase production and keep up with increased demand. Just about that time, a major creditor will run into a snag and will have to slow up payments.

Suddenly the company is caught in a cash crunch—more money is going out than is coming in when it's needed. Then the company doesn't have the capital it needs to help meet customer demand. Despite having a highly profitable profile on paper, the company isn't receiving funds in the timely manner that it needs to pay its bills. Think of it like this: You just ordered a new car because you won $25,000 in the lottery. The dealer wants the money, but the lottery officials just told you that they can't send the check for three months. Uh-oh.

Cash flow problems happen to all of us from time to time. If you plan sufficiently, you may avoid many of those rapids, but not all. This chapter focuses on ways to cope with the whitewater that lays ahead.

What Is Cash Flow?

First and foremost, cash flow is not the profit you make from sales or the difference between expenses and revenue. Cash flow is the flow of money in and out of a business. That's all.

Cash is accounted for as an asset, and there are a lot more challenges related to cash flow than accounting provides. Fortunately, there are also solutions, or at least strategies, to maximize the inflow and minimize the outflow.

Maxim 1

Keep in mind Maxim 1 of modern business:

> *Everything a business does takes longer and costs more than managers could possibly anticipate even in their most liberal scenario. Adjust your thinking accordingly.*

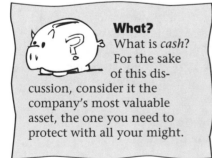

What?
What is *cash*? For the sake of this discussion, consider it the company's most valuable asset, the one you need to protect with all your might.

That's good advice for any department head, no matter what the level of financial involvement. R & D managers might find need for additional research into other avenues affecting market or product, making additional expenditures necessary. Sales managers might suddenly be directed to fire several staff, incurring the cost of training and reduced productivity as part of these unanticipated changes. The product developer may find a need for more complex and expensive equipment, may see a sudden increase in the cost of raw materials, or may suddenly face new legislative restrictions on production.

If either of these individuals or companies haven't made plans to protect their enterprises and reserve against such risks, then the demand for their product won't really matter, because they won't have the resources to meet that demand.

Beware the Cash Crunch!

Businesses, especially new companies or old companies making forays into new enterprises, run the risk of sinking funds into the wrong end of the operation and then not having enough cash when it's desperately needed. Adequately reserving for growth, especially during the early days of the business, is critical. It also helps to recognize the areas where cash can disappear without a trace.

No matter how prepared the business may think it is, unless it is operating in an area in which it has had years of experience—in terms of both the product and the market—the chances of anticipating the majority of risks that could come its way are remote. If managers hope for the best but reserve for the worst, they will find themselves in a better position when those cash-draining contingencies do arrive.

The size, nature, and complexity of a business may indicate up to one, two, or three years of losses before the business starts turning a profit in new ventures. Managers won't know for sure until they have some operations time behind them and have begun retooling based on what the market is really like, rather than on what they think it's like. Once managers have an understanding of what customers think of their products and services, they can make more realistic predictions about expenses, income, and profitability to minimize the chances of getting into a cash crunch.

If the company pays cash for its inventory, it won't be able to restock key products when it comes time. Too many businesses have backed themselves into this corner, suddenly finding themselves with all the wrong merchandise and empty spots on their shelves where their biggest sellers once were because they have run out of cash to pay for the restocking. The next thing to go will be customers and, eventually the business.

Most suppliers understand that no company can sell from an empty store. Therefore, most suppliers usually work out financing arrangements that take into account when the company gets paid by its own customers. In other words, most suppliers have come to understand that when their customers are paid, they'll be paid

Red Flag
No company can anticipate all contingencies with 100 percent accuracy. This is especially true for operations in start-up mode.

Shortcut
When planning cash flow needs for a new business, managers should take their best guess and then double it. Then they should plan to spend three times as long moving into a profitable mode. That way they're less likely to be disappointed. The point: It's sad but true that being a pessimist is probably more prudent than being an optimist when predicting costs and length of time to profitability.

Shortcut
Companies should borrow or set up payment plans with suppliers to pay for all of inventory—or at least part of it—and then actually pay for the inventory using funds received from customers paying their bills (otherwise known as paid off accounts receivable).

Red Flag

Beware of rapid growth. Many companies have grown so fast that demand has out-stripped their ability to pay for increasing inventory or improved services to meet the demand. Remember that demand is not cash. A company should not borrow too much on the expectation that, when it meets demand, it can repay the loans.

shortly thereafter. Otherwise, suppliers know they'll get the unpopular merchandise back anyway when the companies close down—and that's the last thing suppliers want.

Success can lead to failure if you can't master cash flow dynamics. If a company can't keep up with the demand of its customers, it may need to scale down its expectations temporarily and hope to make the most of its growth opportunities later. If a company can't keep up with payments to its suppliers, it should meet and negotiate, and maybe reduce its purchases in the future. Then it should establish better means of monitoring its cash flow and find ways to operate more efficiently.

Time to Cut Costs

If cash flow does become an issue, it's obvious that the company will have to change the way it's doing business if it wants to survive. Does that executive plant service still come in once a week to water the ficus and all the other office flora? As a manager, you may have to cancel the service, buy a $2.98 watering can, and start doing it yourself—or maybe just get rid of the plants altogether.

That may seem a little obvious, but it's amazing how many businesses fall into comfortable patterns during good times and don't see them as unnecessary frills when cash becomes tight.

Looking for ways to decrease operational costs runs hand-in-hand with looking for new and better ways to manage operations. Can the sales team cut down on the number of personal calls by making regular telephone contact instead? In addition to saving sales call time and money spent on automobile wear and tear, the new approach might give a definite market advantage by allowing staff to make more frequent contact. Done correctly, this can translate into better service at a lower cost. Then everyone benefits.

Preserving cash flow is one thing and improving market strategies is another. But sometimes the two can work hand-in-hand for even greater benefit. All it requires is a little better management thinking and a clear understanding of the challenges you face.

Inventory can be a cash eater if it isn't financed. The company should pay the interest required to finance the inventory and keep its cash at hand. The company may need it. To make this clearer: In buying a car, you might have the funds to pay for it in cash, but by financing it, you keep your funds available in case you need them for some situation where it's more difficult to borrow money than to use your cash. Of course, the company should also better control inventory quantities, to minimize its cash investment.

More Ideas for Maximizing Cash Flow

Here are some other ideas for maximizing cash flow:

➤ Buy from firms offering longer payment or consignment terms to maximize cash flow. That may mean changing suppliers. However, current suppliers, faced with this possibility, will often quickly move to accommodate a company's needs for longer-term payment schedules.

➤ Keep a tight control on inventory and turn it over as quickly as possible. The less cash the company has tied up in inventory, the more cash it will have to use for other needs. Deeper discounts on larger purchases from suppliers are nice, but if all that inventory sits on the shelf for a long time, it's not that nice. Unless the company is large enough and its cash flow is secure, it may be better off paying a little more, making a little less and having more cash at its disposal. And if it has old, slow-moving or obsolete inventory, the company should get rid of its as soon as possible before it becomes a serious drain on resources or a burden on the books.

➤ Be vigilant in the pursuit of receivables. Your company should not get caught up in some other company's cash flow scheme while they try to put off payment of amounts owed to your company. The longer the company carries a receivable (an unpaid invoice to one of its customers), the less cash it has. Pursue overdue accounts and offer incentives for payment. Bill on a timely basis. A company that invests in collecting receivables in a timely manner can significantly increase its cash flow.

➤ Be frugal whenever possible and avoid unnecessary indulgences that don't contribute substantively to the bottom line. Legal firms believe oak-paneled offices are necessary to communicate strength, success, and profitability to prospective clients. Maybe they are. Traveling sales people believe lavish expense accounts and expensive

Red Flag

If one of your accounts receivable is having progressively greater difficulty making its payments, look for signs that it may be going bankrupt. If you can't get your money before the account declares bankruptcy, you may never get the total amount owed. Don't pressure all your receivables mercilessly, but avoid being too nice. You may be the last in line to get paid—and stranded when the money runs out.

Red Flag

Two of the biggest causes of cash flow problems for new businesses are failing to ensure adequate capital (to provide reserve funds), and being unable to obtain sufficient credit. Most enterprises suffer several years of slow growth. If a company isn't prepared, that economic desert will dry out the company's deposits and put it on financial skids.

cars give them an aura of success that will translate into greater sales. Maybe they do. But cast a cold, calculating eye on all expenses prior to approval to see if the logic holds. If it doesn't, cut back and increase cash availability. That's sometimes the greatest of all keys to success.

Maxims 2 and 3

Remember Maxim 1 (*Everything takes longer and costs more than managers could possibly anticipate, so adjust your thinking accordingly*)? No matter what the company's strategy to improve its cash position might be, there's one overriding facet that controls all. It's Maxim 2 of modern business:

> *The company must keep its cash flow adequate at all times. The moment managers forget that, financial collapse becomes a possibility.*

This should seem a self-evident law of business, but a lot of business people—in love with their ideas and the opportunities those ideas may open up—set a budget and then charge away, rarely bothering to check to see how the cash drain is running and, worse still, never stopping to retool or rethink the changes that might be necessary. The world of business is a constantly changing scenario. If we're not aware of the way those changes affect our businesses and our cash flows, then we shouldn't be in business.

Cost-cutting scenarios abound, but one account must remain sacred and go untouched as you look for ways to sell the company car and lease back the office equipment. Maxim 3 reads:

> *Payroll is the company's top financial priority. Stop paying the staff, and they won't come back.*

Employee salaries and benefits are probably among your company's and department's top three most expensive cost centers, if not the most expensive one. The ability to skip or even delay a paycheck with the promise of payback in the future seems like it would be the quickest and easiest way out of a cash crunch. Plus, employees are here every day; they can see the challenges the company faces and they're almost family. Surely this is a reasonable solution.

No! Don't take your employees for granted. Because they have other customers, suppliers will forgive and forget, provided the company can crest its financial hurdle and remain a customer. In contrast, your employees are depending on you as the major or sole source of income. The secret to success in managing cash flow in times of crisis is knowing where you can and can't cut. Salaries and benefits is one spot a company had best leave alone.

Journal Entry

Employees can be a company's greatest cost-cutting allies, but don't abuse their loyalty and dedication. Remember: They have their own life scenarios that require positive cash flows—things like mortgages, orthodontia, and college educations. If the company uses their salaries to manage its cash flow, they will never forget. The company will suffer a loss in morale, which could hurt productivity and profitability. Also, the best employees will likely leave to find more reliable wages with a more loyal company.

When Times Get Really Tough

The day may come when cash flow becomes an issue that precipitates a business filing for bankruptcy. Bad things do happen to good business people, including honest and even successful companies and departments that have spun momentarily out of orbit. It could happen to your company, too.

But before managers climb out on the window ledge, turn themselves over to the authorities, or book a flight to Rio de Janeiro, they should ask themselves the following five questions:

1. Have I done my best in negotiating with creditors and suppliers to become partners in helping me out of this cash crisis? Do they understand the severity of my situation? Have I been honest with them in terms of cash availability and payment terms?

2. Have I done my best to collect all current and past due accounts receivable? Have I been honest with them and offered incentives for prompt payments?

3. Have I considered alternative finances, including short-term bank loans, extended credit, and other revenue sources to free up funds?

4. Have I cut loose from non-crucial creditors, paying them just enough to remain legally viable?

5. Have I reduced all unprofitable sides or lines of my business that may have been draining cash and other resources from the organization?

Once the managers have answered these questions, they should be able to come back in from the ledge, forget about calling the cops, and cancel their travel plans. The situation probably seems a little less desperate now. However, if things still seem hopeless, it's probably a good idea to consult with an attorney to discuss bankruptcy. (We'll return to this dismal option shortly.)

Maxim 4

Chances are a company probably will find a few more alternatives it can and should exercise. There's room in almost every area to tighten the belt even more. Every area, that is, except one. And that's Maxim 4:

> *Like employees, Uncle Sam is one creditor a company can't afford to duck. Unlike employees, Uncle Sam won't go away if the company tries to avoid paying its taxes anyway.*

The U.S. government, like all governments, believes a strong tax base makes for a strong country. To that end, it tends to think all payroll and sales tax moneys belong to it, even before those taxes have been computed and collected. In Uncle Sam's eyes, a company is simply holding those moneys in trust until such time as payment is due.

What does that mean? It means that not paying payroll and sales taxes is much different than not paying a supplier's bill. The money belongs to the government; a company cannot use that money for its own purposes. In legal terms, the company is acting in a fiduciary capacity. If the company doesn't send the money to the government on time, the company risks incurring financial penalties and, in extreme cases, suffering punitive damages and having liens attached to its property and its profits. In some cases, management could be held personally liable.

The bottom line: Uncle Sam should be considered one of the company's top creditors and treated with the utmost deference. It's not worth the risk to do otherwise.

Journal Entry

Paying payroll taxes on employee salaries is serious business, and there is no room for negotiation with the government on this matter. However, in terms of income taxes on company earnings, the government's attitude is a little different. There's room for negotiation within reason, particularly if it involves installment payments and a regular schedule of debt clearance. You still will have to pay penalties; but the implied or explicit threat isn't quite as prevalent. The same is true of sales taxes and property taxes, in principle—although local governments may also be rigorous in expecting their money.

Maxim 5

In addition to employees and Uncle Sam, there's one other creditor that a small business owner, especially, needs to put first. That's the owner, and if you're that person, then that means look out for your own interests. And that leads to Maxim 5, one especially important for small businesses or operations you may have set up yourself on the side:

> *Satisfy first the debts you've guaranteed personally. Even if you declare bankruptcy, you will still be personally liable, and you don't want that.*

Often in business, entrepreneurs will borrow money from friends, acquaintances, and others who grant loans based on a personal guarantee. Even if entrepreneurs use the money explicitly for business, and that business falls under protection from the bankruptcy court, any such loans will remain payable in full because they are personal loans—just as if the money was borrowed to take a vacation, get a kid's teeth fixed, or send a child through school. In times of cash crunch, satisfy these personal debts first, then let the wholesale supplier, landlord, and other creditors line up and take their turns.

> ### Journal Entry
>
> If a business has been solvent and successful for a number of years and has had a good relationship with a financial institution, it may, through the good graces of those who hold the money, have options that other businesses may not have.
>
> The bank may continue providing the company with short-term loans if it sees an equitable and relatively quick solution to the cash crunch problem. If the company has been a good risk and promises to be so again in the future, the bank will want to retain this business.

Final Options

If a company has streamlined its operations, cut frills, and stretched its creditors to the nth degree, chances are (if the company hasn't failed) it's once again on solid ground. But if the company is still not solvent, there are still one or two other options managers may consider:

➤ The accounts receivable—income due the firm from outside sources—is a little like money in the bank. A company can sell its A/R to a finance company for a percentage of their face value. The finance company takes over collection and the risk of default. This cash-quick option is called "factoring."

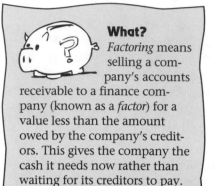

What?
Factoring means selling a company's accounts receivable to a finance company (known as a *factor*) for a value less than the amount owed by the company's creditors. This gives the company the cash it needs now rather than waiting for its creditors to pay.

➤ Consider selling the office furniture and equipment and leasing it back from the company to whom it's been sold. (That procedure is known, logically enough, as "sale and leaseback.") Companies may find they need less than they have, or that they can get by with something a little cheaper. Sound arguments can be made for leasing computer and other electronic equipment that will go out of date in years and sometimes even months. This is another cash-saving option, although it can be expensive. An analysis should be prepared to determine the advantages of leasing versus purchasing.

➤ The company can cut back on space it occupies and various services it gets from outside suppliers. Most companies compute overhead on the square-footage of office space its various departments occupy, along with equipment and services used and supplies absorbed. If, as a manager, you can reduce office space and give back those extra PCs your department isn't using, thus cutting down on service allocation by the MIS support department, you may be able to pare overhead costs, thus saving cash and reducing the drain on the expense side.

➤ Similar to lease backs, asset-backed financing is essentially a secured loan balanced against any assets the company has. Managers should make sure their recovery plan is sound, however. Lenders won't hesitate to seize those secured assets and sell them off if the company misses any payments.

When Darkness Falls

If these strategies still aren't enough, it's time for the firm to contact its lawyer because things will start to take a little uglier turn. Even though the number of bankruptcies has increased dramatically over the past decade, there still is a certain stigma attached to it that makes future dealings with creditors and lenders difficult at best.

Better to get a handle on cash flow early and work through the challenges while they still are small. The opportunities a company ends up with will far outweigh the challenges it faces during the process.

The Least You Need to Know

➤ Cash flow must be proactively managed like other aspects of a business. Managers should stay on top of the cash situation at all times.

➤ Cash must be preserved whenever possible. It's the company's most valuable asset.

➤ Payroll is one of a company's top financial priorities. Stop paying the staff, and they will go away.

➤ Accounts receivable should be managed so that your company doesn't become part of someone else's cost-saving scenario.

➤ Don't try and duck payroll taxes. Uncle Sam takes a dim view of that.

➤ Any debts personally guaranteed by owners should be paid promptly so they don't destroy owners' credit record.

Part 3
Managing with Accounting

Okay, so now you know the basics of accounting and the financial system. In other words, you understand how the numbers are recorded and how the ledgers are linked and coordinated by the general ledger. Now let's move on to what I term "the P chapters"—people, property, profits, and procedures.

No business can function without people, of course. Unfortunately, that also means that no business can function without a payroll system, benefits, taxes, and so on. As a manager, you should know the essentials about the structures and paperwork behind your employees, whether a handful or thousands. And, whether your company is large or small, you've got some property—which means you should know something about inventory control, the art and science of knowing what you've got and what it's worth.

The third P—profits—is all-important. That may not be the only reason why you're in business, but without profits you won't be in business for long. And a major part of calculating profits is determining what it costs to operate your company, so you should know about cost accounting. And, to keep costs down and profits up, you need to consider the dark side of being in business—the occasional dishonest employee. Since every business needs procedures to minimize losses, I discuss internal controls, something every manager should know about and apply.

Managing Payroll

In This Chapter

➤ Establishing a payroll system

➤ Determining the "cost" of paying employees

➤ Understanding withholding taxes

➤ Using a payroll service

➤ Tracking and costing benefits

When it comes to costing out business expenses, payroll and benefits will likely be the highest cost your company has on its books. Employees may be the engine that drives the success of the business, but that's an engine that doesn't run cheaply. Fueling that effort through salary and benefits is costly.

Maybe your payroll function is limited to signing time sheets. That doesn't exempt you from knowing more about your company's payroll system. It's an operating expense like any other—and a costly and time-consuming one at that.

So, too, is setting up that payroll system. Depending on the nature of the operation, your payroll manager may be dealing with something as simple as straight salaries and no benefits or something as complex as a series of piecework pay, overtime, bonuses, or tips that will complicate the payroll and challenge the record-keeping process. Add to that the labyrinth of payroll taxes and reporting requirements, and it's suddenly a system that will take the better part of someone's time to figure out. That's why there are payroll services that do nothing but manage that task.

Shortcut
If your company has employees working in different states, it will be affected by the different state regulations governing the earnings of those employees. By setting up an accounting procedure ahead of time to accommodate those different requirements, your payroll manager can save a lot of time on reconciliation when making quarterly and annual reports.

But whether your company uses a service or manages the function in-house, the basics are still the same. You will need to understand payroll matters if you're going to make any worthwhile contribution to the payroll accounting process.

Establishing a Payroll System

Developing and managing an effective payroll system isn't hard; it just takes time and attention to run it properly. Like much of accounting, payroll is a matter of accurate, consistent reporting and account management. Paying attention to that detail up front can prevent problems during payout. But then most employees aren't likely to let that happen: In most companies, the most important day on the calendar is payday and the most closely read document is the paycheck. So, any company's biggest challenge is proper record-keeping and reporting to the tax agencies, who tend to think of the taxes on your payroll as their money on loan to you.

Steps to Proper Payroll Management

What information should be part of your company's payroll function? Anything that impacts directly on the amount of salary or benefits awarded to employees in compensation for services must be included.

We assume, first of all, that your business office is diligent about having each new hire complete and sign the appropriate paperwork, including a W-4 form. Then, for every pay period, there are specific steps for your payroll manager to follow:

1. Gather all records of money earned and work performed. These can include time cards, piecework description sheets, sales commissions and bonuses, or straight salary records.

2. Compute all payroll changes. These may include new-hire information, salary increases, bonus awards, holiday or overtime pay adjustments, and the like. In the same vein, you'll need to process all payroll deductions, including various taxes, union dues, charitable contributions, and so forth.

3. Compute the actual payroll and draft the appropriate checks to employees and federal agencies. This may mean processing this information electronically for direct deposit.

4. Complete the payroll journal to bring the current record up to date.

5. Make the appropriate entries to the payroll section of the general ledger.

That's assuming that, as part of its payroll function, your company has also established the necessary record-keeping for the accumulation of sick time, vacation days, personal holidays, family-leave time, and anything else required by company policy or state and federal laws.

Journal Entry

If at least some employees are paid on an hourly basis, chances are your company has time sheets and maybe even a time clock and cards that employees punch as they log in and log out. Since the purpose of those cards is to record when employees arrive and when they leave, there should be rules for using the cards. In most cases, those rules are as follows: Employees must have a completed time card if they want to receive a paycheck, no employee may punch another person's time card, and supervisors must verify time card accuracy and sign those cards as proof of verification. The penalties you impose for non-compliance are up to you.

Gathering Types of Salary Information

Payroll information always should require some form of proof before checks can be administered, even if it's just a monthly sheet loosely listing work days, sick days, vacation time taken, and travel days. That's part of your company's internal audit system. But different types of compensation for different types of employees require different levels of monitoring, and thus have different mechanisms for proving hours spent on behalf of the company.

➤ *Professional employees*, it is assumed, do their jobs because they are trained to and represent a higher level of responsibility within the company. Generally speaking, a monthly time sheet outlining the various types of "days"—work days, sick days, vacation days, travel days—is usually enough. If they're not performing, their work will show it and a time sheet usually isn't enough of a measurement tool to bring them to heel.

➤ *Hourly employees*—the clock-punchers we talked about earlier—tend to work at a lower and more closely supervised level. They may not actually punch a clock, but a more detailed record of their work times and comings and goings is preferred. Pay for overtime and holidays, if offered, will be awarded based on pre-established standards as multipliers of the individual employee's salary, such as time and a half, double time, and so forth.

➤ *Piecework pay* is similar to hourly labor in that it's more closely supervised. There's even greater accountability on the part of both supervisor and payroll department in that compensation is based on the actual amount of work completed. Time cards may be similar as far as listing time in and time out, but accurate records will need to be maintained based on the employees' productivity as well. If there's a pure form of pay for performance, this is probably it.

➤ *Sales commission* is another pure form of compensation in that it awards compensation as a percentage of sales. As in the case of piecework, that compensation will require detailed gross sales amounts and details on the appropriate commission split in order for payroll to process the check. In this case, as in the case of professional salaries, the comings and goings of the employee are almost irrelevant from a payroll point of view.

➤ *Performance bonuses* operate through the payroll system, but tend to be determined at management's discretion. The best ones are based on pre-arranged formulae that allow affected employees to understand what they're shooting for. But bonuses also can be awarded by management based on superior performance in a certain quarter; an outstanding idea that has reduced expenses, increased revenue, or improved service; or any one of a dozen factors. As long as accounting has properly reserved funds for these bonuses, payroll simply processes the payments as directed by management.

Journal Entry

When establishing a commission-based payment system, it's important to lay out all ground rules up front, for the benefit of both employee and payroll. A percentage of net sales is the usual way, but some companies are moving toward a percentage of net collected sales. The difference is that under the second scenario, the sales people are paid only on funds received by the company.

Collecting the Necessary Data

Once data-collection methods have been established, what else will be necessary to process payroll accounts? The process isn't difficult, but it requires a lot of information. Data requirements may vary from firm to firm, but at the very least most companies need the following:

➤ Specific payment information for each employee and the process with which that employee is involved. These include sales commission splits, piecework rates, hourly pay or monthly salary, and appropriate bonus information.

➤ Information required by the federal and state governments that affect the taxability of the employee's wages, from the completed W-4 forms.

➤ The employer's tax identification or federal ID number.

➤ The federal and state withholding tables for the current year.

And the Payroll Account Itself?

Shortcut
Bonus awards tend to come sporadically and at the discretion of management. Rather than set up a special account, write a memo indicating the employee's name, bonus amount, and payment date, which should be sufficient documentation for the company's accounting system.

Complete payroll information is the responsibility of the accounting department, which maintains a payroll journal for logging in each type of payment and all other appropriate information. But that information also must interface with the general ledger (G/L), and that requires setting up specific G/L accounts, including:

➤ A payroll account that records the amount of cash reserved for salary administration.

➤ A federal withholding account.

➤ A state withholding account.

➤ A state unemployment insurance account.

➤ A state disability insurance account.

➤ A local disability insurance account.

➤ An FICA account showing taxes paid by the employer and the employee.

➤ Accounts for any other deductions, whether mandatory or elective. These include union dues, insurance and investment deductions, and any garnishment against employee wages.

The Cost of Payroll

Payroll administration costs more than employee salaries and benefits. In addition, employers are responsible for a share of FICA taxes and for state and federal unemployment insurance. The sick and vacation pay companies award as part of benefits programs also are cost items that come under payroll expense, as do any company contributions made to employee pension plans.

Add to that the cost of managing this process and it's suddenly clear why some companies consider payroll services almost a necessity. Not all firms use them and it isn't always a matter of size that guides this decision. It all boils down to resource management, a decision companies have to make.

> ### Journal Entry
>
> Sometimes managers avoid using a payroll firm because they assume the services are expensive. But the cost of payroll processing by outside firms can be surprisingly low. Why? Because payroll firms can make money on the float (a concept we discussed in Chapter 8): they usually require their clients to deposit payroll funds long before the payroll is due, which allows the firm to make use of that money.

To Out-Place or Not to Out-Place?

Payroll services do little more than manage the bookkeeping portion of your payroll function and issue checks. Based on the details discussed, you can see why that may be attractive to some firms. Resource management is the biggest question. Does your company have the capacity to manage the payroll function in-house? Or is it more cost-effective to send it outside?

No matter if you run your system in-house or out-of-house, the system will need to be in place and a certain level of work done by staff before it can be turned over to a service. Let's run a sample scenario to measure the effect.

Company A has 50 employees involved in various types of sales and manufacturing activities. The firm's controller, responsible for that payroll, estimates an average of three hours a month spent doing payroll. Although paid by salary, the controller estimates he makes $35 per hour, so the annual cost of basic payroll administration would be roughly $1,260.

But the costs don't stop there. The controller must also provide quarterly and annual reports to the government as part of the company's payroll tax responsibilities. The controller estimates an additional 15 hours per year generating these reports at $35 per hour, for a total of $525.

In addition, the controller needs to have a trained backup person in the accounting department to handle this process temporarily if it falls during a time when the controller is out. He estimates annual involvement of this person, compensated at $15 per hour, at 25 hours, for a total cost of $375.

How does this break down?

Controller's regular processing	$1,260
Report generation	$ 525
Backup	$ 375
Total In-House Payroll Administration Costs	$2,160

Payroll Service B, competing for Company A's payroll business, offers the following package: a $350 setup fee for 50 employees, plus a cost of $4 per employee per payroll to administer. Since Company A processes paychecks monthly, that means the payroll service will process 12 payrolls × 50 employees for an annual total of 600. Service B's offer breaks down as follows:

Setup charge	$ 350
Processing charge (600 × $4)	$2,400
Total Out-of-House Payroll Costs	$2,750

This, of course, doesn't include the controller's time spent preparing the documents and working with the service firm periodically to make sure things are being done accurately and correctly.

The three questions your firm needs to ask are:

1. Do we have the staff expertise to manage our own payroll?

2. Do we have the time to manage it?

3. How are our resources best used?

The answers you get will help determine if you keep the process in house or look for a payroll processing firm.

Withholding Taxes

Your company has to do it because it's the law. And, as indicated earlier, the government takes a special interest in payroll taxes because they view the money as essentially theirs, and they're simply allowing you to hold. That means when they want it, your payroll manager better have it.

This guide has talked briefly about some of the record-keeping requirements involved with withholding taxes. We will delve deeper into the tax question later, in Part 4 of this guide.

Accounting for Benefits

An important part of any compensation package is benefits—vacation time, sick leave, pension contributions, and the like. These require their own accounting procedure and can be accounted for under payroll as easily as anywhere else.

In many cases, benefits accrue at certain rates for certain employees—one day of sick leave for each month worked, for example, or a percentage of vacation time earned based on seniority, longevity, or both. Accrued benefits must be reflected in the necessary benefits documents—within payroll records certainly, but also on each employee's pay stub—and accounted for when computing reserves, since each benefit represents a cost item to the company.

That's a quick summary of how a company accounts for benefits. The actual processes may not matter much to managers, but the policies providing those benefits may be very important. Consider the following two points, for example. If company policy allows employees to carry benefits over into subsequent years, it defeats the purpose of vacation time when employees hoard the time in hope of exchanging it for its cash equivalent. On the other hand, if company policy states, "Use 'em or lose 'em," most of your employees want to use up their vacation days rather than lose them and your building may become a ghost town every December. But that's a policy decision your company will have to make.

The Least You Need to Know

➤ Payroll and benefits are one of the highest operational costs.

➤ Payroll administration revolves around accurate, consistent, and timely reporting, and good accounting management.

➤ Any information directly affecting salary and benefits administration should become part of the payroll function.

➤ Different types of pay—salaries, hourly wages, piecework rates, sales commission, and performance bonuses—require different forms of administration and reporting.

➤ Measure resource expenditures closely before making the decision to have payroll administered out of house.

➤ Manage benefits—vacation time, sick leave, pension contributions—as a part of your payroll function.

Chapter 11

Inventory Control

In This Chapter

➤ Understanding the importance of inventory control

➤ Establishing an inventory control system

➤ Tracking inventory flow

➤ Accounting for inventory

➤ Computing the cost of goods sold

Whether you're a department head or a company president, your inventory is often one of your company's greatest assets. It's vital to continued profitability.

Businesses use the term *inventory* in various ways. Basically, it's what you sell, in some form or another. A retail business would have a merchandise inventory—the stock of goods on hand to be sold. A manufacturing company would have several inventories: finished goods (its products), materials (what it turns into its products), and work in process (everything in between materials and finished goods).

As an asset, inventory means more to your company's financial profile than just the stuff the workers tote around the warehouse on two-wheel carts. Like other assets, inventory has to be managed correctly if the business is to continue to operate profitably.

That means a company requires good inventory control, from both physical and fiscal standpoints. The result will be minimizing loss and maximizing resources, which translates into greater company profitability.

Identifying Your Inventory

Most people think of inventory as goods ready for purchase, probably because we are constantly assaulted by ads proclaiming "sale on all inventory" and occasionally disappointed when a clerk tells us that something we want to buy is "no longer in inventory." But, as we've noted, inventory is quite a bit more than that.

There are three types of inventory:

➤ Raw materials and supplies used to make products

➤ Goods currently in the process of completion

➤ Completed goods ready for the customer

Depending on your type of company, of course, you might have all three or only one of these types. Consider the widget business, for example. The companies that provide the raw materials—steel and plastic—would have inventories of iron ore, chemicals, processed steel, and plastic. The manufacturer would have an inventory of steel and plastic for making widgets, stacks and stacks of partly completed widgets, and crates of widgets on the loading dock, ready to ship. The widget retailers, in contrast, would have only their inventory of widgets, in crates and on the shelves.

What?
Inventory may include items held for sale as finished goods, goods in production, or raw materials and supplies to be used in the production process.

Whether you deal in widgets or whatnots, each type of inventory is an asset to your company and should be accounted for as such.

Developing an Inventory Control (I/C) System

Inventory is an asset that is by nature always in movement—or the company may not have long to worry about it! So, it's sometimes difficult to create an effective inventory control system to keep track of everything everywhere as it moves through the channels. But approach it logically and all the elements should fall into place. And with current computer technology, inventory tracking can be managed as effectively as your budget will allow.

The first reason to develop an inventory control system is to track the inventory as it progresses through the processes and to assess its value. That may be relatively simple for finished goods—basically a matter of counting boxes, cans, or kegs. The true challenge of inventory is to measure its increasing value as it goes from, say, a pile of oak lumber to a chest of drawers. Inventory control systems help companies understand and measure that value.

The more common use of inventory control is to keep a constant count of finished inventory for sale. More so than the pile of lumber, the finished chest of drawers and other items with retail worth can be better leveraged for financial purposes, have greater market value, and offer a truer picture of a company's net worth. Again, that's a question of the type of business, the quantities of materials and products involved, and the degree of value increase.

Journal Entry

One of the most valuable services inventory control can provide, however, is to assist in computing the cost of goods sold by helping measure the relative cost of the development process and the increase in value as the goods take shape.

None of these are difficult to implement, but keep in mind that the process needs to be multiplied by the number of goods produced or sold. Again, the complexity of your system will depend greatly on your type of business.

For example, if your company produces a single line of luxury automobiles, you probably have less work ahead of you than a company that produces a variety of roofing nails. Cars are bigger, so they're easier to count and harder to lose!

But that's only the inventory of finished goods. For tracking the inventory of materials, the story is completely different: The nail company has large quantities of several types of metal, while the car company has crates and boxes and bags of parts—easily more than several thousand for one make of car—and barrels of paints (dozens of colors) and canisters of acetylene for the torches and... As you can see, data control is a key factor in inventory management. And, again, depending on your business, inventory can be a very valuable asset to manage.

Many companies go through seasons and cycles. Those ups and downs and changes in buying patterns make inventory control even more vital. For example, a retail store could find itself stuck with a warehouse full of summer clothes as the leaves begin to fall if it doesn't keep track of what's on hand. Widgets may sell year-round, but colors come and go, so the manufacturer needs to keep track of its quantities of paint, so they won't get stuck with too much teal when tastes turn to fuschia.

Shortcut

Inventory control (I/C) should link with the other financial components within any good accounting system. A good I/C operation will send and receive information to and from other parts of your system, including the general ledger, accounts payable, materials billing, order entry, and others. An automated linkage will reduce the amount of work and potential errors by reducing the number of repeated entries made for the same materials or goods.

Tracking Inventory Flow

The inventory flow from raw materials to finished products is matched by an information flow that helps track the goods from start to finish—and helps track the value of those goods throughout the process and maintain them at the proper level.

Handling Raw Materials

The raw materials arrive in the warehouse and their value is recorded both in units and dollar amount. The materials, ordered through the appropriate requisition procedure and transaction to accounts payable, are stored in the appropriate spot until needed.

What about the paper work? The accompanying purchase order and packing slip are forwarded to inventory control for recording in the appropriate subledger. Value, again, is recorded both in unit numbers and dollar amounts. At the end of each day, all deliveries are tallied in the subaccount and posted to the appropriate account on the general ledger.

Controlling Materials in Process

The value of those materials increases as they become processed, but so do the costs. The cost of materials, subassemblies, and labor are accumulated for each product through a cost accounting system designed to measure the true cost of each item. As the product completes each processing phase, those additional costs are added to the product. Management should, at any point in production, be able to ascertain the cost of the item to that point.

This may not be feasible for smaller companies or when production consists of numerous stages. However, in general, the more closely a company can account for production costs, the better.

Managing the Finished Products

Once production is complete, the true cost of goods should be known for each item. The finished goods are transferred to the finished inventory—the more traditional and familiar definition of inventory. Inventory control (I/C) closes out the in-process inventory, assigns any remaining costs to the product, and enters the item in the finished product inventory.

As with other aspects of the accounting process, the transfer causes the item to appear as a credit to the in-process inventory (because the in-process inventory is now owed the value of the product) and a debit to the finished product inventory (where it will remain a debit until the product is sold and the income realized).

The procedure is fairly simple once you understand the basic reason: The materials and supplies you buy have a value, and you add to that value as you use those materials and supplies to make products.

Then consider the following three questions:

1. How much value do you add to those materials?

2. How many phases are involved in your process?

3. How closely do you want to track the movement and the increase in value?

It's the answers to those questions that may make inventory control complicated.

Again, the approach described here may be too complicated and too expensive for smaller companies, especially if their production processes are simple. But managers can always use the three questions listed above as a guide. The main point remains: If you don't know how much it costs to go from materials to finished product, how do you know what to charge to make it worth continuing to produce those widgets or pieces of furniture? Sure, you can always charge whatever your market will bear...until a competitor underprices you and steals your customers. Of course, then you can undercut the competitor...and maybe price your company out of business.

The Inventory Control System Itself

The components of a good inventory control system already have been discussed. In summary, note that every system requires a transaction record for each entry in each of the three areas: raw materials, materials in process, and finished goods. And each transaction means a debit to one inventory and a credit to another.

The transaction record should include:

➤ Transaction date

➤ Person responsible for the transaction

➤ Item names and numbers

➤ Origin and destination of the items moved

Red Flag
The inventory balance reported on the books should match the physical inventory. If the *book inventory* is lower, then it's likely an accounting error. If the *physical inventory is lower,* you might have reason to suspect theft—or another accounting error. It's simple: The more tightly you control inventory, the less chance there is of a problem occuring.

Red Flag
Companies transferring inventory control from a manual to an automated system must make sure the new balance matches the old balance and that nothing has been lost in the process. This requires an exact match both in terms of unit counts and dollar amounts.

Once all transactions have been completed, a listing of transactions should be checked to make sure nothing has slipped through the cracks. This is true of automated as well as manual systems.

Accounting for Inventory Control

The accounting entries made to the I/C subledger flow to the appropriate general ledger account. Recap summary sheets listing all steps in the process can be helpful as a way of measuring the process and its results. They are not, however, replacement documents for subledger and general ledger entries.

Policies and Processes

One of the values of inventory control is to help cost (figure the cost of) the inventory process. This may be critical in defending certain expenses during an audit or if investors are interested in your firm. Processes vary, but two rules of thumb exist:

➤ The valuing process must be logical and reasonable to the industry

➤ The process must be applied consistently

Processing costs for what will become a bottle of expensive wine will be very different than those for producing a bottle of mass-market brand beer. The steps may be similar, but the assumed costs or value must be logical to the industry in question.

Costing Inventory

Different methods of costing inventory appeal to different companies. Quite simply, the method your company chooses should be the one that maximizes your net income while minimizing your tax liability. There are four common types:

1. *Average costing.* This method assumes that the cost of inventory is the sum of the average costs of goods on hand when the accounting period began and goods purchased since that moment. If prices are changing constantly or if it's difficult to track slightly varying costs, this method may be the wisest choice, as it tends to level out peaks and valleys.

   For example:

April 1	Inventory	500 units at $1.50	$750
5	Purchased	30 units at $1.60	48
9	Purchased	60 units at $1.45	87
14	Purchased	80 units at $1.30	104
25	Purchased	20 units at $1.65	33
Totals:		690 units	$1022
Average unit cost = $1022 ÷ 690 = $1.48			

   If the inventory at the end of April is 435 units, then the value would be calculated as $644 (435 × $1.48).

2. *Lower of cost or market (LCM).* This more conservative method measures ending inventory value as the lower of the purchase cost of the materials or the present market value. This type of inventory costing may be appropriate for wildly fluctuating goods, like stocks, or heavy investment materials, such as gemstones.

3. *First-In, First-Out (FIFO).* This method assumes that the older goods are sold first. So, the costs of all units in your inventory are calculated according to the most recent prices you paid for any of those units. If there are 75 widgets on the floor, it doesn't matter whether you may have bought them in a lot of 200 three weeks ago at $5 each or in a lot of 100 last week at $6 each—you calculate their cost at $6. In an environment of rising prices, FIFO will provide a lower cost of goods sold, thus increase net income (and tax liability!) at a faster rate. Warning: This method is criticized for accentuating the effects of a business cycle on income.

4. *Last In, First Out (LIFO).* Just the opposite of FIFO, this method assumes that you're selling the goods most recently purchased. When prices are rising fast, this method increases the cost of goods sold, reducing the net income. The result is a tax advantage for companies that need it. But when prices are declining, income is increased. This method softens fluctuations in the business cycle, but it could give an unrealistic account of the current value of inventory, since the valuation reflects earlier prices.

Journal Entry

Different factors affect the value of inventory, including annual changes in inventory quantity, obsolescence, and changes in styles and tastes. Complicated, huh? Just remember that inventory is not a static item and must be aggressively managed like other aspects of your business.

Measuring the Cost of Goods Sold

An example of a small business might work best for the next point, showing how a perpetual inventory system helps a business owner keep better track of what's hot, what's not, and what it costs to be selling that merchandise.

Lee owned a liquor store and there was nothing he hated more than taking inventory. Each January, after the holiday rush, his staff would dust and rearrange all the bottles on the shelves and in the bins, weeding out slow-moving items for discount and promotion in the close-out bin. Lee would order just enough of the bare necessities to get by from week to week. Slowly his leftover holiday stock would begin to dwindle.

What?
The formula for calculating the *cost of goods sold* is opening inventory plus purchases, labor, overhead, and any other costs incurred in getting the goods to the customer, minus ending inventory.

Red Flag
No matter how sophisticated inventory accounting may become, there are still problems with inventory "walking away." If you make the warehouse manager responsible for all inventory loss, that problem will improve quickly. If you establish a policy to not blame workers for items that get broken accidentally, you're more likely to get reports of any breakage. Such a policy can't prevent breakage, but it would allow for adjustments as accidents happen and mean fewer discrepancies when you do a physical inventory.

Lee was heading for May 1, the day on which his state assessed its dreaded "floor tax," a tax on the wholesale value of each item on the sales floor. Needless to say, that was also a good time to perform the necessary "new year inventory" exercise, the annual counting of the bottles.

Many companies still perform a physical inventory of some type, which is critical at least as one form of measuring the cost of goods sold. But relying on a physical inventory delays knowing the cost of goods sold—and thus the company's operating margin—until the end of the operating period.

A better method might be an ongoing measurement of cost of goods sold, using one of the four methods for costing inventory (described earlier) to compute the value of items as they are purchased or produced. By using existing data instead of a physical count, the gross margin figure is available for each and every item as it's moved through inventory. You have information available at your fingertips on problems and opportunities without having to wait and then frantically wade through a physical inventory.

Lee found that out. By installing a scanning system that read the data for each purchase as it went through the register, he not only improved traffic flow, but was able to tally his gross margin at the end of each day from sales information measured against inventory data. His staff still had to dust the bottles and rearrange shelves, but the inventory process and resulting May 1 floor-tax requirements proved much easier to manage.

Use of a perpetual inventory system cannot eliminate the necessity of doing a physical inventory after the accounting period ends. Records show what should be in stock, but there may be losses from theft, breakage, spoilage, and other causes. So, it's a good idea to check out the inventory the old-fashioned way. The records are adjusted for any losses with a credit to merchandise inventory and a debit to the cost of goods sold.

Tracking Inventory Performance

The real question behind inventory management is tracking inventory performance or turnover rate—the speed at which a company converts its investment in inventory into sales. To operate a business, you need to have inventory at every phase in your business process. If you manufacture widgets, for example, that might mean a materials inventory of plastics and metals for phase one, springs and fasteners for phase two, paints for phase three, labels for phase four, and packaging for phase five. But to generate revenues, that inventory needs to keep moving. Inventory that doesn't move is almost worse than no inventory at all, because it becomes a financial liability on your books. Unless inventory has investment value—like fine wines, objets d'art, or precious metals—the faster it turns over, the better.

Turnover rate can be computed by dividing the cost of goods sold by the average inventory. Inventory turnover rates change throughout the year and good managers anticipate the fluctuations in their industry and respond by stocking accordingly.

That's how Lee managed his liquor store and, for the most part, he was successful. He would never stock collector decanters until October, and then he would stock fewer than he anticipated he would sell. He may have lost a sale or two, but he was never caught with the little monstrosities in hand when the May 1 floor tax came around. That also helped keep his gross margin up, which meant he wasn't working as hard for his money. I/C planning made the time he spent with his customers more profitable.

The Secret to Inventory Management

Things have changed over the past decade, with the increased emphasis on supplier service and the rise of "just in time" inventory management. Companies no longer want to stock excessive amounts of inventory without reason. All those discounts from buying larger quantities are lost if the inventory doesn't turn over in a reasonable amount of time. Inventory is assets that don't work until sales are made. Turning that inventory is critical to financial growth and success.

Lee knew that and, although he occasionally found himself stuck with a dog, he knew his customers and their tastes well enough to be able to buy from his wholesalers beverages and accessories that he could turn over rapidly.

That knowledge is the primary criterion for successful inventory management. No formula exists for all industries, although each industry has criteria. No magical mathematical equation exists for determining just the right amount of inventory based on previous sales.

It's all in your knowledge of your customers, your understanding of your products, and making wise management decisions. Remember: More is better only if you can sell it. Otherwise, it may significantly reduce your gross profit margin.

The Least You Need to Know

➤ Inventory is defined as raw materials, goods in process, and finished products.

➤ Inventory controls exist to track inventory through your business and allow you to compute the cost of goods sold.

➤ The information flow that matches the inventory flow can tell you a lot about the financial side of the process.

➤ Inventory control requires its own subledger, connected to order entry, purchase order processing, work order processing, bill of materials, cost accounting, accounts payable, and, of course, the general ledger.

➤ Different methods of inventory costing result in different values and different advantages and disadvantages for each business.

➤ Generally, the faster you turn over your inventory, the more profitable you'll be, if you set your selling prices appropriately.

➤ One of the secrets to inventory control is customer knowledge backed by good management.

Cost Accounting

In This Chapter

➤ What is cost accounting?

➤ How cost accounting affects your company

➤ Understanding cost accounting systems

➤ Organizing your general ledger for cost accounting

➤ Correctly accounting for overhead

In Chapter 11 we discussed ways to find the cost of goods sold. That's a good start to discovering the cost of operating your business and determining the true cost of products produced or services offered. Measuring those true costs is the purpose of cost accounting.

As a department manager, you're aware of the cost of materials, supplies, and labor involved in your operation. Chances are you also have overhead allocations for space and direct telephone charges, but has the accountant also assessed fees for the administrative overhead that pays for you and the rest of the management team? That's also part of cost accounting.

What?
Overhead is the indirect, general costs of doing business, to be shared by every unit of the company, according to some system of allocation. Put in this category only those costs not directly adding to or readily identifiable with the product or service constituting the main object of your operation.

Shortcut
One of cost accounting's most important functions is to allow managers to control production costs. This is done by determining what those costs should be, compared with what they really are, based on cost accounting applications. Most accounting systems should provide the necessary information to help you make the appropriate adjustments.

Everything Costs Something

When it comes to determining the value of what a company produces, the only reliable way is through cost accounting, which measures all costs associated with doing business.

These costs include materials, some types of labor, and sometimes distribution—getting your products out to the market. Those are known as direct costs.

But cost accounting also covers facilities—the costs of paying the rent, keeping on the lights and heat, cleaning, maintenance, depreciation, property taxes, and insurance—marketing, some types of labor, and administration—the costs of back office operations such as accounting, human resources, and quite possibly your salary. These are known as indirect costs or overhead.

In order to stay in business, much less succeed, you will have to account for all the costs of the products you produce. Procedures may vary and allocations may not be divided equally, and that will be a decision you will make as management. But the basics of cost accounting must be applied.

A Manufacturing Example

Oakleaf Furniture was proud of the method by which they turned their pile of oak lumber and crates of hardware into beautiful chests of drawers. Production managers at Oakleaf were equally proud of the way they managed their resources. In doing an analysis for each item, in fact, the production department came up with the following cost per unit, as shown in Table 12.1.

Table 12.1   Oakleaf Furniture: Chest of Drawers Production

Cost Elements	Cost
Oak lumber	$ 44
Brass hardware	$ 12
Miscellaneous supplies	$ 3
Total materials cost	$ 59
Labor (3.5 hours @ $18/hr.)	$ 63
Shipping (paid by client)	0
Total cost per unit	$122

The production department was pretty proud of its modest investment and recommended increasing Oakleaf's normal profit margin on this product, coming in at the low end on cost and really cleaning up.

Then management pointed out that the overhead allocation had yet to be applied. The production team could not make the product without the machines they used, so there was the cost of machine time, maintenance, repairs, and depreciation. They could not manufacture the product without having a facility in which to work, so there was rent, utilities, property taxes, and insurance to pay. And there were also administrative costs, including the cost of support, sales, and administrative staff. Even a piece of the production manager's salary and benefits package had to be figured in.

The adjusted unit cost analysis, then, looked something like what is shown in Table 12.2.

Red Flag
Beware of applying overhead and indirect costs arbitrarily to the production of goods. It makes good sense to try to define indirect costs as clearly as possible. This may be a problem, especially when there are considerable differences among product lines or building facilities and when managerial responsibilities are blurred or overlap.

Table 12.2   Oakleaf Furniture: Chest of Drawers Production

Cost Elements	Cost
Oak lumber	$ 44
Brass hardware	$ 12
Miscellaneous supplies	$ 3
Total materials cost	$ 59
Labor (3.5 hours @ $18/hr.)	$ 63
Shipping (paid by client)	0
Sales commission (approx.)	$ 20
Administration/overhead	$ 28
Total cost per unit	$170

That's quite a difference—$48—making the cost per unit almost 40 percent higher!

This adjusted unit cost meant a considerably lower profit margin, but it was a realistic calculation—and it still kept the retail price within the market and resulted in a healthy profit. The production crew was disappointed to realize the true cost of their products, but vowed to continue improving the production process to reduce costs. The production manager was happy just to see that he was still getting paid.

Remember: The goal is to determine the most accurate calculation of costs. That includes overhead, of course, but resist the temptation to take the easy route. Sometimes managers simply pool rents, utilities, and salaries and benefits for support staff and management. Then they allocate them across all departments in the company according to square footage of each department or the number of employees in each department, rather than according to actual contributions to the products or services. In many cases, this approach falsifies the cost figures, and may lead to resentment among employees who end up shouldering more than their fair share.

Tracking Cost Flow

The purpose of cost accounting is to track and assign costs, as appropriate, to the production, administration, marketing, and distribution of the products or services your company offers. It involves classifying, recording, allocating, summarizing, and reporting current and prospective costs. That's how you compute the true cost of goods sold—and it's necessary for your company's survival.

The previous chapter on inventory management introduced the rudiments of cost accounting during the production phase. In addition to those direct costs for the raw materials and labor necessary to produce goods, true product costs also contain an allocation for indirect and overhead costs.

Although we may use examples here that involve manufacturing, other types of businesses need cost accounting to help track and control the cost of goods and services.

Consider, for example, the neighborhood service station. In the old days, the cost of a gallon of gasoline included the services of the smiling, uniformed attendant who cleaned your windows and checked your oil while he pumped the gas. That attendant may now be just a memory, but a gallon of gas is still a gallon of gas, albeit much more expensive. But the cost of that gas would be significantly higher if it still included that attendant. The product hasn't changed, but the service that was once part of the price has changed.

Cost System Types

Different businesses adopt different types of cost accounting systems. Some systems are informal, while others are almost scientific. The choice depends on the business, its sensitivity to costs, the general nature and place of the accounting function, and the concerns of management.

But there are some more formalized systems to consider:

➤ Process costing

➤ Job order costing

➤ Joint product costing

Let's take a closer look at each of these systems.

Process Costing

If your company's production runs hundreds or thousands of widgets each day, week, or month, *process* costing is likely the system for you. Cost measurement focuses on the operation, or process, and then that production cost is divided among the number of pieces produced during an individual run. Since there are several production steps involved for each widget—casting, tooling, assembly, and packaging—each step is costed separately. The cost of each step is divided by the number of widgets produced. Then the individual unit costs for each step are added together to arrive at the total cost per widget.

As with our examples for inventory control, the costs at each step are credited and debited to the proper accounts—notably, a work in process inventory, a materials inventory, and a labor expense account for each step and, for the final step, a finished goods inventory—as materials move from one step to the next and additional materials and labor charges are added at each step. Finally, the total cost is reported on a statement of goods manufactured.

Job Order Costing

What works for a widget manufacturer producing thousands of similar items won't work for a custom manufacturer, such as a home builder. He or she produces custom products often designed to buyer specifications. In this case, *job order* costing is a better way to go.

Job order costing attaches relevant costs to the individual products produced. In addition to direct costs—the price of the land, all materials, all labor, all subcontractors, permits, and other related costs—the builder also should attach a percentage of overhead costs, including office administration, advertising, fixed assets (tools and trucks, for example), and other costs.

Similar to this is a method called *job lot* costing, a method appropriate when a supplier produces a batch of custom items for a client. A house-label wine produced for a hotel or restaurant is an example of job lot costing. The costing process is similar to the job order costing process: The supplier calculates the direct production costs (such as private labeling in this case), then adds the allocated indirect costs. That total cost is then divided by the number of units, to arrive at a cost per unit.

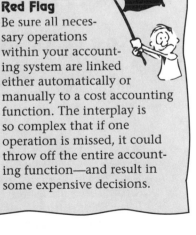

Red Flag
Be sure all necessary operations within your accounting system are linked either automatically or manually to a cost accounting function. The interplay is so complex that if one operation is missed, it could throw off the entire accounting function—and result in some expensive decisions.

Joint Product Costing

Some industries make different products from the same raw materials. Unfortunately for our accountants, those products need to be costed individually. To do that, accountants will use the *joint product* costing system.

Oakleaf Furniture bought oak lumber by the ton, usually winding up with a certain percentage of waste wood not up to their exacting furniture production standards. In addition, the manufacturing process resulted in large piles of oak shavings and wood chips.

Rather than treating these as waste products, the production crew cleaned and packaged them. The waste wood, if it was of suitable size and length, was marketed as cord wood for home fireplaces. The waste wood that didn't measure up was ground up and added to the wood chips, which were then sold as mulch for home garden use. What once had been trash that Oakleaf paid to have hauled away was now a small profit center for the company—an example of turning lemons into lemonade.

The secret to costing these items is to do so at the point the materials are spun off. Since Oakleaf knew the relative cost of its lumber per pound, the person responsible for the spin-off profit center weighed the bags of wood chips and stacks of cord wood and estimated their value. Not surprisingly, the profit margin on the former waste products was about as high as the profit margin on the finished furniture.

> ## Journal Entry
>
> When accounting for byproducts in joint product costing scenarios, remember to give each byproduct its own line on the financial statement, and treat it as a separate item when allocating indirect costs. In addition, subtract the byproduct sales revenue from the cost of the main product to get a true picture of the gross margin.

Full-Cost vs. Limited-Cost Accounting

All three systems—process costing, job order costing, and joint product costing—involve full-cost accounting. That is, all direct and indirect costs are assigned to each product or service.

Companies often use limited-cost accounting, choosing to ignore or reduce overhead costs for certain lines—new or weaker products or services—so they can come in with a positive bottom line. In companies where decisions are based on figures alone, this may be a way of "going with a gut feeling" to keep a product alive until it has time to become profitable. There may be factors other than finances driving the decision to use limited-cost accounting. Sometimes, unfortunately, it can simply be a question of political games among managers who are engaged in "turf wars." When managers pride themselves on the number of products and employees and dollars under their control, limited-cost accounting may allow them to defend their fiefdoms on paper.

The important thing to remember about limited-cost accounting applications is that those indirect costs are being paid for somewhere else. And such situations quickly can get out of hand and cause accounting problems, provide misleading information, and undermine employee morale. Use full-cost accounting wherever and whenever possible.

Setting Up the General Ledger

The cost accounting effort may best be handled by establishing cost centers in the general ledger. These require their own subledger entries, which are tied to the general ledger, of course. They can be as detailed as necessary, but the various categories in the numbering system should at least be broken out, as shown in Table 12.3.

Table 12.3 Oakleaf Furniture: Chest of Drawers Production

Chart of Accounts Number	Cost Elements	Cost
10-123	Oak lumber	$44
10-223	Brass hardware	$12
10-323	Miscellaneous supplies	$3
	Total materials cost	$59
20-100	Labor (3.5 hours @ $18/hr.)	$63
00-100	Shipping (paid by client)	0
30-500	Sales commission (approx.)	$20
30-700	Administration/overhead	$28
Total cost per unit		$170

Note that the materials costs begin with the prefix 10-, followed by a three-digit description that ties to the company's ordering mechanism and inventory. Direct labor costs begin with the prefix 20- and indirect costs and commissions are indicated by 30-. (Since shipping is paid by the client, there's no entry for it in the chart of accounts, and so the prefix 00- is used. The three-digit number for labor—100—is used, as the most convenient and logical category for shipping.)

A system like this will help keep the individual expenses separate and easy to tally. More important, those expenses also will be easy to trace. That way if the cost of goods increases dramatically, the system allows a check to see if materials, labor, or administration are what's making your company less competitive in the marketplace.

Cost Center Management

This type of system will also help feed information to cost center managers responsible for managing expenses for that particular group. They can study each of the costs, then consider reasons and remedies.

Is the cost of labor increasing more than the market will bear? The person in charge of the production crew must determine if this change is due to higher costs for salaries and benefits or to slower production. It's then that person's responsibility to rectify the situation or recommend changes to management.

Is the cost of materials rising too quickly? Maybe it's time to find another supplier or to consider buying in larger quantities to benefit from discounts, focusing more on profit margin and worrying less about cash flow. It's a question of balancing the general interests of the business with cost center management.

System Integration

Like all components of the accounting system, the cost accounting function must be integrated with the other functions. Different accounting tools react differently to the process.

Cost accounting examples seem to revolve almost entirely around inventory control (I/C), and it's clear I/C has one of the strongest relationships to the cost accounting function. Sophisticated computerized systems link the two so that an entry made to one has the proper reaction on the other. If your company is posting by hand, be sure to make the proper credits and debits to the various cost centers as materials move through production.

Direct and indirect labor are involved in costing products; therefore, the payroll system also will be affected. The costs associated with employee time may be attributable to several products or processes, but the proper adjustment should be made once the payroll has been completed. If there are employees who are involved with several products, it may be wise to have them use time sheets to record the amount of time they spend on each product. In normal situations, this might be just a temporary requirement, to allow the managers to determine average time distributions for each employee.

Shortcut

Consider pre-printed cost detail sheets as a way to more accurately capture direct cost information. This detailed record should be completed during each step of the process to show all cost items that go into each step of production. The best ones also show which costs should be administered so that production managers can compare actual costs with ideal costs.

Purchasing also becomes involved, especially when the cost of goods is directly related to a product or process that's part of the cost-accounting structure. In many cases, purchase accounts represent a direct expense, but companies also tie purchasing to cost accounting as a matter of course.

Purchasing ties in directly to accounts payable, which records the cost of raw materials purchased and the amount owed the supplier. Automated systems often move invoice information directly from accounts payable to the appropriate production accounts. In addition to the costs of materials, fees and other external costs are recorded to the appropriate production accounts and transferred from those accounts to the work-in-process inventories or the finished goods inventory, the statement of goods manufactured, and the general ledger.

Accounts receivable (A/R) comes into play for companies that do progress billing as the product moves through the production stages. These partial payments, to be completed upon product delivery, originate in the production process and are assigned to their specific product before being sent to A/R for collection.

The general ledger (G/L) may be the most important component of the cost accounting system. Cost information is posted to the G/L as frequently as it makes sense to do so. But the more frequently those costs are transferred, the more accurate the production costs are at any point in time. Current figures allow more accurate cost tracking and adjustment if needed.

Journal Entry

Effective cost accounting requires time, effort, and care in the reporting and recording of costs associated with production. The secret to an effective cost accounting system is the proper recording of cost transfers as credits and debits in the appropriate accounts as materials move from one process to the next.

Accounting for Overhead

Overhead—one of the most misused and maligned terms in any business, yet a necessary expense—must be correctly calculated and allocated if a company intends to stay in business. True overhead costs must be distributed among all profit centers.

The term is misunderstood because it is often applied to all expenses that aren't direct costs to the production of a particular item. There are really two categories of overhead to consider when assigning direct and indirect costs:

➤ *Real overhead*. The correct use of the term applies literally to the roof overhead and attendant utility costs. It also might apply to employee overhead, such as benefits and insurance. Real overhead costs are more easily computed when treated as an annual expense, similar to rent. The most accurate way is to apply a portion of overhead costs to each product produced or to each cost center.

➤ *Labor overhead*. Although payroll can be considered an overhead cost, salaries should be allocated based on the type of labor provided. Direct labor responsible for helping produce the product in question should be directly attributable to the cost of that product. Indirect labor that supports production at a distance may be allocated based on the amount of contributions made. Commissions from selling the product, for example, should be considered almost as a direct cost and their full amount allocated. However, the sales manager responsible for supervising that sales person may have other responsibilities as well. His or her time should be allocated by percentage to all appropriate cost centers.

Shortcut

Costing can be simplified, as long as you use an approach that's systematic, honest, and fair. Do you want to allocate overhead according to the profits generated by each product? Or according to the chunk of your business represented by each product? Or more heavily on mature products, to allow new products a greater chance to prove themselves? There's no single right answer—just do whatever seems to work best for your company.

Red Flag

Never assume standard costs, either direct or indirect. Over time, things change, especially in fast-growth markets. Staff should always take the time to compute actual costs if the cost accounting system is going to work properly. An hour or two here, a half-dozen employees there…it all adds up, so it's vital to know the figures.

Standardizing Costs

Large companies like General Motors and Microsoft have armies of professional staff trained to cost out products and processes. These professionals measure all direct and indirect costs and apply scientific theorems to arrive at the most accurate cost of goods possible, so that prices can be developed to ensure the highest levels of profitability.

Most companies don't have that luxury. The job of costing often falls to someone in the financial office who wins the title by virtue of his or her access to the accounting system. But that person still can develop and administer a system that is accurate, timely, and more than adequate. How? By following several simple rules:

➤ *Identify all the resources*—materials, preparation, machine usage, and labor—that go into one unit of each product. If the labor rates differ for the various steps, identify those rates and apply the costs accordingly.

➤ *Assign a direct cost to each product* and extend that cost to all items produced.

➤ *Assign overhead allocations* based on a consistent method, such as the amount of revenue or the percentage of production represented by each product annually, and divide by the number of units.

➤ *Add up the costs.* This will give the cost of goods sold for each line of product produced, allowing it to be priced competitively without going below the cost that it takes to produce.

It's that simple—at least in principle. Depending on your business, it can be much more complicated. But it's one of the best investments of time and effort your company can make. Or, to put it another way, if you don't do it right, it's perhaps the easiest way to ruin your business.

It's basic business: You want to make a profit by selling your products or services for more than they cost you to provide. But how can you be sure of doing that if you don't know the actual costs? That's the reason for effective cost accounting.

The Least You Need to Know

➤ Direct costs apply to product production, while indirect costs apply to functions that support that production. Both must be considered in cost accounting.

➤ Cost accounting helps track as closely as possible the cost of goods produced.

➤ Different types of cost accounting scenarios benefit different companies. Choose yours based on management technique and the products you produce. Then, don't hesitate to change as your situation changes.

➤ The cost accounting function interacts with many different components within your accounting system.

➤ Calculating and allocating overhead is critical in determining the true costs of production.

Managing Internal Controls

There's an old story about the company controller who was so dedicated to her job that she never complained, never asked for assistance, barely took time off for holidays, and didn't take a vacation in her 20 years of employment. In recognition for her years of selfless service, management forced her to take her first vacation and even bought her a ticket for a Caribbean cruise. She had worked hard, they said, and she had earned it.

It was only after she left that the managers made a startling discovery—the controller, who had sole responsibility for all accounting, had managed to embezzle $2.4 million during that 20 years. A quick check with the cruise line showed that she had never shown up to enjoy their gift.

There are numerous variations on that story, but they all lead to the same conclusion: Your company needs an effective system of internal controls to protect its assets. Certainly not all controllers are like the one in this story—but how many dishonest controllers would it take to hurt your company?

And while it may not fall within your authority as department manager to oversee the controller or the financial function, there's value in understanding the reason for and function of internal controls. It may even help you supervise your own employees. After all, for every controller who embezzles $2.4 million, there are probably 2.4 million employees who are occasionally pocketing office supplies, borrowing tools, or even driving home with furniture or computer equipment. That not only means a decrease in assets and an increase in the costs of equipment and supplies, but also undermines production—and it may even undermine the integrity and morale of your honest employees.

An Ounce of Prevention

It's not within the scope of this chapter to review all possible security breaches and internal threats your company may face. Those are worth a book or two of their own. Instead, let this chapter set some basic guidelines for your company's internal control mechanism as well as offer a few particulars that affect the financial management function. That will at least get you started in safeguarding your company's property.

Situations differ based on the type and nature of various companies, but there are two absolute rules for all firms.

Rule One: All Companies Need Internal Controls

By working through to the end of the accounting section of this book, you've come to understand that the accounting function is a series of checks and balances, consisting of ways to monitor expenses and prove financial results. That's one of the purposes of the general ledger, as a matter of fact: to serve as a master account against which all subledgers must balance.

So, too, with internal controls. Without that mechanism, company assets will be exposed to unscrupulous employees and their cronies who may devise ingenious schemes to steal funds or other assets right out from under your nose. The vast majority of staff are honest and hard-working, but perhaps not everyone. Those are the individuals against which internal controls are designed to protect your company.

Rule Two: The Best Internal Controls Are Preventive

It does little good to detect a problem after the fact. Someone may be caught in the act of embezzlement, but by that time the assets may have been spent and the chances of recovery are long gone. Preventive plans are the better option.

Above all, employees should know about these preventive measures. The whole idea is to deter staff from even thinking about stealing from the company. There may be those who will try, but the marginal types will look for a softer target that's more easily penetrated.

To be effective, your company's internal control system must begin with a commitment from management to make security a priority, as well as to outline, implement, and abide by security procedures. Components of security procedures may vary based on the industry, but the purpose of all such procedures is to create an environment that makes stealing difficult.

One of the greatest contributors to a sound security plan is your company's accounting system and the measures it has established. By its very nature, the accounting system should provide an environment that identifies, classifies, and verifies various assets. Done right, the system will track funds disbursal and in general create a paper trail to follow when tracking finances. In short, your accounting department is a key component in your security procedures.

Red Flag
Announcing company internal controls is an effective part of the deterrence mechanism; people tend to be more honest if they know they're more likely to get caught. But never broadcast the details of the plan. Those experienced in security issues know that clever criminals will find a way to bypass systems if they truly want to. The less they know about the particulars of a security system, the better.

Establishing Internal Controls

Unless a company has hired a security expert or is large enough to have a security force that protects both your facilities and your workers, the accounting department is probably responsible for establishing and maintaining internal controls. Your firm may also have an internal auditing department that checks these procedures. Either way, the system depends on standard accounting practices.

No matter how large or sophisticated the internal controls department may be, the key responsibilities for every company are about the same:

Red Flag
Most accounting systems offer their greatest measure of control when transactions are entered into the system. It's not unusual for someone to make an occasional error; in fact, it's only human. However, a constant flow of errors means something else is going on and needs to be investigated.

➤ The plan must provide for a separation of operational responsibilities within departments, particularly for the accounting function. Had the controller in our opening scenario shared accounting responsibilities, chances are she never would have had the chance to embezzle anything. Of course, there's always the possibility of collusion, but that's less likely than for one apple to go bad.

➤ Staff experience must match their responsibilities. This is especially true for smaller firms, where the head of internal controls might be simply the manager who drew the short straw. Most companies wouldn't want an inexperienced person to design and produce their products. Why, then, would you choose someone without the proper qualifications to be responsible for your security?

➤ A company needs a system of effective policies and procedures, including strong authorization and recording procedures. Companies that have been following good accounting principles all along probably already have this in place. As much as feasible, policies and procedures must address all possible contingencies.

➤ Finally, and perhaps most important, keep recording and custody of assets separate. If one person is responsible for the paperwork and another is responsible for signing checks, allowing credits, and handling petty cash, for example, you close the door on significant opportunities for wrongdoing.

The Bottom Line: Cost

Shortcut
A simple method of internal control for larger companies consists of rotating employees in accounting and other areas of greatest risk. A person is generally less likely to play with the figures if he or she knows someone else will be handling those figures as well. In some companies, job rotation is routine, for several reasons. This one makes sense —and dollars.

There's always a cost to any system of internal controls. But that cost is far less than the loss of assets left unprotected. If you're not sure, ask yourself how much your business risks losing: $10,000? $100,000? If it's less than the cost of establishing internal controls, don't worry about the system—just take the losses as they come. But if a loss of assets would really hurt your business, it's worth investing in internal controls.

One of the best security safeguards available is a fidelity bond, bought to cover employees who have access to funds. Bonding guarantees the employee's past exhibits no evidence of wrongdoing such that it would impact your company's financial safety. (If there is evidence of wrongdoing, the provider will not bond the employee.) A bond also is an insurance policy. In the unlikely event that the bonded employee does steal, the bonding company will pay the victim and then go after the perpetrator. That's a nice ally to have.

Setting Up a Control System

Accounting systems offer different avenues for fraud and embezzlement. Here's a look at some of the more vulnerable areas, as well as some ideas on how to avoid trouble.

Monitoring Accounts Payable

Accounts payable is one of any company's most vulnerable areas for fraud. Although not a source of liquid cash, it is the company's primary source of outflow of funds. Payment to vendors who have never provided the service for which they're being paid, false invoices, or totals that have been altered all require a little more savvy than merely dipping one's hand into the till. But pilferage of accounts payable is well worth the effort for enterprising employees.

As we noted earlier, the best bet is to separate functions, such as payment authorization, accounting, and disbursement of funds, and have different people handle each one. This will reduce the opportunity for fraud and better safeguard company assets. (Of course, the more business a company does in cash, the greater the risk of fraud.)

Consider the following scenario:

➤ When workers are unloading a shipment at the warehouse, the receiving clerk verifies that the goods match the invoice and the workers are storing them properly.

➤ The accounting staff enters invoice amounts into accounts payable, reviewing purchase orders for invoice accuracy. A second person's signature may be required to verify entry accuracy.

➤ A third party, someone external to the accounting function, holds the prenumbered checks and delivers them to the accounting officer. Checks are cut based on the payment schedule established by the accounting officer.

➤ The disbursement officer—perhaps the chief financial officer—signs the checks after reviewing the work done by the accounting staff. The unused check stock is returned to the third party who verifies the number of checks used and the number of checks remaining.

It is assumed at this point that the accounts payable subledger agrees with the general ledger. That, too, is an important safeguard. The check-writing process should never have gotten this far if the two disagree.

Shortcut
Your internal control system requirements will change as conditions and staff change. Make sure all bank records and especially official signatures are updated and ready before you need them.

An Eye on Accounts Receivable

Once again, separation of duties is the key to safely managing accounts receivable (A/R). The person who makes the sale, of course, is not likely to record the sale in A/R. That should be done by the accounting staff, taking care to make sure the amount is recorded accurately. The sales invoice is a primary milestone along the A/R paper trail here.

When it comes to receiving payment, it's wise to assign two separate staff to processing: one person to handle the actual payment and another to post it to the general ledger. The check recipient, who may be stationed outside of accounting, should log the payment, prepare the bank deposit, and provide the necessary documentation to A/R. This may include deposit receipts, check stubs, and photocopies of the actual checks.

This method has two advantages. In addition to reducing the chance for misappropriation of customer payments, it also speeds the check through processing.

Keeping Tabs on Inventory

The biggest problem here is inventory that walks away in the night. The best internal control mechanism is the comprehensive record-keeping that follows materials through to their completion as finished goods or a perpetual inventory system. If you've been following the appropriate steps outlined in our chapter on inventory control, you will have an extensive string of checks and balances against which to compare physical stock.

Of course, that requires a physical inventory against which records can be measured. But a more frequent check of your inventory should reduce the incidence of pilferage and theft. It also might help to remind the warehouse manager of his or her responsibility for any missing inventory. Generally, the more concern you show about your inventory, the less likely employees are to be casual about it.

Red Flag

In most cases, the chief financial officer and other company officers are charged with managing internal controls. However, if any of them are undergoing extreme personal problems, particularly of a financial nature, they should not have that authority no matter what their level of seniority. Sometimes a crisis can alter judgment and cause an otherwise honest and trustworthy person to make a mistake.

Watching Payroll

Improperly or illegally completed time sheets and time cards punched by someone other than the employee are probably the most common forms of payroll theft. Incorrectly completed piecework reports are another area of abuse. There even have been cases of several employees conspiring to create a fictional employee and then sharing that person's paycheck.

Suffice it to say a close eye, strict accountability, and swift punishment are necessary to keep this form of petty pilferage in line before it adds up to significant losses. Two adages to bear in mind are:

➤ A trickle of water, unchecked, becomes a stream.

➤ One bad apple can spoil the whole barrel.

Handling Internal Cash Accounts

Despite the fact that this area often offers the smallest amount of remuneration, internal cash accounts, and especially petty cash, come under everyone's watchful eye just because the opportunity for theft appears so evident. Some guidelines for petty cash are:

➤ The imprest system is perhaps the best. A petty cash fund is established for a set amount, then reimbursed periodically to return the balance to that amount.

➤ Appoint one individual as keeper of the cash, responsible for monitoring the balance.

➤ Appoint a second person to be responsible for distributing petty cash.

➤ Require written approval from management for any petty cash disbursement. (That's the paper trail again.)

➤ When the fund is reimbursed, the total of the amounts approved for disbursement should equal the difference between the original amount and the current balance. In other words, the paper trail should cover the missing cash.

➤ Minimize the amount of money passing through petty cash. Some businesses do a lot of small cash transactions. That may not mean they need a large petty cash fund. They might be able to lower the set amount and reimburse the fund more frequently. Or, if they're paying out cash to certain recipients regularly, they could try to arrange running a tab, so they could pay by occasional check rather than with petty cash.

Shortcut
One of your best resources for controlling fraud is making sure all subledgers and the general ledger balance, something that needs to be done anyway as a part of general accounting procedure. If they're out of whack consistently, chances are something is wrong. It may not be much, but how much can you afford to lose? Of course, the reason may be poor accounting practices and errors, but that's also a problem you'd want to resolve.

In terms of short-term cash investments, the role of separate responsibility comes into play once again. Make sure the officer investing the cash does not have the authority to record the transaction. It also is wise for the investing officer not to have a personal account with that same investment firm. The chance of an inadvertent transfer of company funds to a personal account is not as likely as the prospect of collusion between the officer and the broker, but why take unnecessary chances?

Can You Beat the System?

There's always the chance, and occasionally the opportunity, for some enterprising employee to beat the security checkpoints that have been established. Consider just two examples in the headlines recently: credit cards and computers. No matter what security measures credit card companies and computer network administrators take, someone finds a flaw in the system. No system is perfect.

Smart companies are always looking for ways to improve internal controls even before the need arises. By preempting criminal strikes, they can protect assets and keep employees from being tempted into fraud. Such systems require several things:

➤ Managers who understand what's at risk and are committed to protecting the company's assets

➤ A solid accounting system that provides an adequate system of checks and balances and a comprehensive paper trail for all transactions

➤ Proper division of duties, to keep employees from both the temptation and the opportunity for wrongdoing

There's no last word when it comes to internal controls, but following these guideposts would be an excellent start.

The Least You Need to Know

➤ All companies, large and small, need effective internal controls.

➤ The best internal controls are preventive, aimed at reducing the possibility of fraud.

➤ Key control factors focus on separating operational and custodial responsibility and establishing effective policies and procedures.

➤ The cost of any internal control system is likely to be less than the amount of loss from not having one.

Part 4
Sources of Funds and Acumen

No business can run without an adequate supply of capital. Your company will likely need an infusion of funds from time to time to underwrite capital purchases or pursue new markets. That's normal business.

In fact, companies with smart managers can leverage other people's money in order to grow in size and profitability. Everybody knows about how developer Donald Trump built his empire around money from outside sources. He's just one example of knowing how to make money work. With the right management, your company may be able to make some smart moves, too.

This section introduces the basics of several sources of funds and expertise. If your company can pursue the right source of finance the right way, chances are it will have all the capital flow it needs when it's needed—even if you don't have Donald Trump calling the shots.

Chapter 14

Managing Commercial Lenders

In This Chapter

➤ Learning the role of commercial lenders in business

➤ Understanding the different types of financing

➤ Picking a lender and getting a loan

➤ Knowing what to do after the paperwork is signed

➤ Deciding what to do if the banker says no

In the past, if you said the words "commercial banker," the image that immediately came to mind was of a gray pinstriped suit, a steely gaze, and a big stogie clenched between the teeth. Today that image is no longer accurate. Most bankers prefer smaller cigars.

Seriously, your banker—let's say "lender," because these days business funds come from all types of sources—can be one of your company's greatest allies. As a financial partner, a reliable lender who is familiar with your company's business and understands your industry may be the one resource that keeps your operation afloat during hard times. And, like any resource, your company's relationship with its lender must be handled with the proper care and feeding.

Business Is Business

Make no mistake. The lender may personally like your executive team and admire the company's goals. But ultimately the lender will provide money for your company because he or she sees it as a sound financial decision that provides the appropriate returns. Your executive team, in turn, may like and respect the lender. But first and foremost, your company should go where the rates, terms, and expertise are most advantageous to the situation.

That's the way business works. Companies and lenders that do business otherwise are not likely to remain in business for long. Their alliance is based on a matching of financial interests and trust: The lender trusts the company to pay the loan and the interest, and the company trusts in its own ability to make the loan pay for itself and more. Let that reality help you keep things in proper perspective when dealing with lenders.

You may not be directly responsible for seeking loans from your company's lender. That task may be reserved for your chief executive officer or chief financial officer. But it helps to know what they're doing, so you and your department can help make the company the most appealing loan customer possible.

Are You a Good Candidate?

What?
A *small business loan* is traditionally defined as a loan to a company with less than $5 million in annual sales. (It's the business that is small and not the loan, which could start at $100,000.) Often such loans can be handled by the lender's small business loan department. If your company does better than that, it would probably seek a commercial loan.

Lenders love any business that guarantees a good return with limited risk. Who wouldn't? That's why many lenders prefer reliable ventures with a proven track record that offer good reward with little risk. Unfortunately, that practicality makes it more difficult for new and young businesses.

How can your company improve its chances of getting a loan? To increase your appeal as a loan candidate, keep these basics in mind:

➤ Positive cash flow is critical to the company's image of stability.

➤ Valuable collateral—such as real estate, operating equipment, and even a reliable list of accounts receivable—also increases loan opportunities.

➤ A strong management team is vital. If a company demonstrates it has the personnel to make best use of the loan, the lender is more likely to make the loan.

Types of Loans

Different lending institutions offer different types of loans based on a variety of factors. The details will be found in their brochures. But to help you make sense of all those details, you should know some essential things about the following kinds of loans:

➤ Basic commercial loans

➤ Term loans

➤ Lines of credit

➤ Time/sales financing

Basic Commercial Loans

Commercial loans are granted for growing a business. They are usually due in one year or less. They can cover anything and everything—real estate, equipment, or inventory, for example. The loans can be in any amount, with the larger loans often requiring approval from the lender's loan committee. Some smaller banks may need help to underwrite larger loans; they can work with correspondent banks, which serve as sources of additional lending capital.

Loans can be secured or unsecured. If a loan is *secured*, the borrower pledges collateral to offset the loss to the lender in case of default. If a loan is *unsecured*, there is no pledge of collateral, and the loan tends to cost more in terms of higher interest rates because of the greater risk to the lender. (Banks generally accept the risk of unsecured loans only with well-capitalized and profitable companies, not with new or smaller companies.) The collateral pledged to secure a loan might be anything of value: real estate, equipment, and inventory. In some cases, your accounts receivable also can be used as collateral.

Term Loans

If you need money for a longer period, between one and five years, what you want is a term loan. These are like commercial loans in that they may be either secured or unsecured by collateral. There is a difference: Term loans require periodic repayments.

Companies often use term loans to finance their growth strategies. A savvy lender will draft a term loan to fit a company's specific needs, making it easier for the company to borrow—and for the lending institution to earn more interest. (Lenders may be nice, but they've got to take care of business!) Customized term loans also tend to cultivate a better relationship between the client and the lending institution, an assurance of more business in the future. That's an advantage for both the borrower and lender, as business allies.

However, lenders are likely to evaluate companies very carefully before issuing term loans. Over time, fortunes change. Since term loans often take several years to mature, the borrowing company could run into financial difficulty, compromising the lending institution beyond its comfort level. Many companies find short-term commercial loans easier to get than term loans for that very reason.

> ### Journal Entry
>
> Chattel mortgages are another sources of funds. More familiar in the manufacturing world, chattel mortgages allow companies to borrow against the value of specific business assets, such as manufacturing equipment, for example. The equipment, or "chattel," is used to secure the loan.

Lines of Credit

A line of credit is an open source of funds that may be drawn as needed to a maximum level agreed to by the lender and the borrower. The amount and terms of the loan are set in advance and based on the company's situation and asset balance. Companies use this source of capital for seasonal needs, most often to lay in stock for sale around the holidays or to make it through a period of slow sales. They can generally pay off the debt within a short time.

Lines of credit are handled in different ways, but most are executed through renewable 90-day notes. In most cases, the balance is due within a year. In addition, the lender may require that the credit be supported (for example, by deposits or checking accounts at the institution). The lender may also require that the borrowing company, after paying off the loan, refrain from using the credit line for one or two months. The rate usually depends on the financial strength of the company, the size of the loan, and the value of the collateral. It's often one or two percentage points over the prime rate for established firms and slightly higher for new firms or in other situations of greater risk.

Time/Sales Financing

Have you ever bought an appliance on a time plan with no payments due for 90 days? Then you know about time/sales financing—at least from the outside.

This may be an option for your company if it offers time plans as part of its sales approach. Companies that do this regularly can't afford to carry the full financial burden required by such plans. So, the companies sell and assign the time plan contracts to a financial institution, which makes money servicing the loan—what buying on time is, essentially—until it's paid up or interest begins to accrue.

The financial institution usually purchases such contracts at a discount and takes as collateral the business's interest in the conditional sales contract. As the institution receives payment from the customer, it pays the business, often withholding a percentage (five to ten percent is common) until the customer has paid the entire amount, as further protection against default. Rates and ratios are adjusted as the accounts receivable change in value due to depreciation of the collateral.

Journal Entry

Another source of business funds—almost the flip side of time/sales financing—is through trade credits. Simply put, trade credits result when a business is given 30, 60, or 90 days to pay for goods or services. That payment period amounts to a short-term loan from the provider. Depending on the industry, trade credits can make up a significant percentage of the liabilities listed on the accounts payable side of balance sheets for non-financial companies.

Picking a Lender

Choosing the right lender for your specific business needs is a lot like choosing any partner. The terms and conditions have to be right—and so do the personalities.

Because of the advantages of finding the best fit, your company should shop around before settling on a particular lender. The largest or best-known bank in the community may not be the right one for your firm. Your company should define what it wants and decide what it can offer as collateral, then go out and find the partner.

Journal Entry

The best time to shop for a commercial lender is not when debts are past due and the wolves are at the front door. At that point company financials look their worst and the borrower appears to present the greatest risk to lenders. Shop instead when conditions are calm and cash flow is strong. Your firm will make a better impression and generate better terms.

Be Choosy

What are some of the criteria when choosing a banking partner? Here are a few:

➤ *Fit the lender to the size of your company.* Your company's lender must have sufficient capacity to meet the borrowing needs of your company, of course. But consider the other side of the equation as well: Your company and its needs must be big enough to attract sufficient attention from a lender. Finding the right-sized lender is part of making the best fit.

➤ *Pick a lender that understands your business.* Industries differ, and an institution with a clear idea of what it takes to produce your particular kind of widgets stands a better chance of serving your company than one that doesn't understand.

➤ *Find an institution that takes a proactive stance in helping manage company finances.* Today, institutions need to be more than passive sources of loans. The best ones look for ways to help their client companies better manage cash flow, finances, and other elements of their business. These services may be available for a fee, in some cases, but sometimes they may be just a value-added benefit of dealing with a particular lender. Whatever the case, a proactive institution will be a better investment of company time and money.

➤ *Look for a positive personal chemistry between your executive staff and the lender.* People like to do business with people they like—that's basic human nature. It's especially true when that business involves money or credit. Make sure the lender's knowledge and professionalism meet your company's standards. The lender should be reliable, honest, and available when needed. Your executives must be generally comfortable with the lender—and the lender should feel the same about your executives. If there are personal differences, there likely never will be professional comfort.

> **Shortcut**
> You want money, of course, but what else? Is your company usually profitable, but now caught in a particularly difficult time? Is your company solid, but beginning to consider expansion strategies? Is your company generally well-managed and seeking capital to finance a project? What you need in a lender will depend on your answers to such questions as these.

> **Shortcut**
> Check any lender's references before embarking on a relationship. Past performance with other similar businesses is the quickest way to determine if the match is right for your company. Again, this part of the process should involve the company's accountant.

Looking for Mr. Goodloan

How does a company go about finding that lending institution? First of all, your borrowing staff should get recommendations from other professionals—accountants, attorneys, and others you know and trust in your industry. As they shop for the institutions, the staff should meet the loan officers with whom they would be working, and interview the loan officers while they themselves are being interviewed. Above all, check the lender's references with other businesses the lender has served. This prospecting should involve the company's accountant and attorney.

For the most part, a lending institution's safety and soundness will be guaranteed by the FDIC or other government agency, so your executives don't need to worry about that question. But they should work at uncovering the rest of the information.

Getting the Loan

Like any business procedure, there are certain steps borrowers must follow when applying for a loan. Some occur before the fact, some during the transaction, and some after the funds have been received. But all are important and the better they're managed, the more professional impression your company will make.

That impression is no substitute for having the right numbers in the book, of course, but it can't hurt.

But First...

Here are some things you need to do before taking the loan:

➤ Know how much the company wants to borrow, how it's going to use that money, and how it will pay it back. Loan requests based on strategy are granted far more readily than loans accompanied only by fuzzy ideas and financial need.

➤ Make sure that corporate profiles are up to date and strategic plans are in place and operational. Your company's strategic plan is the single most important tool in proving to lenders, venture capitalists, and other funds sources that the company is a good investment because it knows what it's doing. What's more, the knowledge is all down in black and white.

➤ Outline all necessary conditions, including amount, terms, rates, and conditions. Ideally, loan conditions should be part of your strategic plan. At the very least, they should be adding to, not subtracting from, the company's cash flow or net worth.

➤ Have the company's CFO or accountant prepare a projection that demonstrates borrowing needs and a repayment time frame. Since it takes time to obtain a loan and receive the money, it's important to plan how the business is going to operate in the interim period.

➤ Select a lender and find out everything possible about their operation, lending philosophy, and other facets of character that will affect your "loan-ability."

➤ Put the loan request in writing and rehearse the key points of the presentation. Your executives may have to sell the lender on why the company should receive this loan, and that means clearly identifying what's in it for them, both in terms of revenue and future business. If your execs impress the lender by providing more than mere background information—thus making the lender's work easier—so much the better.

Shortcut
Making the loan decision easy for the lender is probably the quickest way to get the money. When meeting with the lender, your executives should have ready cash flow projections and a schedule of operating and asset needs. That will help the lender decide if you're a good risk or not.

Meeting and Greeting the Lender

Your company's first contact with the lender likely will be by telephone: That's the first opportunity to sell him or her on your company and its goals as they relate to the loan in question. In the case of commercial loans, borrowers should be prepared to describe the nature of the business as well as past financial particulars. If the company or its principals have provided all the financing up to that point, then the borrower should be in good shape. If the business is heavily leveraged or plagued with debt, your executives might find themselves facing a little greater challenge.

The lender's going to ask a lot of questions, many of which may, at first, seem personal to your executives requesting the loan. But the lender needs to know these things in order to make a sound loan decision. Questions may include:

➤ *"What are you going to use the money for?"* No, the right answer is not "None of your business!" The lender needs to know because that will tell him or her more about the company's capital position and what type of return the institution can expect. Companies that need funds to invest in the future are quite a bit different from those that need the money to pay off the past. Your company's reasons will help determine the rates and terms of the loan.

➤ *"How much do you need?"* This is not the same as "How much do you want?" This question helps identify the company's true financial condition and forces a certain conservation of resources. As long as the loan offered is enough to get the job done without leaving your firm hanging halfway through a project or process, a little less might be a better strategy, because it will force you to do a little more with what you already have.

➤ *"When do you need the money?"* Again, "Yesterday" is not the best answer, because it says a lot about your company's financial management. Don't borrow when you don't need to, but don't wait until the last minute. That brings an air of desperation to your plea, resulting in less favorable terms, since the lender is likely to feel less confident in your company's management skills. The end result often is higher interest rates and shorter terms.

➤ *"What is your payback plan?"* This is the most obvious question. Most lenders allow greater room for negotiation on commercial loans than they would for consumer loans. Your company's executives should know exactly how the company plans to pay back the loan and how it expects to generate the funds to make those payments.

What's the single most effective tool you have to answer these and other questions? If you answered "business plan," you've obviously been paying attention.

> ### Journal Entry
>
> Although your emphasis should be on planning, you should come to your meeting with a potential lender prepared to negotiate. Know how much you can scale down your expectations. Again, this means knowing both how much you want and how much you need. It also means prioritizing amount, time, and terms. If you have to choose, which is most important to you? How important? You may want to work out several alternative plans, detailing amount, time, and terms: $A at B percent for C months, $D at E percent for F months, and so forth.

The Five Cs of Credit

When it comes right down to it, lending is a science based on the following five foundation pillars, known as The Five Cs of Credit:

➤ *Character.* The lender has a fiduciary responsibility to his institution to make good loans. Thus, the character of the borrower is one of the strongest determinants of whether or not the loan is granted. Lenders will make loans only to those they believe will repay the debt on time and according to the set terms.

➤ *Capacity.* Simply put, will your company be fiscally able to repay the loan if it is granted?

➤ *Capital.* Do your company principals have an adequate financial stake in their own business? If not, chances are they won't work as hard to protect those assets and make both the business and loan succeed.

➤ *Collateral.* What will your company pledge to secure the loan? Will that pledge be adequate to cover the loan's value if your company defaults? If your company is an established business with a great performance record, you may qualify for an unsecured loan, in which case, you don't need to worry about collateral.

➤ *Conditions.* Even well-established businesses suffer from difficult conditions from time to time. These might include—or even be dominated by—conditions beyond the company's control, such as market fluctuations, product devaluation, and other critical changes that may reduce the value of the company product. Borrowers should be wary and try to anticipate such trends. The lender must also do his or her best to anticipate such conditions. Neither your company nor your lender wants to be taken by surprise.

> ### Red Flag
> Are the company's books in order for previous years? Taxes all paid up? The lender may want to see proof. Not having it ready may delay the loan.

The Paperwork

We've emphasized throughout this chapter that your company and the lending institution are business partners. Here's where that relationship changes—or at least where the question of perspective enters.

For your company, the primary purpose of a loan is to obtain capital. But from the lender's point of view, the primary purpose of a loan is to make money through interest on that loan. It's not surprising, then, that the lender drafts all loan documents with covenants attempting to tell the borrower what he or she can and can't do. Some of these covenants may be negotiable, while others may be non-negotiable. Those that are too restrictive, however, may actually lessen the benefits of the loan—for both partners—if they forestall company growth.

> **Red Flag**
>
> When it comes to loan covenants, beware the conditions. Some lenders put constraints on additional borrowing, while others may restrict you from acquiring additional assets or hiring new managers. Make sure your company can live with the terms asked before signing on the dotted line.

The conditions of the loan covenant should be calculated before the agreement is signed, to determine that the company can comply with the covenants. This should be done as part of your negotiations. It's simple: Understand completely what you're signing and make sure all the terms are written down in black and white.

Remember that your company and the lender are allies—but on opposite sides of the table. Have your attorney and your CPA review the loan agreement carefully before you sign it. Don't hurry to get the money at this point; you may regret your haste.

Personal Guarantees

The lender may also require personal guarantees from the company owners to ensure that the loan will be repaid in full. Requests for personal guarantees usually come if collateral for the loan is insufficient, if the company's relationship with the lender has suffered in recent months, or if there have been management changes, performance problems, or other conditions that might raise questions for the lender.

Personal guarantees are dangerous, because in the event the company runs into trouble, the guarantees personally obligate the individuals who give them. Under adverse conditions, lenders may be quick to call the loan, which can mean the individuals who signed guarantees may need to liquidate personal assets to pay the debt, regardless of what the business is capable of doing. So, be aware of the danger of personal guarantees—but know also that many loans now require them.

Building Lender Relationships

After warning you about all the problems that can arise over a loan, we should assure you that most loans serve their purpose without any complications. In fact, many form the basis of excellent relationships between businesses and lenders. The most savvy borrowers build good relationships with their lenders, sharing information and further establishing themselves as good financial risks and solid contributors to the business community.

The key to this scenario is open and honest communication with the lender, both when you're negotiating a loan and throughout the course of your relationship. Share both good news and bad when appropriate, and your company may be surprised at how the lender comes to its aid, if only to protect his or her financial interests. Invite the lender to visit your company operations and meet the management team. The more comfortable the lender is with your company, the better your business relationship will be. The bottom line: No one likes surprises, so communicate information—whether it's good or bad—on a timely basis.

And if the Lender Says No?

The world of finance can be a hard place. Many companies in search of loans get turned down. That's the way the business operates. The first thought is simply to visit another lender, and that may be the most logical option. But there also may be some lessons to learn from rejection.

If a lender denies your loan application, here are some questions that you might want to consider:

➤ Is your loan request logical, reasonable, and appropriate at this time? Is there another way to get beyond this financial hump other than borrowing?

➤ Did you document and present your loan request properly? Do company executives need to review the information shared and their style of presentation?

➤ Are there aspects of your company's financial condition that executives should be more concerned about? Does the financial statement represent the true picture? If so, is that picture sending lenders signals to which your company's managers should pay more attention? In other words, are there problems that money can't remedy? If so, take care of them or you may continue to be frustrated in your search for a loan.

If a lender denies your loan application, you should calmly and tactfully ask him or her to explain why. You may not get an answer—or an honest answer. But if the lender feels comfortable with you and if you show you're looking for problems that you can then fix, rather than hoping to bully the lender into granting the loan, you should be able to learn something about why the lender didn't find your company worthy of a loan.

The bottom line: We often learn more from our mistakes than from our successes. That's as true when applying for a loan as it is for anything else.

The Least You Need to Know

➤ A lender can be one of a company's greatest business allies. Choose a lender that matches the company in size, capability, interest, and expertise.

➤ Positive cash flow, good collateral, and outstanding management are all critical to being an attractive commercial loan client.

➤ Commercial loan types vary and should be chosen based on a company's specific needs.

➤ A company's strategic plan is its single most important tool for securing funds. This should include projections and cash flow requirements.

➤ Understand the Five Cs of Credit and adhere to them as much as possible.

➤ Bear in mind that loan documents are written to protect the lender as well as provide funds for the borrower. You're business allies, but with different interests.

➤ Build a strong relationship with the lender and adhere to your projections. Doing so will help future loan transactions proceed more smoothly.

Chapter 15

Utilizing Venture Capital

In This Chapter

➤ Understanding that it's an investment, not a loan

➤ Knowing what to expect from venture capitalists

➤ Finding the venture capital firm for you

➤ Attracting the interest of venture capitalists

➤ Making the presentation

➤ Watching for red flags involving venture capitalists

Loans from standard commercial lenders tend to be fairly common among businesses of various sizes and shapes. But the terms and limitations of such loans don't always satisfy every need. Sometimes more capital is required to make the engines of business hum, while at other times the purposes for which the funds are needed just don't satisfy commercial lenders. This is most often because a company has insufficient collateral or a poor or limited performance record, or because the need for the loan involves greater risks.

Enter the venture capitalist. It's the role of this person or firm to provide both the financial resources and management expertise businesses need to get a leg up on the competition. Some businesses, especially startup firms, owe their lives to venture capitalists. It's no wonder those investors are also called "angels."

It's essential for business managers to understand the difference between angels and standard financiers. The opportunities created by venture capitalists may be greater, but the involvement is very different. And so is your company's obligation to that angel.

What?
An *angel* is generally anybody who backs a project financially. In the world of business, that usually means a venture capitalist.

An Investment, Not a Loan

Unlike a bank, a venture capitalist does not loan money to a business, but invests money in it. So, as an investor, the venture capitalist is part owner of your firm. Your company's interests are his interests and your company's successes his successes.

Venture capitalists tend to be individuals or groups who have succeeded admirably in their own businesses and now are looking for a place to invest excess capital. They will take greater risks than commercial lenders, but they will require greater rewards in return. They're interested in your company's financial plans, goals, and demonstrated skills, but they also will more closely consider your product, the market, and the likelihood of your company growing.

In the end, the venture capital firm will be interested in a company's success because they will be sharing that success. The lender, on the other hand, will be interested mostly in how and when the borrower is going to repay the loan.

Journal Entry

The slam-bang 1980s saw a dramatic increase in investment capital available to companies. The more conservative '90s have done little to diminish that boom. The trend began in 1979, thanks to an overall reduction in capital gains taxes. A decade later the market had 80 times the amount of investment capital available than when the trend began. Estimates differ, but today some 600 venture capital firms have $32 billion in investable capital available to those who know where and how to look.

What to Expect from Venture Capitalists

Venture capitalists come in at the high end, usually picking up where Small Business Administration (SBA) loans leave off. The average SBA loan maxes out at around $750,000, while most venture capitalists won't even become interested until an investment of $250,000 is required. Anything less and the cost of investigation isn't worth the effort. Their involvement may range up into the millions if the idea is right, if the management team looks capable, and if the market appears lucrative.

But as you might have expected, qualifying for venture capital can be challenging. Depending on its size, a venture capital firm may receive up to several thousand proposals each year. The vast majority of proposals are rejected immediately because they don't fit the firm's specific criteria. Venture capital firms, like other businesses, have their areas of interest and expertise and tend not to operate outside them.

Journal Entry

On average, an effective venture capitalist expects a return of three to five times the original investment within five to seven years. That seems like a lot, especially when compared with the lower rates of interest on loans. But the venture capitalist can't expect this return on all investments, while the lender—with the exception of the rare loan default—obviously can. That means the reward must match the risk.

The proposals that aren't rejected are explored thoroughly by the firm before it makes any commitment. Such exploration may take months and may involve several layers of expertise, including evaluations of management, the market, and the product itself. The firm may hire consultants and conduct studies. The firm may invest several thousand dollars or more in investigating your proposal. The proposals that survive this initial investigation must undergo more rigorous investigations involving comprehensive background checks of the principals and studies of the market.

After all, your company may be asking these firms to become investing partners in a dream. They want to know all they can about the chances of that dream becoming a reality.

Like anyone else, venture capital firms prefer the most predictable risks and the highest rewards. That means established firms often have an edge over startups. But there are firms especially geared to helping startup companies or specializing in new product launches. If they can see ample reward for their level of risk, they just might invest in your company's proposal. In the end, the risk-reward ratio is the venture capital firm's bottom line.

Red Flag

Begin the search for investment capital before you need it. Anticipate your cash flow needs and plan accordingly. Wait too long and your company may be out of cash at the time it needs it most.

Finding the Right Venture Capital Firm

There are distinct steps your company will want to take in searching for the right venture capitalist. Like the commercial lenders described in the previous chapter, some will be better than others for your company:

➤ *Look for an investor capable of providing both the capital and expertise necessary.* If a company underestimates its financial needs, the impact can be disastrous to its business. The same holds true when choosing a venture capital firm. In addition, you'll want a firm that can participate meaningfully in managing those capital funds within your business. One of the key resources venture capital firms can bring is expertise. Like all resources, the more they can offer, the better off your company likely will be.

➤ *Look for a firm that understands your company's business and knows the market.* If you manufacture microchips, for example, your needs are different from those of an import firm or restaurant. The more the firm knows about your company's business before beginning the relationship, the more effective that relationship can be.

➤ *Require that the firm be reputable and ethical.* Ask for references or other proof that the firm is not a fly-by-night outfit—a partner your company will later regret.

➤ *Consider firms with proven track records.* The venture capitalist will expect a demonstrated level of expertise from the company, so there's no reason the company shouldn't expect the same from the venture capitalist. Effective firms have mastered a unique set of skills that involve both financial investment and business consulting. Your company will want a firm that won't shortchange it on either count.

Shortcut
Companies looking for quick growth and generous cash infusions may want to consider venture capital firms first because they tend to invest big and allow more time for a return on their money.

➤ *Look for venture capitalists with whom your executives can get along.* It sounds obvious, but most executives don't even give this one a thought. For the duration of their involvement, the venture capital firm will be your company's financial and perhaps even operational partner. Personal difficulties will get in the way of a professional relationship. Consider the pending partnership as you would a marriage. If it doesn't look like the two parties will be able to get along, don't get involved.

Don't Discount Informal Investors

Despite what we've just said about the need for reputable, well-known firms, there may be a place for informal investors in your company's growth scenario. These often are self-made individuals who can be tapped for cash or expertise for a smaller or limited-term endeavor.

Perhaps yours is a high-tech firm in need of a special prototype, the cost of which doesn't require full-fledged venture capital support. Perhaps your import business wants to expand to a new region of the country and you need funds for a temporary distribution infrastructure. In either scenario, an informal investor might be a better option.

Many business owners know such individuals personally. If you don't, however, make sure you investigate them thoroughly and clearly spell out their involvement and your obligations. That's just common sense and good business.

Attracting the Interest of Venture Capitalists

We've already briefly described some of the fundamentals of approaching venture capitalists. Once the venture capital firm accepts your company's initial proposal and launches its own investigations, however, the going tends to get tougher.

The best place to start is with a comprehensive business plan. The following elements will help lay the necessary groundwork for writing a good business plan:

➤ An executive summary and concise analysis of your company's current situation, to help bring the venture capitalist firm into your company's mind set.

➤ The concept behind your company's products or services and its development strategy.

➤ A description of the market and any appropriate segments.

➤ A comprehensive customer analysis, showing where the product or service sits in the public eye.

➤ A competitive analysis demonstrating your company's relationship with its competition.

➤ Your company's product and positioning statement that distinguishes it from the competition.

➤ Advertising and promotion strategies illustrating how the company plans to grow market share.

➤ A sales strategy that takes into account all competitive and market components.

➤ Product and market development plans that chart expected future growth of your company.

➤ An outline of company operations and an introduction to key staff. These will be especially critical in helping venture capital firms decide if you have what it takes to succeed.

➤ An up-to-date financial statement that shows your company is currently financially sound. Venture capitalists are unlikely to invest in a firm on shaky financial ground.

➤ A payback plan. In other words, when and how do you expect the investment to pay off for the venture capitalist and what terms do you propose for ending the partnership? This step may be the most critical to some investors, because it will answer their ultimate question: When can we count on getting an appropriate return on our money?

If your company has developed a comprehensive business plan, you should have answers to all the basic questions the venture capital firm might ask. Some answers will be of greater interest than others. Try to anticipate the biggest questions and address those up front.

Journal Entry

Another variation on the venture capital theme is the formation of strategic alliances between and among complementing companies to better capitalize on a specific skills set. This approach to business—which you may recognize as "supply chain management"—may offer great advantages. The financial investment for the collaborating companies may be lower and they can make better use of their resources.

If any of the above factors stand out as most important in attracting the interest of venture capitalists, they are the following:

➤ The competence and experience of management

➤ The product or market elements that distinguish this company or its proposal above all others

A well-organized, professional, and well-led management team is essential for continuing the company's operation and safeguarding the venture capital invested in it. The distinguishing market or product characteristic is what puts the company ahead of the pack. Together, these two elements are what most likely will drive the success of the firm and protect the investment.

Knocking on the Right Doors

Finding a venture capital firm is not like finding buyers for your widgets. Companies' executives can't walk through the front door, announce their interest in doing business, and wait for a thumbs-up or a thumbs-down. They also don't want to take a scattergun approach, sending out a proposal to every firm they happen to come across. It's considered bad form and word can get around.

Think of the proposal process almost as a dating ritual from ages past. If your company's executives have prepared diligently and identified the five to ten firms they think might be the most likely capital investors, the next step is to arrange for an introduction. That may come through an attorney, accountant, banker, or other professional who's familiar with both parties and able to arrange a meeting in a suitable way.

Your company may have to contrive such a meeting or employ the services of an intermediary at anywhere from five to ten percent of the total deal price. That intermediary will examine the proposal and help you decide which venture capital firm is the most likely to buy into your company's goals and ideas. The whole procedure may sound a little archaic and slow, but keep in mind the importance of your goal and your chances of securing the funding—one in ten on average. The rewards should make it worth the extra effort.

Red Flag
No matter how likely it is the relationship will succeed, assume the deal will not close. That way you'll be on your toes throughout the solicitation process and you'll be planning alternative sources of financing.

Fine-Tuning Your Presentation

Once your company has gotten through the door—or, if yours is a going concern, you've likely gotten your prospective partner through your door for a site visit—the success of your oral presentation will be critical for closing the deal. Here are a few dos and don'ts for the executives making your pitch:

➤ DO be well-versed and well-rehearsed in all elements of your operation as well as with your proposal. The venture capitalist should by now be familiar with the proposal and may have questions that go beyond that document.

➤ DON'T be slick to the point of emphasizing style over substance. Venture capitalists are highly sophisticated and will be turned off by whatever feels like a snow job.

➤ DO anticipate the venture capitalist's questions and prepare answers. The less time your representatives spend digging through papers in their briefcases, the more confident and in control they will seem.

➤ DON'T assume the venture capitalist understands the unique nature of your company's product and its presence on the market. Be prepared to provide an interpretive presentation that takes everyone's basic understanding to the next level.

Red Flag
Once you've courted and won an investor, they may want to close the deal with the execution of a terms sheet that outlines the specifics. But the terms sheet doesn't guarantee the investor has money in the bank. Insist on checking the investor's references before signing on the dotted line. Otherwise, your company may be tied to someone with the desire but not the means to finance your venture.

➤ DO have available supporting documentation, literature, even product prototypes that will help make important points more clearly.

➤ DON'T rely on just one of your company's representatives to do all the talking. Venture capitalists often will note not only how their questions are answered, but also who answers them, as a way of measuring the company's expertise. If the executive team sits mutely by while the marketing vice president fumbles for answers, that may send the wrong message to potential investors.

After the presentation, there will be a lag time in which the investor will launch his or her investigation. During this period your company may want to approach other firms and make similar presentations, but do so discreetly. If a firm is hesitating for any reason, knowing you are checking around may be all they need to reject the proposal.

Final Considerations

Your executive team may have designed a riveting proposal and made an outstanding presentation. But two final factors will ultimately decide whether the proposal will become a plan:

➤ *Your company's finances.* Are they sound? Is the company saddled with debt? Does it have the financial wherewithal to make this deal work?

➤ *The terms of the deal.* What's in this deal for the investor? Is what's being offered well worth what's being asked? Will both parties prosper in the end?

The right responses here will make all the difference. What responses would be right? That depends on the investor. If you've gotten enough information about the firm, you should be able to come up with the right answers to these questions. Your company's finances should be generally solid (that goes without saying, for any prospective investor).

Red Flags Involving Your Venture Capitalist

The venture capital firm will spend from three to six months doing market share analysis, poring over your company's financial statements, and talking with employees, customers, and competitors. The firm is looking for your company's shortcomings, the things the team purposely chose not to share.

Meanwhile, your executives chew their fingernails and hope for the best. But they should be considering a few questions:

➤ Did the executives find it difficult to get through to the major partners of the venture capital firm when they needed to reach them? Chances are it will get only worse once the two parties become involved.

➤ Do the investors/partners seem to want to micromanage your business? That's the type of relationship your company will want to avoid.

➤ What does the venture capital firm's portfolio look like? Are their past relationships successful? Or do you see a lot of struggling or failed companies?

➤ Does the venture firm have a steady source of capital? Or do partners come and go through an endlessly revolving door? The latter could signal a lack of cash when you need it.

➤ Does the venture capital firm's management team have the real-world experience and maturity you will need? In most cases, a new MBA with no real experience, no matter how promising, is still just that—promising. Only time will tell if that person can deliver.

And the last thing you can afford from your venture capital firm is to buy a pig in a poke. Or even an MBA in a poke, for that matter.

The Least You Need to Know

➤ Venture capitalists don't lend money; they make an investment in a business. There's a big difference.

➤ Venture capitalists favor investment opportunities of $250,000 and up. Most consider anything less as not worth their time and expense.

➤ Venture capitalists accept only ten percent of all business proposals presented to them, meaning the competition for dollars is stiff.

➤ Choose a venture capital firm that meets the special needs and has the product knowledge of your company.

➤ Companies need comprehensive business plans to attract venture capitalists.

➤ Management competency and your company's unique product or market position are two key elements of interest to venture capitalists.

Chapter 16

Proprietorship, Partnership, or Incorporation?

In This Chapter

➤ Weighing the pros and cons of sole proprietorships

➤ Deciding when to partner and when to pass

➤ Incorporating businesses of any size

➤ Filing for incorporation

➤ Stepping stones to incorporation

The structure of your company's business will help determine both its financial risk and reward, but it is also a legal question. The amount of liability your company's principals can afford to carry is somewhat related to the amount of capital they can afford to pledge to their business. For most business leaders, the days of building a financial empire with their own two hands are well past. Today, they need to consider other options.

Business Building Blocks

Every business is somewhat different in its structure, but the basic business building blocks break down into three distinct types:

➤ Sole proprietorships

➤ Partnerships

➤ Corporations

Whatever your position in the company, you should be familiar with its structure and basic characteristics. Of course, knowing the fundamentals about the three types of structure also helps you to understand better how your vendors and business customers—and competitors—operate.

Red Flag
The biggest advantage of a sole proprietorship—that you're on your own—is also the biggest disadvantage. The proprietorship is the same legal and economic unit as the individual who forms it. In other words, the owner receives all profits, but he or she also bears unlimited liability. That means suffering all losses and being liable for all the obligations incurred by the proprietorship.

Sole Proprietorships

If you've always wanted to run your own bait and tackle shop on the shores of Lake Ketchabigwon because the last thing in the world you want is to answer to a boss, then you're a prime candidate for a sole proprietorship. You're your own boss and your only limits are those imposed by state and federal regulations, your financial wherewithal, and your imagination. Sure, you have responsibilities. But no one is going to tell you how to meet those responsibilities except you.

Many businesses in the United States are sole proprietorships. As you might guess, most of them are small businesses. Yet even a large company with hundreds of employees can be a sole proprietorship. Look below the surface and see what's there.

Partnerships

Perhaps your ideal business venture involves one or more like-minded friends who share your passion for fishing or widgets or oak furniture. Perhaps none of the gang has enough money to start that business on his or her own. That's where a partnership structure comes in.

The law defines a partnership as "the association of two or more persons to carry on as co-owners of a business for profit." The partners may be equal or unequal, silent or active, and the structure may follow any one of dozens of variations. None of the partners enjoys as much personal freedom as he or she would have as a sole proprietor, but together they have more assets, a wider range of ideas, and greater depth of expertise from which to draw.

Journal Entry

Although partnerships generally begin as an agreement among several people who share an interest, it's important to remember that they need to agree also on how to share that interest. We've all experienced the frustration, disappointment, hurt feelings, and even anger that can result when several friends decide to spend a weekend camping or traveling. They realize that they may have quite different ways of preparing, of doing the same activities, and so forth. Now, imagine those sorts of differences arising within a business venture. Unless the partners understand each other and work out in advance what they want and how they intend to get it, the results can be disastrous.

Corporations

If primary liability is not your style and you have the vision, acumen, and legal support to develop a company that you expect to grow considerably, then incorporation may be just what you need. Incorporation removes direct liability from the principals, but it's a complex legal entity that requires a lot more structure and compliance than either a sole proprietorship or a partnership.

Unless unbridled personal freedom is your primary reason for going into business, then incorporation is the most likely choice for your company's structure. It's certainly a good choice if you have any concerns about whether you have enough capital and skills to make it as a sole proprietor or whether you could bring together partners and keep them thinking and acting along the same lines.

In most cases, incorporation is the most common structure among larger, successful firms. Quite often, a sole proprietorship or a partnership, as it grows in size and complexity, will decide to incorporate. That's generally a wise move for the owners.

What?

A *corporation* means forming a body: The owners decide to create a business entity that is legally separate from any and all of them. They may not even run the corporation, at least not directly, leaving operations to a board of directors. Their ownership is represented as an investment in shares of stock, which is also the extent of their legal liability.

Summary...and More

There are financial advantages to all three structures, depending on what you want from your business. There are also differences in the way the companies can operate. You've

Shortcut

It's not difficult to change from a sole proprietorship to a partnership to a corporation as your business develops. A business should start at a level that the owners can manage, or it could wither and die. Then, as it grows, the owners can change its structure and legal identity as appropriate.

probably noticed that you can sometimes do business with a sole proprietor at a lunch meeting and on a handshake. The same business deal with a partnership might require a series of meetings. If you're trying to work with a corporation, it could mean formal presentations in a board room and involve accountants and attorneys, depending on the size and structure of the company.

This chapter should give you a good working knowledge of business structure. But if you're thinking about starting your own business, remember that each structure also requires its own legal identity. Don't attempt to legally establish any business—particularly a corporation—without the help of a very good lawyer.

Considering Sole Proprietorships

For entrepreneurs who like to go it alone, a sole proprietorship is often the business structure of choice. It's also the easiest to start, because to get up and running, it merely requires securing the necessary permits—if any—from the appropriate local, state, or federal agencies. And you don't have to twist any partners' arms to get a consensus on anything—although you should certainly consult with an accountant and, as we recommended earlier, an attorney.

What's more, all the profits belong to the sole proprietor. Taxes can be declared on the standard 1040 IRS form, using Schedule C: Profit and Loss from a Business or Profession. (Sole proprietors will also need to complete Form 1040 ES: Declaration of Estimated Tax for Individuals, and to make quarterly estimated payments in January, April, June, and September.)

Sole proprietors have complete control over making decisions, greater flexibility when responding to market demands, freedom from bureaucracy, and direct control over expenses and revenues. But sole proprietors also live more fragile business lives, with only a single point of view. They say it's lonely at the top, but it can be just as lonely at the bottom, if you're a sole proprietor facing a business decision.

The success of a sole proprietorship is often directly dependent on the health and well-being of the proprietor. If you feel tired or you want to play hookey, you can't just call in sick and expect the business to thrive without you. Raising capital is sometimes a problem, so it's harder to get over financial obstacles and to take advantage of opportunities. Finally, as we mentioned before, the proprietor is directly responsible for all debts incurred—including any damages resulting from lawsuits.

Certain types of individuals and businesses thrive as sole proprietorships, while others crumble to dust. Anybody thinking about going it alone should definitely not arrive at that decision alone.

When to Partner and When to Pass

In some ways, partnerships are the most difficult of business structures, in other ways the most accommodating. As in so many aspects of life, one key to survival and maybe even success is having the right attitude. But it's also essential to establish and maintain a clear understanding of who does what, who's responsible for how much, and—because partners won't always agree on everything—who's in charge and who makes the tie-breaking decisions.

Partnerships have a legal definition under the law, of course, but no hard and fast criteria about what constitutes the partnerships. Different individuals bring different elements to the table, including financial support, ideas, expertise, labor, and other resources. How ownership of that partnership is distributed is up to the partners to decide. Determining the value of all but financial involvement may be difficult, but it can be done.

There are two very important points to remember about a partnership:

➤ In general, any partner can legally bind the partnership to a contract or other obligation.

➤ If there are financial obligations beyond the pooled resources of the partnership, the partners may be legally required to use their personal resources to pay those debts.

Just remember the cardinal rule of partnering with family or friends: The relationship will stay alive as long as the business thrives. Hard times ahead mean the relationship may soon be dead. There are variations on the saying, but you get the idea.

As long as we're discussing death, we should point out another hard fact: If a partner dies or otherwise leaves the partnership, the partnership must be dissolved. (The same is true if a new partner joins.) If the business is to continue, it can do so only if a new partnership is formed or the owners decide on another structure for their business. Prudent partners can avoid problems of change and dissolution by constructing their partnership agreement to cover the various situations that might otherwise cause them to dissolve their partnership. The agreement might state, for example, that if one of the partners dies, the remaining partner(s) will buy that partner's share of the business from the surviving beneficiaries at book value.

Red Flag

Because of the changing nature of human beings, a partnership can actually be more unstable than a sole proprietorship, which depends on the welfare of only one person. Partners, even those who know each other, should spell out the criteria completely and legally and make sure all involved understand their rights and obligations under the law as outlined in the agreement.

Types of Partners

The law recognizes several types of partners:

➤ An *active partner* is just that, someone actively involved in your business.

➤ An *ostensible partner* is someone who, while not actively involved, is known publicly to be a partner in the business.

➤ A *silent partner* is inactive, but may still be publicly known as a partner.

➤ A *secret partner,* unlike a silent partner, is active but unknown. Unless you are violating some legal or ethical requirement, there's nothing wrong with secret partners, provided their identities and involvement are known to all other legal partners.

➤ A *dormant partner* is considered inactive and may not be known to the public.

➤ A *subpartner* and a *limited partner,* two different classifications, both participate as less than full partners in the venture.

Journal Entry

While it's easier to dissolve a partnership than a corporation, there often is trouble agreeing on distribution of assets and liabilities, even when the partnership agreement spells out everything in black and white. Hint: If your partnership is simple or you expect it to have a limited life, consider a sole proprietorship first, perhaps with your business associates in the role of investors rather than partners. You can always form a partnership if your business situation changes.

Partnership Advantages and Disadvantages

Like sole proprietorships, partnerships are easier to form than corporations and offer direct rewards to the principals involved. Except where there are a lot of different partners or the operational structure is hazy, partnerships tend to be similar to sole proprietorships in that they generally offer greater flexibility.

Partnerships may also be similar to sole proprietorships in that one person may be designated to bear the brunt of responsibility as agent for the company, with unlimited liability. Plus, this person is legally responsible for all the business-related actions of the other partners. (This is generally the best way to run a partnership, unless you like the excitement of knowing that any of the partners can commit the partnership to anything at any time.)

Remember: Business is finances, but it's also people. Because it pools the resources—fiscal, material, and intangible—of several people, a partnership can be a more stable financial structure than a sole proprietorship. On the other hand, having more than one person involved can make the partnership a more unstable social structure.

Of course, if things don't work out, in terms of the finances or in terms of the people, the partners can agree to dissolve the partnership, or some partners may choose to buy out the other partners. That may be complicated and even unpleasant, but it may be better than staying together in a bad relationship.

Like sole proprietorships and corporations, partnerships have their advantages and disadvantages. For people who want a highly flexible company in which they pool their expertise and assets and share responsibilities, risks, and rewards, then a partnership may be the right structure.

Going Corporate

When it comes to financial and legal stability and setting a trajectory for long-term growth, the only business structure to consider is a corporation. Businesses of just about any size can incorporate, even your bait and tackle shop.

Since corporations are distinct legal entities, forming one can be a complicated procedure. It takes more than just securing the right operating permits, unlocking the front door, and putting up a sign. There are significant restrictions placed by laws and charters governing the corporation. There's also the matter of double taxation: Being a legal entity, a corporation pays income taxes; then, because after-tax earnings are distributed as dividends to its stockholders, that income is subject to individual income taxes. If the corporation is owned by just a few people and the earnings are healthy, those dividends could be substantial and the taxes considerable. (We'll consider the tax situation in Chapter 19.)

On the other hand, the owners of a corporation assume limited liability for company debts—the opposite of the situation faced by sole proprietors and partners. As we noted earlier, all they can lose if things go bad is the amount of their investment.

In forming a corporation, the owners create a separate legal entity. They contribute their money and nothing else, directly. The corporation is run by a board of directors. The owners may do no work at all in the corporation: It's their money and other assets that work—the very essence of pure capitalism.

If the corporation needs more capital, it can expand to include other investors, as a private corporation, or it can go public and sell shares. Either way, there are more owners or more stockholders who can vote on company policies—meaning less control for the original owners. Of course, stockholders in a public corporation wield a power greater than their periodical votes. If stockholders lose confidence in how the board of directors and other corporate officers are running the business, they can sell their shares. In large

169

Shortcut
Whether the business is a partnership or a corporation, you enjoy the greatest advantages if you maintain majority ownership, at least 51 percent. You'd be surprised how much extra weight that one percent can wield.

enough numbers, their sale of shares could drive down the value of the stock and, consequently, the corporation.

Because incorporation means sharing ownership and control, many people with an entrepreneurial spirit are wary about incorporation. It's like riding in a big bus when you'd rather be driving a little car.

But there are definite financial advantages. The corporate tax rate is often lower than the tax rate for a sole proprietorship or a partnership. (Rates vary and laws change, so you'd be wise to check out your particular situation before you decide on your business structure.) Also, a corporation of any size tends to have a more imposing business presence. A company that goes through the rigors of incorporation will be viewed as professional in every sense of the word. That may make your firm more appealing, both as a vendor and as a customer.

Journal Entry
If the corporate tax burden or shareholder obligations are a concern, there are several types of corporate structures that may help alleviate those concerns. An S corporation, as defined by the IRS, allows income to pass through directly to shareholders and be taxed on a pro-rata basis, provided the corporation meets certain criteria for size. This allows the owner to bypass double taxation on both profit and dividends.

Filling Out the Forms

Despite the legal hoops, some entrepreneurs file for incorporation without the benefit of legal counsel. It's a way to cut down on legal fees, of course, but it may be a foolish way to save a few dollars. It's a wise investment to have an attorney explain the benefits and liabilities, so the principals can make the right decision about incorporation. Also, unless you're fond of legal paperwork, you may want to leave that to your attorney. All in all, involving the attorney from start to finish may be money very well spent.

Articles of incorporation, filed with and approved by the state in which the company operates, usually require the following information:

➤ *Company name.* Choose a name, then follow it with the words "Incorporated" (or "Inc.") or "Limited" or ("Ltd.")—terms that indicate the level of liability to which each shareholder is held. The name needs to be reserved to make sure there isn't another company already using that name, a process that takes 90 to 120 days. A small fee also will be required.

➤ *Address.* Check in advance whether your particular state allows a post office box to serve as the address. Your firm may need an actual street address to file for incorporation.

➤ *Purpose for the business.* Certain states require lengthy elaboration of the purpose of the business and its goals, while others require significantly less. Additional documentation may be required or allowed to further explain the purpose.

➤ *Information on stock issues and share par value.* Depending on whether the corporation is public or private, the articles of incorporation should include information about the value and types of stock. Companies with two or more series of stock must offer a comprehensive description of each class, including rights, restrictions, and preferences that accompany each class.

➤ *Information on the board of directors.* This should include a list of names and addresses for all directors. In many states, only one director is required and that will be the owner or principal stockholder.

➤ *Incorporator name and address.* That's likely the owner or principal stockholder. If that person also is the registered agent, he or she will need to be identified as such.

➤ *Date of incorporation.* When did it all begin?

What?
If approved by the state, the *articles of incorporation* become, in effect, a sort of contract between the principals (or incorporators) and the state. That contract is known as the company charter.

Some states require that all legal signatures be witnessed and notarized by a notary public. That may not be a bad idea, even if it's not required.

Boards, Bylaws, and Banking Resolutions

Once the state approves the articles of incorporation, your company is a legal entity within that state and free to operate as a corporation. There's no specific methodology by which to do that, but there are certain requirements and recommendations to consider.

The first step is to establish a set of bylaws by which the company will be run. Among other things, the bylaws should indicate time and place of shareholder meetings as well as voting procedures for shareholders, assuming you will have some. State and federal laws govern the way we do business, but bylaws often offer the methodologies. More important, directors and officers who have faced legal challenges have been either saved or sunk depending on whether or not they adhered to the bylaws of their own companies.

Shortcut
One of your safest investments may be in your own corporation. As an individual, you can lend money to your company, with all the rights and privileges of any other investor. As long as your company is solvent, your investment is safe. And if the corporation starts running into financial difficulties, you can get your money out—if you can sell your stocks before the value drops. Of course, it's the market that determines the return on your investment.

Once those bylaws have been adopted, the board will need to determine the company's fiscal year and adopt a set of banking resolutions that will determine its financial institution relationships. The banking resolutions will describe banking procedures in detail, as well as who is legally allowed to sign checks and make withdrawals.

Along those same lines, the corporation must obtain a tax ID number from the IRS and a corporate seal from the state's Secretary of State office. It's also necessary to know about state and local business regulations, including various code requirements for the particular type of business, and about such accounting matters as payroll taxes—more good reasons to be working closely with an attorney—and finding a good accountant.

The whole process of setting up a corporation is very complicated. In fact, you may not feel like continuing with this chapter. But you should spend a few more moments checking out what happens next, if only to help you deal with corporations in your business affairs, but especially if you intend to form a corporation.

Corporate Liability to Shareholders

Quite a lot can be written on board and corporate obligations to shareholders. But we won't do that here. At this point you need just a few basics.

Some states and industries allow boards to operate without liability, while others impose stiff restrictions, including criminal and civil money penalties for directors convicted of not exercising their fiduciary responsibilities. Before becoming a director, research thoroughly the rights and obligations of directors under all regulatory bodies.

The most basic obligation directors have to shareholders is to run the company safely, soundly, and profitably. The director also has an obligation to:

➤ Hold board and shareholder meetings on a regular basis. That's a legal obligation to the owners of the corporation.

➤ Take accurate and comprehensive minutes from those meetings and make them available, as appropriate, to shareholders. As mentioned earlier, minutes of procedures, actions, and votes become legal documents—and minutes have been used to convict directors of negligence or fraud.

➤ Advise shareholders of elections and board actions that affect their portfolio. Give them the opportunity to vote for directors and provide them with comprehensive information on candidates. Notify them of any changes that will affect the value of their stock beyond the normal ups and downs of the market.

And directors must not forget to pay their taxes. That's critical for the company's continued well-being and operational guarantee.

The Least You Need to Know

➤ The basic types of business structure are sole proprietorships, partnerships, and corporations.

➤ There are advantages and disadvantages to each type of business. Understand both sides before making a choice.

➤ Define partnership roles, rights, responsibilities, and shares up front to avoid difficulties later.

➤ Corporations take more time and effort to set up, but in the long run may be worth it.

➤ If incorporating, establish and adhere to bylaws. It's a smart move from both a legal and operational standpoint.

➤ The board has fiduciary responsibility to shareholders and needs to operate with that in mind.

Part 5
Your Company's Tax Obligations

As the Beatles were making their millions, they came out with a song about tax collectors—and made even more money. We all complain about taxes, but they're the price of success.

And, although our founding fathers were praised for their protest against taxation, it's not likely that your company would be heralded as heroic if it tried to shrug off its tax burden. Quite the opposite, in fact.

In this section, I'll look at business tax fundamentals—the stuff every manager should know. I can't provide you with comprehensive coverage of business taxes. That's beyond the scope of this book. Besides, the information changes from year to year and sometimes even from month to month. There are many excellent sources on the market to help you pay the least amount and, perhaps, with the least pain. But if all you need are the basics to understand what your company faces when considering its tax obligations, read on.

Chapter 17

Your Business Obligations to Uncle Sam

In This Chapter

➤ Keeping track of business income

➤ Reporting business income

➤ Understanding Schedule C taxes

➤ Making the most of professional deductions

In life there are only two inevitabilities: death and taxes. And medical science is making great headway with the former.

The moment your company's founders hung out their shingle and unlocked their door, their tax obligations to Uncle Sam changed. Dramatically. When they still were Joe or Jane Private Citizen, your company's founders were concerned primarily about getting all the right deductions and exemptions for themselves. Once they became employers, however, their lives became more…well, taxing.

This chapter shouldn't be considered a comprehensive guide to the latest information on each of the tax laws and requirements. That's a task for a tax professional, especially since tax laws change often, even if just in the small print. In this chapter we simply offer some valuable basics and miscellaneous information that may help you understand what your company is up against.

Right now, managing the company's tax obligations may not be among your responsibilities, but understanding what must be done and how it must be handled will help you provide the necessary information to the appropriate company staff. And, if the day ever comes when you find yourself settling into the chief executive officer's chair, the background information you pick up here will be well worth the effort.

Let's start with some basic business tax rules.

First Step: Hire a Competent Tax Professional

Business taxes are going to be one of your company's greatest burdens in terms of both costs and operations. And while your chief financial officer and accounting staff may have a great understanding of tax concepts, an outside tax accountant who works with hundreds or thousands of such returns and arrangements every year is going to provide better service. It's probably the best consulting money your company will ever spend.

A certified public accountant (CPA) specializing in tax issues is the best choice. If there's one familiar with your industry, so much the better. Ask for references from regular clients and, as we advised in Chapter 14 regarding the process of choosing a lender, look for a good match—not only in the type of business your company is in, but also in revenue size and operating similarities. The more closely your company matches the other clients served by a particular CPA, the better.

Accounting for Business Income

Red Flag

Never consider the IRS as you would other creditors. The IRS should be paid first, even during times of severe cash crunches. Vendors tend to forgive payment delays if the company remains a good customer. The IRS will levy fines and penalties and, in the end, seize company property if taxes aren't paid. The IRS will also proceed against an owner personally if payroll taxes are unpaid. Don't mess with the IRS!

The federal government has a simple way of looking at taxable business income: Businesses are taxed on income when they receive it and should deduct expenses when they incur them. (That's how it goes for businesses that operate on an accrual basis. For those businesses operating on a cash basis, the situation is slightly different: They deduct expenses when they pay them.) Life, in the government's eyes, is simply that easy.

But business procedures aren't that easy, and the IRS admits that there are finer points to be considered when managing business funds. That means, as a business, your company has a choice of reporting income on either a cash or an accrual basis. And if your firm holds inventory, the choice is even simpler. Companies with inventories *must* use accrual accounting. No ifs, ands, or buts. If only all matters related to taxes were that easy!

Reporting on a Cash Basis

This simple equation is made only slightly more flexible by the recognition that cash may be received but not processed during the same payment period. This is called a *constructive receipt* of funds.

Consider a scenario in which your company sells a line of products and receives a check from the purchaser just before the year-end holidays. Even if that check isn't deposited until the new year begins, that payment is regarded as constructively received during the old year. So, you pay the tax on that transaction just as if you'd actually processed the check before the ball dropped in Times Square.

Since you're not in charge of accounting, you don't need to worry about the details here. But it's good for you to at least be familiar with this accounting principle and the term "constructive receipt."

Red Flag

Some companies attempt to pay rent charges for the upcoming year, to gain the expense deduction for those charges in the current year. The IRS says no deal. Rent is an expense incurred as the rental property is used, not in advance. However, a court case has offered a different resolution for insurance prepayments: Those may be deducted during the previous year. Go figure!

Cash Accounting Limitations

Cash basis accounting can be used if a company meets the numerous requirements set by the IRS. In fact, the IRS allows cash accounting for certain C corporations (what we generally mean when we use the word "corporation") and S corporations, if they meet specific requirements. Professional offices or practices—such as doctors, lawyers, and accountants—are exempt, if all stock is owned directly or indirectly by the employees. Other businesses with gross receipts of $5 million or less can also take advantage of cash accounting.

Advantages of Accrual Accounting

It can be summed up in two phrases:

> Accrual accounting offers greater flexibility.

> Accrual accounting provides a better matching of costs and revenues, resulting in a more meaningful financial statement.

Let's assume that, as the year is ending, a business ally is planning a new venture and wants to tap the expertise of your company's marketers. That firm contracts with your marketers to consult during the following year and makes a sizable advance payment on the upcoming consultation fees just before the holidays. In what year is that income for the marketing department taxable?

According to the IRS, your company will need to pay taxes on that advance payment only when the marketers are actually doing the work. In other words, since the payment is for consultation scheduled for the new year, the marketers are not providing any value in exchange for that payment until they begin working. Thus, your company pays taxes on that income as the work is being done. That type of value recognition and flexibility is one of the advantages of accrual accounting.

On the other hand, that business ally would be deducting the advance payment as an expense in the year in which it made the payment, even though the marketers had not yet started consulting. There are exemptions for recurring expenses, and your company specialist will want to consult fully with your tax advisors or attorney on this matter.

Those cold, hard facts of taxes may cause some businesses to engage in a flurry of deals in December. And you thought it was just the holiday spirit…

Now, let's put those talented marketers in another situation. Assume they started providing consulting services for that business ally during the old year, but their services will not actually bring income into your company until the new year, after they've finished their consulting. At that time your company will receive compensation in full for those marketing services. Although your company did not receive any payment until the new year, it must report that part of the income earned by the marketing services provided during the old year.

Again, you don't need to know all the ins and outs. But you should certainly understand the basic principles involved, so you can appreciate the timing involved in business conducted around the end of the tax year.

Journal Entry

If your company is reporting on a cash basis and wants to change over to an accrual basis, the IRS will allow that change, provided you file Form 3115 within 180 days of the beginning of the tax year, whether or not the company's fiscal year mirrors the calendar year.

The $10,000 Business Cash Question

Most successful business owners are not criminals, but easily could become criminals if they're not aware of reporting requirements and restrictions for cash receipts of more than $10,000. For amounts this size, businesses must complete IRS Form 8300. That form is used largely to help track criminal activities, particularly drug trafficking and money "laundering."

The IRS requires that Form 8300 be filed within 15 days of such a transaction. Also note that none of the fee can be deferred or split into smaller payments in order to avoid completing the form. Uncle Sam will assume your firm has something to hide and, if he finds out, will pursue it with a vengeance.

Failing to file because your tax specialist forgot or didn't know can cost the company $50 for each instance, although, based on circumstances, the penalty can be rescinded at the judge's discretion. For businesses that fall below the $5 million ceiling, those fines can't exceed $100,000 per year. Businesses over $5 million can pay up to $250,000. Ignorance and a faulty memory can be very expensive!

However, if the IRS determines the failure to file Form 8300 was intentional, then the penalty is either the amount in question or $25,000, whichever is greater. What's more, criminal penalties apply. That, after all, is how the feds nailed Al Capone.

Filing Schedule C Taxes

Large-scale corporate tax preparation is beyond the scope of this chapter and the intent of this book. (After all, if you're involved in such preparation, it's likely you're not a complete idiot about finances.) But if you're involved in an entrepreneurial business, it may be helpful to know about Schedule C.

Schedule C-EZ is not an option for many entrepreneurs, but if your business operates with an expense level of $2,500 or less, then you qualify. However, your company can't carry inventory nor claim a home office expense. A single individual must be sole proprietor, with no employees, no prior-year suspended activity losses, and no depreciation.

That's quite a lot of limitations, but there are people and businesses who qualify. Executives who also earn money from consulting or professional speaking fall into this category. The form also is perfect for full-time sales persons and commission drivers, employees who derive their primary income from this activity.

> ### Journal Entry
> If you suffer a business loss that exceeds your present income, you may be eligible to recover all the taxes you paid in the prior three years.
> If that tax rebate doesn't fully cover the loss, you can use the remaining amount to reduce taxes for up to 15 subsequent years.

Professional Deductions

No matter the size of the business, it will have deductions for professional expenses that support that business. A good corporate tax advisor knows to take full advantage of those deductions available.

What constitutes such expenses? Here are some examples:

➤ *Professional association or organization dues and subscriptions to professional journals.* Development education for professional staff is a legitimate deduction, providing the membership, participation, or subscription matches professional profiles.

➤ *Rent and utilities for office space.* Rent is obvious, but make sure you include telephone, heat, water, and other basics involved in the business habitat.

➤ *Supplies and other professional resources.* Paper clips can be a tax write-off, as well as professional resources, libraries, and information services with a useful life of one year or less.

➤ *Staff salaries.* The total amount your company pays its employees is a very real business expense.

➤ *Expenses for operating and maintaining vehicles used on professional calls.* If most of the time spent in the car or truck is on business calls and careful mileage records are kept, write-offs can be significant.

There also are some expenses that may seem to fit, logically, but *not according to the IRS:*

➤ *Expenses if you are an employee.* If you are a professional—say, a physician—but you're an employee rather than a proprietor, you may not deduct professional expenses on Schedule C, which is for sole proprietors only. There are other forms and requirements for you.

➤ *Expenses paid on behalf of clients.* A lawyer, for example, who pays her clients' fees may not deduct them as she would her own fees. Those are considered the expenses of the client, no matter who pays them.

Red Flag
Remember: This book is a general guide to finance and accounting. We cannot possibly cover every detail of tax law; that would take stacks of books that you'd never read! Always discuss tax matters with your tax advisor.

➤ *Professional development and preparation.* If you decide you want to go back to school and become a lawyer, then you'll have ample opportunities to pay all kinds of taxes and take all kinds of deductions in the future. But while you're in school you may not deduct tuition and related educational costs as a business expense.

➤ *Daily business lunches.* It doesn't matter if you talk shop. The IRS is onto that game. You can't deduct your regular meals. But the occasional business meeting lunch may be deductible. There are also specific regulations governing travel and entertainment deductions.

New Business Deductions

Many entrepreneurs and corporations don't take advantage of potential deductions for the time and resources spent investigating a new business. Obviously, there are travel expenses as principals visit a business they're considering purchasing and talk with clients and partners. But there also are other expenses that relate to the business after it has been purchased.

In fact, major costs of investigating a new business can be amortized for up to 60 months. This is true either for a business acquired from someone else or a new business created from scratch. This includes things like market segment exploration, product development, labor force development, fees and salaries for consultants and attorneys, and other sizable expenses.

Keep this in mind if you find an opportunity for your company to grow. Exploring those opportunities may not cost as much as it might seem. Uncle Sam will help you open the door when opportunity knocks.

What if It All Falls Through?

Even the best-laid plans sometimes go awry, even when they involve considerable time and money—or often simply because the time and money are too considerable for the potential benefits. If your firm has gone through all the effort with due diligence and taken the allowed amortized deduction, chances are you'll wind up the proud owner of that new business. But if those best-laid plans fall through, the expenses can be deducted as a capital loss. Your company still gets its deduction, as well as the opportunity to consider lessons learned along the way.

Amortize Organizational Costs

If you're developing either a partnership or a corporation, those costs also may be amortized over a 60-month period. That allows you to spread out the tax benefits of all those expenses, to better match them against your income.

For a partnership, such expenses include legal fees for negotiating an agreement and fees for accounting, consulting, and management. But expenses linked to marketing or issuing shares, including the costs of producing a prospectus and of syndication, are not included.

If you're forming a corporation, it's much the same. The cost of organizational meetings, incorporation fees, and accounting and legal fees qualify. However, costs involved in selling stock or securities do not.

There are other expenses that may not be amortized. These include loan interest, taxes, and research or experimental costs.

183

You may be feeling overwhelmed by all these tax details. Again, we've touched upon them just to show you how many things should be considered when you're considering ways to help your company grow. Remember: Professionals hire professionals. Just as you are paid for your training, experience, and judgment, you should not hesitate to pay a tax advisor or an attorney for that person's training, experience, and judgment.

The Least You Need to Know

➤ Hire a competent tax professional who has experience with your size and type of company.

➤ Income and expenses can be recorded and reported on either a cash or an accrual basis. Accrual accounting allows for better matching of income and expenses.

➤ In accrual basis accounting, income is taxed at the time it is earned and expenses are deducted at the time they are incurred.

➤ There are limitations, based on corporate size and structure, affecting firms wanting to use cash-based accounting.

➤ Cash transactions of $10,000 or more require completion of IRS Form 8300.

➤ Schedule C tax forms, although subject to significant limitations, may be right for single entrepreneurs or independent salespeople.

➤ Take advantage of all professional deductions available to your company. Understand and maximize deductions for developing new areas of business.

Chapter 18

Sharpening Company Tax Smarts

In This Chapter

➤ Managing employment taxes

➤ Managing corporate income taxes

➤ Paying other types of taxes

➤ Depreciating your assets

➤ Using first-year expensing deductions

There are many ways to look at taxes. Maybe the best way is to recognize that the more taxes your company pays, the more income it must be earning. That may be overly optimistic, but you get the idea.

Businesses can't dodge their tax obligations, but they can minimize the damage. There are legal ways to minimize the amount you send to Uncle Sam each and every quarter. The government, in fact, expects businesses to take a smart approach to taxes, so there's nothing wrong with trying to pay the least possible, provided your tax-minimization strategies fall within the confines of the law.

But there also are internal strategies that can help minimize the impact of taxes on precious company resources. There are even ways you, as a manager not directly involved in financial operations, can help your company keep its tax obligations to a minimum. And after this chapter, you're going to appreciate even more the job your accountants are doing!

This chapter will take an overview of business tax obligations and look for ways to get the most out of the situation. What follows should help most companies start getting smarter.

Accounting for Employment Taxes

Red Flag

Companies must also complete an I9 form from the Department of Immigration and Naturalization. That doesn't have an impact on the financial side of a business—unless it's discovered that the business has hired some illegal aliens. Then penalties and other costs could be severe.

Red Flag

What could be worse than having to withhold taxes for your employees? Withholding too little. Even if the IRS gets it all eventually, they will believe they have been cheated out of the earning potential on those funds throughout the year. Right or wrong, the government will sock the company with a penalty if it withholds too little in employment taxes.

Unless your business is of a significant size, chances are you have an outside firm managing the payroll function, as we discussed in Chapter 10. If that's the case—or even if it isn't—you should have an outside firm manage payroll tax requirements. Your company will be further ahead than if you attempt to manage it yourself.

The process of managing employment taxes begins with having your new employees complete federal W-4 forms (including that all-important social security number!) and whatever state-level tax documents may be required.

At first glance, the steps for payroll tax computation seem clear and easy:

➤ Use federal and state withholding tax tables from the correct year.

➤ Determine gross pay for each employee on whatever payment breakdown scenario your company uses— weekly, semi-weekly, or monthly.

➤ Scan the columns on the tax table to determine the proper amount of withholding for each employee.

➤ Consult the alternative tables on the flip side of the tax table if the gross pay exceeds the upper limit listed on the table.

Sounds simple, right? Determining the proper tax level isn't challenging, provided you have the necessary information. The challenge comes in staying on top of reporting requirements to the satisfaction of the government agencies being paid. Like other facets of the taxation equation, flexibility is very limited. And it doesn't pay to upset the IRS.

When to Hold 'Em and When to Fold 'Em

Some companies submit withholding taxes on the same day they distribute paychecks. That's certainly a simple way to schedule. But many commercial tax preparers hold onto the funds a little longer, earning interest until the very last minute. This is one of the ways commercial preparers make money and are able to offer such low rates to some companies. (With new electronic filing requirements, this may no longer be possible. There's a price to pay for progress.)

There are statutory time limits past which companies should no longer be keeping employee withholding taxes. Limits are based on payroll frequency and can be determined by consulting federal and state tax tables. Hold onto those taxes too long and your company may end up paying a fine.

Red Flag

If yours is a service industry, remember that tips must be reported as regular income. The IRS would like employees to report cash tips to their employers who then add them to gross income paid. Tips can be used to bring employees up to the minimum-wage level, otherwise the employer will have to make up the difference.

Payment Requirements: A Question of Timing

One of the most important things the tax preparer needs to consider is keeping the necessary paperwork current. Quarterly payment reports should contain all withholding tax information and can be used to verify payments. These same reports automatically compute the employer's contribution to unemployment taxes, which usually constitutes a small percentage of the total payroll.

Social security and FICA payments are handled in much the same way.

Keeping track of the employment tax payment schedule can sometimes be frustrating, because the payment window changes as companies increase in size. New companies are allowed to pay every month; but as companies grow, the frequency of payment increases—first to every two weeks, then to weekly. The largest companies have an obligation to pay within 24 hours of the payroll. Certain employers may even be required to file electronically.

Paying Corporate Income Taxes

If your business is incorporated, it must file and pay federal and, in some cases, state and local taxes. If your company is an S corporation, through which income and losses are passed on directly to stockholders, those stockholders pay federal taxes in the same way. Some states tax S corporations directly, while others follow the federal approach.

The IRS is very specific about when corporate taxes are due: The 15th day of the third month after the close of the fiscal year. If your fiscal year ends December 31, the corporate income taxes are due March 15. If your fiscal year ends August 31, taxes are due November 15.

187

> ## Journal Entry
>
> Since sole proprietorships and partnerships are not separate legal enti-
> ties, as we remember from Chapter 16, the IRS taxes the owners directly.
> Most states take the same approach. But all business entities must pay
> taxes. And your tax consultant should tell you how much and when you need to
> contribute to the government coffers.

Ah, the price of success! Corporations (including S corporations) that owe $500 or more in income tax for the tax year must make estimated tax payments during the following year or be subject to a penalty. Payments of at least 25 percent are due on the 15th day of the fourth, sixth, ninth, and twelfth month of the company's fiscal year. That's April 15th, June 15th, September 15th, and December 15th if your fiscal year mirrors the calendar year. And this is an area of total equality: Whether the company is a corpora-tion, a partnership, or a sole proprietorship, it must make estimated payments. (Partner-ships are different because of their structure. A partnership does not pay federal estimated tax as an entity, but the partners individually may pay estimates.)

Taking Care of Other Taxes

Employment and income taxes are just two of the types of taxes for which your business may be responsible. There are others, almost too numerous to mention, but we'll list a few more of them.

> ## Red Flag
>
> Your company may be liable for local sales taxes on merchan-dise sold in states where it doesn't have a physical presence. Mail-order houses are subject to local regula-tions, and municipalities have taken companies to court to collect their fair share from catalog sales made in their jurisdictions. Your company's accountant or legal advisor will have further details.

Sales Taxes

Sales taxes are one of the most common types of taxes that businesses must collect. With limited exceptions, sales tax must be collected on just about every item sold to anyone anywhere.

And what are those "limited exceptions"? Items sold for resale, if the wholesaler or retailer holds a valid reseller's license. Sales to public institutions—such as schools, libraries, or some government agencies—are also tax-exempt.

Some states require sales tax be paid on the sales of goods only, while other states require sales tax be paid on services as well. Finally, your local government may also take its share from every sale. Here again, check with your state and local authorities. They'll be glad to help you help them.

Usage Taxes

This is the flip side of sales taxes. Usage taxes usually apply to businesses that purchase from mail-order houses or other out-of-state sources that don't charge sales tax. Under this scenario, since the seller didn't charge a tax on behalf of the government, the buyer pays the sales tax directly. Again, the level of demand and threat depend on the municipality in which your company is located.

Property Taxes

Just like you pay property taxes on your home (either directly or through a landlord), your company must pay property tax on any real estate it owns. The company may also find itself paying taxes on leased property, depending on how the lease has been written.

Out-of-state businesses that aren't careful may find their property being assessed at an exorbitant rate. That's one way municipalities have of keeping property tax at a more comfortable rate for local businesses. Your company should review its assessment carefully and talk to its legal counsel about what to do if it suspects the assessment is unfair.

And All the Rest

Different industries draw different taxable demands from local, state, and federal authorities. There are specialized taxes on equipment and durable goods some businesses use to operate. There are room and entertainment taxes tacked onto the price of a hotel room in various cities. Some communities tax the sale of periodicals, while others do not.

The best advice for corporate tax specialists is to keep their eyes open and their purse strings drawn. If the authorities can find a way to tax your business, they certainly will.

Using Depreciation of Assets

Another tax strategy for saving money is through depreciation of tangible business assets—equipment, machinery, computers, and other items that have a measurable life over which their value can be depreciated. This works for most business situations, although rarely for personal or pleasure materials. The saleswoman can take depreciation on the green Ford Taurus she uses during the week to make her sales calls, but not on the snappy red Trans Am she tools around in on weekends. The one is clearly for business and the other for pleasure—and Uncle Sam frowns on mixing business and pleasure.

Shortcut

Companies looking for ways to lengthen tax payment cycles should examine their business profit cycles. Companies that find a large income stream toward the end of their fiscal year may want to change that fiscal year, so the income stream comes in the middle. That will allow more time to pay taxes on income, allowing the company greater investment time and earning opportunity. A company can't change its fiscal year with every change in its fiscal situation, however.

What?
The term *depreciation* does not refer to physical deterioration or a decrease in market value. It means the allocation of the cost of an asset over the period during which benefits are derived from that asset. In a way, it's like buying on time, but instead of spreading out payment for an item, the accountant is gradually converting the cost of the asset into an expense.

Not all tangible business assets can be depreciated, however. Since land is considered to have an unlimited life, your company can't take depreciation on the real estate on which the business sits. But it may be able to depreciate the landscaping surrounding the business if it appears that it would be destroyed if the building were ever razed.

Determining depreciable life has become more complicated in recent years. Fortunately, you likely won't have to worry about that—it's a matter best left to accountants. Your tax professional can offer counsel based on your company's specific situation.

There is a special form you must use for depreciation allowances. Form 4562 can be used regardless of the item or its age. If you're depreciating pre-1996 assets, Form 4562 isn't necessary: Depreciation is entered on line 13 of Schedule C.

First-Year Expensing Deduction

Just how much depreciation a business can deduct during its first year—a time when cash flow may not yet be at the desirable level—is a decision your company must make in conjunction with its tax advisor. The IRS sets a ceiling every year: For 1997 the limit was $18,000. (This is called Section 179 election.) If the business is located in an "enterprise zone," the first-year ceiling is raised to $37,500. Another example: The most that traveling salespeople can deduct in auto depreciation during the first year is $3,060.

What?
An *enterprise zone* is a district established by a government to promote business growth and opportunities in an economically distressed area, through tax and benefits and other incentives. For more information, contact the USDA EZ/EC Team at 800/645-4712 or 202/619-7980; e-mail: ezec@rurdev.usda.gov; Web: http://www.ezec.gov.

In order to qualify for first-year expensing deductions, the amounts must be applied to items bought for the business during the tax year in which deductions are taken. Expenses incurred prior to 1996 don't qualify for first-year deductions, even if 1996 was the first year in which the property was used for business purposes. Again, we advise consulting with your tax advisor.

It all goes back to the basic IRS rule of paying taxes in the year in which the income is earned, and claiming expenses in the year in which those expenses are incurred.

There are a lot of other restrictions that can limit first-year expensing. Partners and S corporation owners, for example, fall under scrutiny from two angles—business taxes and personal taxes. Deductions may be allocated among the partners or shareholders, but may not exceed the net taxable income earned by the partners.

But there are limitations. (Are you surprised?) Businesses may not qualify for the expense deduction if the property has been acquired from a direct or linear ancestor, related either by blood or by marriage, or if the acquisition is the result of foreclosure or other similar action. Other related transfers of property by family or existing partners are subject to IRS scrutiny and may not qualify for the first-year expense.

However, if the appreciable business use of an asset falls to 50 percent or less of its worth before the end of the year in which it is expensed, the business owner may elect to "recapture" it and claim the deduction. Like other aspects of IRS requirements, this is a fine point and may be better left to a discussion between you and your tax counselor.

Red Flag

First-year expense deductions, even when valid, may not exceed the net taxable income from all the businesses your company owns and operates. The deduction is designed to help new business or investment cash flow, not serve as a blanket write-off for businesses trying to manipulate their worth.

The Least You Need to Know

➤ Take advantage of all tax minimization strategies available under the law.

➤ Abide by all withholding tables and payment guidelines, but make them work to your company's benefit whenever possible.

➤ Tax payment windows change as the company grows both in size and taxable income.

➤ The IRS assumes ownership of all payroll taxes from the moment the money is earned by the employee.

➤ Corporate income taxes are due on the 15th day of the third month after the close of the fiscal year.

➤ Depreciation is allowable on items used for business purposes only.

Chapter 19

Partnerships, S Corporations, and Limited Liability Companies

In This Chapter

➤ Knowing the advantages and disadvantages of business structures

➤ Reporting partnership profit and loss

➤ Understanding taxes and the S corporation

➤ Defining limited liability companies (LLCs)

Earlier chapters have discussed the tax impact on standard corporations (also known as C corporations), as well as some tax strategies for maximizing business resources. But other business structures have their own reporting challenges, specifically partnerships, S corporations, and limited liability companies (LLCs).

Why should you care? After all, your responsibilities don't include tax matters. And maybe your company isn't a partnership or an S corporation or an LLC. But if you know about managing the tax burdens, you might be able to come up with ways to minimize taxes and maximize opportunities, which could really impress the boss. Also, the chances are good that you do business with at least one partnership, S corporation, or LLC. The more you know about how those structures work, the better.

Structures, Structures, Structures

As we mentioned in Chapter 16, the easiest and cleanest way to operate a business is as a sole proprietorship. All revenue and debts belong to one individual and there's no concern over elaborate profit-sharing plans or corporate tax structures.

What?

Sole proprietorships, partnerships, most LLCs, and S corporations are known as *pass-through* tax entities. This simply means that all business profits are reported on the individual tax returns of the owners. By contrast, C corporations are tax entities separate from their owners, so they file corporate tax returns and their owners file individual returns.

In terms of taxes, a sole proprietorship is also the easiest structure. The other business structures require more tax time and cost. We've already discussed C corporations and their taxes. In this chapter, we'll consider what taxes mean for partnerships, S corporations, and LLCs.

Partnership Profit and Loss Reporting

When a partnership is formed, chances are each individual brings some different level of financial participation to the arrangement. The IRS recognizes that and taxes the partners appropriately based on their stake in the company. A partnership files IRS Form 1065, which informs the IRS of the company's partnership status.

Since a partnership is a "pass-through" entity, it pays no taxes. Each partner, however, reports his or her share of the income or loss on Schedule K-1. In most cases, allocation of the partnership income or loss among partners is based proportionately on each partner's financial interest in the company. Losses are subject to basic liabilities and at-risk rules. (We won't go into technicalities here. We'll leave that to your tax advisor.)

If partners draw a salary, they each report that salary as ordinary income, despite any ownership arrangement. Partners are required to pay self-employment tax on whatever they collect from the firm, subject to limitations. Limited partners or others who don't draw any income aren't required to pay the tax.

Special Allocations

If the financial participation of a partner changes at any point—whether through a greater contribution of capital, a transfer of his or her share, or another financial move that will have an impact on either the partner's ownership of shares on his or her participation in the company—the IRS must be notified of that change within 30 days.

In the same vein, the IRS may allow changes in the relative distribution of income, loss, deductions, or credits among the partners. The downside is that the IRS won't issue prior approval of a plan to change partnership participation; it will simply allow or disallow the changes after they've been made. Working with a tax advisor prior to making significant changes will help ease the pain and increase the gain.

Loss Limitations

You just can't lose! At least, that's the word from the IRS.

Any partner's share of a partnership loss may not exceed his or her financial interest in the partnership. In the event that does happen, the partner cannot deduct that loss until the partnership shows enough revenue to cover the loss. The IRS computes the value of a partner's financial interest in a partnership as the amount of the original financial involvement minus withdrawals from the partnership plus accumulated taxable earnings that haven't yet been withdrawn.

That's fairly straightforward, as taxes go.

In Case of an Audit...

Partnerships, like other types of businesses, are subject to audits. In the case of a partnership, that means an audit not just of the partnership but of all the partners as well.

If your partnership is selected for an audit, it's in your best interest to choose the partner who knows the most about tax matters to be the primary spokesperson for your business. If you don't choose a representative, the IRS will do so, usually choosing the partner with the highest level of financial interest in the company. That may not be the person who can best represent the partnership's interests to the auditor. (The person with the most money is not always the person with the best grasp of tax matters or the coolest under pressure!)

> **Shortcut**
> Remember that a partnership is not a legal entity. It's treated basically as a pool of individuals, so auditing the partnership means auditing each partner.

But that representative doesn't face the auditor alone. The IRS requires all of the partners to participate in the audit and it treats each as an individual entity. That means if there is a discrepancy, the IRS may offer settlement terms to some or all partners.

If you don't like the results of the audit, there is an appeals process. It's up to the partner who represents your partnership for the audit to file the appeal with the tax court no later than 90 days after the IRS mails its decision to the partnership. If your representative doesn't do this, individual partners have an additional 60 days to file their own appeals.

There are other appeal options through federal court. But the bottom line is that no matter who files what appeal, all partners will be bound by the final decision.

Journal Entry

Understanding and mastering your tax obligations is an important part of managing your business, of course. But you certainly don't want to make decisions that will affect the growth of your business based solely on their tax implications. Your tax burden, despite all else, is a sign of your profitability: more taxes mean more profits. If you fail to do something because it will mean more taxes, you're reducing your profits. And profits are the very reason you're in business, right?

Taxes and the S Corporation

The big advantages of forming an S corporation are:

➤ The owners are protected from unlimited personal liability.

➤ The S structure pays no corporate income tax.

Red Flag

The financial structure of an S corporation may have disadvantages at tax time. If a stockholder is paying individual taxes at a rate higher than the corporate tax rate would be, the S corporation structure might actually cost that stockholder more in taxes because of the pass-through characteristic. The owners might be better off with the more traditional C corporation, even though they would then be paying taxes twice—as a corporate entity and as individuals.

Taxes on earnings are paid directly by the shareholders, just like in a partnership. This helps owners avoid the double hit of corporate income tax and personal income tax as stockholder-employees.

This structure may be especially attractive during the early years of the business, when the balance sheet shows more losses than profits. The S corporation structure passes those losses on directly to stockholders who, with any luck, have income from other sources to offset those losses. (If they do not have sufficient income, perhaps it might be wiser to fully incorporate.)

S corporations, much like partnerships, are required to pay estimated taxes on projected losses and earnings of its stockholders. Returns are filed on IRS Form 1120S.

Reporting Income and Loss

As in a partnership, stockholders in S corporations share financial responsibilities individually. That means certain income, losses, and deductions are passed through to stockholders relative to the amount of stock they hold in the company, including:

➤ Tax-exempt interest, which remains tax-exempt, but increases the value of the stock held. Other dividends also may qualify under this proviso.

➤ First-year expense deductions and tax preference items.

➤ Income and losses from capital asset exchanges. Interest and dividends on corporate investments and losses also fall into this category.

➤ Foreign corporate taxes paid and income or loss from off-shore sources.

Red Flag
S corporations act like partnerships in terms of passing on profits and losses to shareholders, but shareholders who work for the corporation are treated as employees for FICA tax purposes. They don't pay self-employment insurance. Make sure your accounting function reflects that fact.

Shares May Be Subject to Change

An important thing to remember, too, about this structure is that the pass-through of profit and loss will change the basis of the share-holder role and equity in the company, but will not change the company itself. By their structure, S corporations have no earnings and no profits. Those are held by the stockholders and may be subject to change as income and losses ebb and flow.

In addition, stockholders may come and go during the tax year, so profits and losses will have to be allocated in a way that makes sense to owners and stockholders both old and new. Profit and loss can be allocated for each period of time the ownership was different, on either a daily basis or a percentage basis. The tax implications for both types of allocation differ, so all options should be reviewed before a decision is made.

Becoming an S Corporation

Despite the complexities, you may be interested in forming an S corporation, because of its big advantages—limited liability for the owners and no income tax for the business. So, how do you do it?

It's not just a matter of filling out forms, although there is some paperwork involved, of course. There are a few requirements a business entity must meet to qualify for the S corporation structure:

➤ S corporations formed before 1996 may have no more than 35 shareholders, all of whom agree to the S corporation designation. Starting in 1996, that limit rose to 75 stockholders. Husbands and wives are counted as one shareholder, but both must consent individually to forming an S corporation.

➤ Shareholders must be U.S. citizens or residents or represent certain estates or trusts.

➤ An S corporation is limited to offering only one type of stock. You can't offer both common and preferred stock if you want to be an S corporation.

Entities wanting to become S corporations should plan on completing and filing IRS Form 2553, complete with the signatures of all shareholders. If the form is filed after the start of the year for which the corporate structure is to be effective, consent forms also must be filed by individuals who held shares in the business in the prior year, even if they've sold those shares.

Shareholders who become partners after the S corporation is established don't need to file their consent with the IRS. (After all, it's assumed they know what they're getting into.)

Shortcut
S corporations are generally required to operate on a calendar year basis, unless there is a sound business reason to have a different fiscal year. If you don't have a compelling reason to depart from the calendar year, plan on following IRS directives here.

Losing S Corporation Status

Breaking up is so hard to do—but not in this case.

If the majority of shareholders decide to do so, they may choose to revoke the S corporation status. They do so by filing a revocation form that will take effect at a future date, which they may specify. If no date is specified and the revocation is filed before the 15th day of the third month of a tax year, the status will be revoked for that tax year. If filed after the 15th day of the third month, the revocation will take effect the first day of the following tax year. (It's actually easier to do than to explain!)

The S corporation status also may end if the company no longer qualifies under the requirements listed above.

What Is a Limited Liability Company?

If the owners of a company are interested in involving more shareholders than are allowed under S corporation guidelines, they may want to consider a limited liability company (LLC). The structure offers the advantages of profit and loss pass-through of a corporation, with the extra flexibility of allowing profits and losses to be allocated in any manner, regardless of how the stockholders are invested in the company. In addition, as you could assume from the term LLC, the partners also enjoy a semi-corporate structure with limited liability.

LLCs offer many of the advantages of S corporations with fewer restrictions. In fact, as LLCs have become more widely recognized by law, S corporations have declined in popularity.

However, some state laws differ when it comes to liabilities and responsibilities for LLCs in their jurisdiction. If you're interested in forming an LLC, before you take the plunge, carefully review the laws that would apply wherever your LLC would operate.

The Least You Need to Know

➤ Sole proprietorships may be the easiest structures to manage, but partnerships, S corporations, and limited liability corporations offer certain advantages.

➤ Partnerships and S corporations allow pass-through of profits and losses to shareholders.

➤ Partners may not claim more in deductions than they earn through their share in the partnership.

➤ The tax codes clearly define "pass-through items" for S corporations.

➤ S corporation structures are defined by strict limitations.

➤ Limited liability corporations (LLCs) offer the advantages of both partnerships and S corporations.

Part 6
Strategies for Growth

When it comes to business finances, mastering the basics is critical to a company's success. Any business needs a strong foundation from which to grow its success. Without that foundation, the company likely will crumble.

Business, like nature, is always in flux. Companies that don't change with the business climate—finding new ways to do things and ways to do new things—may find the business climate changes them…for the worse. When a company chooses to stand still, when the managers don't lead, it begins losing ground. That's just the way things are.

The remaining chapters in this book contain a few more basics, as well as some more advanced strategies for growth. Managers in companies of any size can benefit from these chapters—if those managers are willing not only to learn what they need to know but also to apply what they learn.

Developing a Financial Plan

Ludwig Mies von der Ohe, who worked for Chicago architectural giant Louis Sullivan, is probably best known for the quote, "God is in the details." That phrase has been applied to industries of all stripes and fits financial management as well. (You're probably more familiar with the flip side: "The *devil* is in the details." Just two ways—optimistic and pessimistic—of making the same point.) Readers who haven't yet mastered the details should go back to square one...or at least Chapter 1 of this book.

Actually, it wouldn't hurt to read Chapter 2 again, about business plans, because we're going to get into developing a financial plan. That's a more sophisticated concept that requires some basic financial knowledge.

In this chapter we'll look at how much money an enterprise needs to start a business function and then keep it going and growing. It's a little more complicated than just having enough money to pay the first month's rent and turn on the lights. Even if you're not thinking about ever starting your own business, you should still understand the basic financial start-up process, because more than likely it's the foundation on which your firm was built. Also, knowing about financial plans will help you if your company assigns you the opportunity to start up a new operation.

Types of Required Capital

This country is a nation of Horatio Algers, poor boys and girls who manage to rise to the top of the heap through a combination of inspiration, dedication, and perspiration. Their success stories have motivated many an entrepreneur. The sad part is that many of those entrepreneurs, despite their personal qualifications and drive, have not been able to make it. Unlike Horatio Alger, they are not the stuff of legend.

It's obviously not enough to be inspired by heroes and their success stories. The important thing to remember is that it's a question of the right place and the right time as well as of the right person. The chance of succeeding on willpower alone is slim at best—and it seems to be growing slimmer every day.

They say the best things in life are free, but not in the business world. Anyone venturing out there needs to have enough capital on hand, or at least available, for the hard slog that lies ahead.

There are three kinds of capital for three levels of need:

➤ Initial or start-up capital

➤ Operating capital

➤ Reserve capital

Red Flag

Statistics from the U.S. Department of Commerce show that the vast majority of businesses that fail do so during their first 18 to 36 months. One of the key reasons for this failure: too little capital at the start.

To get started, any business requires an ample supply of initial or start-up capital—funds designed to cover such expenses as inventory purchases, equipment and supplies, rent and security deposit, utilities, legal and licensing fees, advertising and marketing, and any other costs you'll need to get your business going.

There may be areas in which a resourceful entrepreneur can scrimp and save a little, such as through begging and borrowing and cutting corners. Those who take extra risks to compensate for a shortage of capital may end up paying high costs in terms of additional stress.

Once a business opens its doors and hangs out its sign, it needs a steady supply of operating capital to keep the shelves and warehouses full, to keep the employees producing and promoting the products, and—of course—to continue paying rent and utilities and other overhead costs. One cardinal mistake new business often make is assuming revenue will cover expenses during those first few critical years. Until the business has established a financial pattern, it may find itself caught short when it needs a financial boost the most.

Finally, a business also needs reserve capital to cover unexpected contingencies as well as those little additional necessities that would strain the operations budget. Too many entrepreneurs again assume their profits will cover such needs. Not likely, at least during the first few years of business. Even after that, some entrepreneurs get spoiled by their success: They forget they have to keep working at it and assume things will continue as they are. So, when there's a problem down the road, some entrepreneurs may not have enough set aside to cover the costs.

Shortcut
For most types of businesses, you can get general guidelines from folks with experience. They can tell you how long you should expect to go without making a profit, and how much longer it might take before your profit covers the start-up costs and losses.

Of course, it's not always an expense that causes problems. It may be an opportunity. And if you can't afford to open the door when it knocks....

So How Much Capital Is Necessary?

The answer to that question depends on how much income your company thinks it will be able to produce during its initial year or two of business. For a biotech firm that will spend the next two years perfecting some disease-resistant strain of sweet corn, chances are the answer will be, "None at all." On the other hand, a corner hardware store likely will have some level of income from day one.

The amount of capital necessary to get started will depend on the business itself, of course, as well as a variety of other factors, including:

➤ *Product demand.* Is there currently a market for what the company produces? Or will you need to create that market as you are developing the product?

➤ *The competition.* How saturated is the particular market? How are your competitors positioned? Can your company muscle its way in easily? Or will it be a pitched battle from day one?

➤ *Personal expertise.* How much of the first two years of business will company executives spend learning the market? How much time will be

Shortcut
Businesses with an inadequate track record in their areas find that establishing a sales target helps them better manage their reserves. The sales target puts the pressure on performance, not reserves, to strengthen the company's financial wherewithal. Reserves should be treated like an insurance policy: It's there if you need it—and you do your best not to need it.

spent on personal growth and education by the staff to learn the new industry and its responsibilities? Companies that have been down this road before and know what's ahead will be better able to maneuver the bumps in the pavement. Those who haven't been here before should reserve funds for inexperience.

In emphasizing the need for capital, we don't mean to suggest that it's necessarily the key to success—or the only key. The success of your company, in your market, against your competitors, may depend primarily on creativity in research and development, for example, or on marketing acumen. But then, so often getting the right people means paying the right money.

Be Realistic

If you're starting a business, you're likely to be enthusiastic and optimistic about the future of your venture. That's great! After all, how many successful companies have been started by pessimists?

But you should force yourself to be realistic when it comes to calculating your company's financial needs. Follow this operating advice:

➤ *Estimate sales (revenue) conservatively.* Any business will want to be able to weather any market downturns, both expected and unexpected.

➤ *Budget expenses generously.* During the first few years of business, it's vital to monitor and control expenses—because you're not likely to have much income to manage. By budgeting generously, your company should have enough money to meet unanticipated market conditions. Then, if you spend less than budgeted, you can add to your reserves.

Remember: If you're realistic in your planning, then you have good reasons to be optimistic in your expectations.

Establishing a Schedule of Start-Up Costs

Every new business will have different start-up costs. But new businesses are alike in that they all require some form of computation to help establish estimated levels of financial needs. Call this the start-up financial worksheet or schedule. Compute it on printed forms or a sheet of notebook paper. The name and format really don't matter, as long as the following items are included in the plan:

➤ *Anticipated fixed costs.* Rent, utilities, equipment and furniture, licenses and permits, office supplies—the basics for getting up and running generally fall into this category.

➤ *Variable costs estimated realistically.* These costs involve serious thinking and a good understanding of your dream. If your company is planning on selling a lot of merchandise, you better also plan on buying a lot of raw materials. If the market is highly competitive, you should plan generously for advertising and marketing costs. If you expect your company to grow rapidly, plan on payroll expenses increasing dramatically.

The bottom line here: The more realistic your cost estimates, the better your chances of succeeding.

The following start-up costs worksheet should be adapted to your specific needs. It's designed to help determine how much a company can expect to pull from income and reserves for each item, until the business gets established. Include all categories specific to your industry.

Shortcut

You don't need to go into great detail. It's more important to make sure not to forget anything. Remember that wisdom about not being able to see the forest for the trees? Locate all your forests and size them up, but don't waste time and energy counting all the trees.

Revenue and Expenses Worksheet
A. START-UP COSTS (ONE TIME)

Item	Total Cost	Amount from Income	Amount from Reserves
Legal/professional fees			
Fixtures/equipment			
Cost			
Installation			
Licenses/permits			
Marketing/advertising			
Inventory (initial)			
Supplies, materials			
Cash, receivables			
Facility costs			
Security deposit			
Initial rent payments			
Remodeling/renovation			
Utility security deposit			
TOTAL START-UP COSTS			

continues

continued

B. ESTIMATED MONTHLY INCOME (START-UP PERIOD)

Item	Total Cost	Amount from Income	Amount from Reserves
From sales			
From service			
Other			
TOTAL ESTIMATED MONTHLY INCOME			

C. ESTIMATED MONTHLY EXPENSES (START-UP PERIOD)

Item	Total Cost	Amount from Income	Amount from Reserves
Rent			
Utilities			
Electricity			
Heat/AC			
Telephone/on-line service			
Wages/salaries			
Managerial			
labor/hourly			
Insurance			
Taxes			
Income			
FICA			
Social security			
Maintenance/service			
Cost of goods sold			
Raw materials			
Manufacturing procedures			
Inventory costs			
Shipping/billing			
Legal/professional fees			
Miscellaneous			
TOTAL ESTIMATED MONTHLY EXPENSES			

Based on this worksheet, you can prepare projections. After all, it shows only what your business will be earning and spending. Projections show you where your revenue and expenses will be taking you and help you determine where you can take your business.

Where will you stand financially in three months, six months, a year, two years, five years? When you have your projection for each step into the future, ask the question, "Then what?" What should you expect? What should you plan? Invest in more inventory? Hire more workers? Design new products? Create new services? Without projections, you may be moving but not going anywhere.

The Balance Sheet

One of any company's key financial management resources is its balance sheet—the summary of the assets, liabilities, and net worth of the business. The accounting chapters in Part 2 discussed the impact of the balance sheet on the various components of the accounting system, and its role as a balancing mechanism for the firm's financial and accounting statements.

The true value of a balance sheet comes through its use as a financial tool to help keep not only the company's books in balance but also its finances in line with its operational needs.

If a sample revenue and expenses worksheet is one end of the financial management spectrum, then the balance sheet is the other. The worksheet will tell where a company is going. The balance sheet describes how well it's doing in getting there.

Journal Entry

Before we review a sample balance sheet, let's review some of the basic terms.

The left column, assets, groups all items of value owned by the company. This includes cash, inventory, fixtures, and accounts receivable.

The right column, liabilities, refers to all debts owed by the company. This includes accounts payable, start-up expenses owed to investors, and other minor debts. Ongoing expenses, such as rent and utilities, are not considered owed until the bills come due. At that point they enter the accounts payable category.

The balance sheet also indicates the company's capital, its net worth computed as assets in excess of liabilities. For a sole proprietorship or a partnership, this might be called owner's or partners' equity. For corporations, outstanding capital stock value would be listed at its original price of issue.

The interplay among all these components should become clearer on the sample balance sheet that follows.

XYZ Business: Balance Sheet, December 31, 1997

Assets		Liabilities	
Current Assets		Current Liabilities	
Cash	$2,000	Accounts payable	$14,686
Accounts receivable less bad debt allow.	1,585 ($158)	Accrued payroll taxes	2,165
Inventory	75,995	Notes payable (1-year or less)	7,800
TOTAL CURRENT ASSETS	$79,422	TOTAL CURRENT LIABILITIES	$24,651
Fixed Assets		Long-Term Liabilities	
Real estate parcel	$10,250	Three-year notes	$13,500
		Six-year notes	$8,900
Facilities less depreciation	46,660		
Equipment less depreciation	24,456		
TOTAL FIXED ASSETS	$81,366	TOTAL LONG-TERM LIABILITIES	$22,400
TOTAL ASSETS	$160,788	CAPITAL	$55,000

Computing Profit and Loss

There's one more component in the basic financial plan—the profit and loss statement. That provides a very basic measurement of your success.

How often should you do a profit and loss statement? That depends on several factors. Conventional wisdom says that profit and loss statements should be computed at least once a year. Many businesses do them more often, either quarterly or even monthly.

Constant monitoring of this critical component is vital to business success. Unfortunately, what's good for most companies is not necessarily good for all. Sometimes companies become too focused on their profit and loss. But running a company is like driving a car. Remember what you were taught in driver's ed class: Get the big picture. Steering a company requires similar forward thinking. Know where your company is in terms of dollars and sense, but keep your thoughts on the road ahead and your chosen destination.

Whatever the period you choose for your profit and loss statements, you calculate them with the following formulas:

➤ To determine net sales for the period:
gross sales – returns and allowances

➤ To determine gross profit:
net sales – cost of goods sold

➤ To determine operating margin:
gross profits – operating expenses

➤ To determine total income before taxes:
operating profit + any other income

➤ To determine net income or loss for the designated period:
total income – reserves for income taxes

Shortcut
Prepare ahead of time your estimated balance sheets and profit and loss statements for the first year. In addition to helping you form a good business habit, the exercise allows you to develop your ability to plan for the inevitable ebbs and flow of business.

Here's a sample profit and loss statement in full detail. The amount of that detail may seem excessive at first. But the more you know about the finances of your business, the better you can control those finances.

XYZ Business: Profit and Loss Statement

September

Gross monthly sales	$28,927
Less returns/allowances	632
Net Sales	$28,295
Cost of Goods Sold	
Inventory value 9/1	$24,101
Purchases during Sept.	4,488
Shipping	78
Total Costs Handled	$28,667
Less Inventory 9/30	$16,050
Total Cost of Goods Sold	$12,617
Gross Profit	$15,678
Operating Expenses	
Salaries	$4,512
Rent	1,100

continues

continued	
Utilities	670
Marketing/promotion	300
Telephone	225
Supplies	135
Miscellaneous	200
Depreciation	175
Total operating expenses	$7,317
Operating profit	$8,361
Provision for income tax	$2,090
Net Income	$6,271

Watching your profit and loss trends may help you bring those expenses under tighter control. And that might mean the difference between success and failure for your business.

The Least You Need to Know

➤ Businesses must have enough capital before opening their doors for business.

➤ There are three types of capital—initial, operating, and reserve. Companies need them all to support the first several years of operation.

➤ Err on the side of realism in both revenue and expense budgeting.

➤ The balance sheet should be considered a primary financial management tool.

➤ The more managers and employees know about their company's profit and loss trends, the more likely it is the business will succeed.

Chapter 21

Forecasting Your Future

In This Chapter

➤ Understanding the dynamics of projection

➤ Weaving together the sales projection and profit and loss statements

➤ Developing an accurate expense measurement

➤ Measuring cash flow

Every business, new or old, thrives on growth. Being able to project that growth accurately and meaningfully is one of the most difficult tasks a company faces. Managers in every department face their own version of it whenever they forecast revenues or expenses. This chapter explains both the theory and technique of forecasting.

This guide has already offered a strong dose of accounting and financial management, both of which are critical to business success. But financial projections are as different from accounting practices as yesterday is different from tomorrow. Accounting practices deal with numbers from the past—existing revenue and expense figures. Financial projections look into the future, using past information to create another set of numbers, a set of possibilities that may become realities. And that's just about as easy as it sounds.

The purpose of financial projections basically boils down to determining how much money a business will need to maintain an even cash flow, and when that money is required. Simple? Not really.

The Dynamics of Projection

A lot of businesses develop effective stand-alone projections based on past sales activities, inventory maturation tables, economic forecasts, and lots of other data available to them. That is one way to develop financial projections. As Abraham Lincoln would say, if he were a business advisor, it works for some of the companies all of the time and all of the companies some of the time. Companies that have been following that track and are satisfied with where it has taken them should stick with it.

> **Red Flag**
> Companies will know if their banker is savvy by the level of sophistication he or she requires in financial projections. A projection should produce a balance sheet and an income statement, to show where the company will be at a certain point. A banker may also want a cash flow statement, which shows the company will have the wherewithal to get to that point.

But as shown through accounting procedures, business finances are an integrated, dynamic network of relationships in which activity at one end of the spectrum likely will have an effect on activity at the other end of the spectrum. For example, if you post expenses to the general ledger without similarly debiting the appropriate subledger, it throws the books out of balance.

So, too, with financial projections. Because projections are ways of playing with the future, there is some latitude for approximation. But the more play you allow in that particular rope, the greater the danger. The reality of a financial situation might suddenly slip the noose at a time when control is needed the most. That's where a more integrated approach proves its value.

The Illusion of Reality

In the world of business finance, there are two great assumptions that are as widely accepted as they are *incorrect:*

➤ *Assumption 1:* We know our business, we built our budget, so we understand the numbers inside and out.

➤ *Assumption 2:* With the right software and spreadsheet program, we can predict with pinpoint accuracy our company's financial future.

Regarding the first assumption, realize that it takes a truly extraordinary individual to fully understand the ins and outs of his or her company's finances through this simplistic approach. With a little effort, it's not that hard to create an integrated financial projection that brings all the salient elements into play to create what seem to be perfectly logical assumptions.

The big question concerns what the company's system is logically and rationally projecting. Just an error in judgment here and there, just a wrong turn can make a great difference. Business can be compared to an English hedgerow maze, where each path looks equally logical and rational—until it leads to a dead end. What you expect logically and rationally may just as logically and rationally surprise and disappoint you.

And if Assumption 1 can be misleading, then Assumption 2 is downright dangerous. Software and spreadsheets are, after all, merely tools to be used. Without the right information, they will still offer some form of projection, because that's what they were programmed to do. But it will be up to the person, not the program, to provide the necessary information as accurately and completely as possible—and then to decide if those projections make sense.

Projections can be done effectively. People do them all the time, sometimes quite accurately. But it's important to remember that projections are simply assumptions based on certain information that can be manipulated by formulae to come up with an approximation of the future. That's really the best any company can hope to achieve. That and a little bit of luck.

What's Next?

The process of integrating financial statements to make effective financial forecasting possible is something that must be cultivated over time. There will be procedures that become part and parcel of the way a specific company or an entire industry does things. You will find some procedures that are most valuable, while others will provide projections that are merely interesting or even simply misleading. Better projections require time and experience.

For right now, let's trace a likely path through the various financial statements and other record-keeping tools available to you. As we've noted in previous chapters, financial statements, balances sheets, and other documents are more than mere records of activity. If you use them properly, they can be dynamic tools that will help your company achieve its goals.

Journal Entry

In developing any kind of financial statement, certain knowledge is assumed. In some cases, those assumptions are safe.

For example, companies that plan to sell more products will need to budget for more raw materials. They will also likely need to hire more workers at a later date, and then still later perhaps even rent or build a larger facility.

You may want to put those assumptions in writing, as a record of the logic behind the projections. It helps to spell out your assumptions in an attached document, so there's no confusion down the road—especially if the assumptions are not so routine.

Don't assume everyone will understand why sales were expected to double. If you're basing that projection on a growing awareness of your products or on recent training for your sales reps, for example, you should put your thinking into black and white.

Building an Assumption Statement

Keep in mind that the more specific and accurate you make your research and projection development, the better the results. Most financial forecasting begins with a sales projection derived from market data, past sales performance, and, occasionally, just the need to balance an already budgeted expense.

Shortcut

We talk a lot about assumptions, because we need to make them and because we need to avoid making them when we can use facts instead. I'll never forget what my Uncle Ned taught me about being careful when I assume anything. He divided the word "ass u me."

"When we assume something," Uncle Ned explained, "it can easily make an ass out of you and me." That was one of my first and best business lessons.

An assumption statement weaves together elements of both the sales projection and profit and loss (P & L) statement, resulting in a comprehensive projection based specifically on a demonstrated—or at least budgeted—expense statement. A good P&L statement already should have taken these elements into account, but many don't. The assumption statement ensures all elements have been considered.

The assumption statement links to the balance sheet projection, cash flow projection, and other revenue measurement instruments within a company's financial system. That simply means that the net income—derived from subtracting expenses from sales on the income statement—should relate to the equity—derived from your assets minus liabilities on your balance sheet. Retained earnings will be derived from that net income and contribute to your cash flow statement.

If the proper lines among all your statements don't mesh, you're likely to wind up with a financial mess. It's not enough to be just close: After all, the words "mesh" and "mess" are close…

Composing a Better Sales Forecast

Sales forecasts can be developed in one of three ways:

➤ Careful budgeters can *underestimate* sales income, creating an accompanying expense budget, forming a budgetary safety net that, in effect, rewards marginal or merely adequate performance.

➤ High-flyers, on the other hand, can *overestimate* sales income, hoping the resulting projections will drive sales staff to meet artificially high goals. Even if those goals aren't met, the accompanying expenses may still create a safety net, albeit a smaller one, to help cradle the crash-and-burns.

➤ Realistic budgeters can use empirical data and a knowledge of sales history to create a *realistic* sales income forecast that allows latitude for growth without chewing up staff in the process. This is generally the most difficult of the courses, because it requires just the right level of effort and expertise.

No matter which sales scenario is followed—and different ones may make more sense at different times in a company's life—accurate expense measurement should play an important role. Then, if you deflate or inflate the figures, it's by intention, not by error, by strategy and not by stupidity.

Unexpected sales growth is sometimes a happy problem to have. It can wreak havoc on the budget, but will bring more income into company coffers. But the budget should be able to project those added costs and should reserve sufficient capital to meet those sales needs.

If a regional sales rep suddenly comes across a motherlode client whose orders will demand doubling the company's annual widget production, will the company have sufficient funds to cover production costs? Yes—if it has reserved sufficient capital based on a multi-tiered sales projection that forecasts the level of likely sales, along with "optimistic" and "pessimistic" sales figures as well. Otherwise, those widget orders may later go to a competitor—and you may lose your talented but frustrated sales rep as well.

Journal Entry

The income statement will tie to the sales forecast, but provides more detail. Similar, again, to the P&L statement, the income statement projects earnings over time, usually a year, balanced by relevant expenses. The income statement may not always be able to project an unexpected doubling of production need, so both the revenue and expense sides of the income statement will have to be amended to reflect sales and the costs related to meeting those sales.

Controlling Cash Flow

Despite such happy sales news, the company may have concern about its ability to produce the necessary additional widgets to meet the order and satisfy this new, obviously profitable client. It's not a matter of desire, certainly, but it may be a matter of cash flow. And cash flow management may be the most critical factor affecting companies, especially new ones.

Measuring cash flow is not the same as measuring sales. Cash flow is the amount of cash moving into and out of your company. Increasing sales are important to the company's long-term growth, but good cash flow management is critical to those problems facing you today and tomorrow.

Take our widget sales example. If that widget contract is worth $4 million in sales, that's great. But if payment for those widgets is to come after the whole order of widgets is delivered, which could be six months from the start of production, the profitable sale

Red Flag
Negative cash flow isn't always a sign of poor business planning. Start-up companies often budget for negative cash flow, knowing it will take them several years to become established. If that's part of the plan and funds have been reserved sufficiently to cover expenses, there should be no problem. If it's not part of the plan, a company could go under quickly.

could be tying up lots of cash in raw materials—cash that's urgently needed for payroll and for taxes over those six months.

The cash flow statement isn't designed to replace the balance sheet or income statement. But it may add a dose of reality to an otherwise rosy projection, showing you in advance that, in order for the company to break a million in sales by the end of the year, it will need some significant financial shoring up around months six and seven.

And that's really the purpose of all the statements discussed in the last two chapters. Like the others, a cash flow statement can help predict problems before they occur, making it easier to head them off long before they become crises. And predicting and preventing problems are as important in financial forecasting as they are in projecting revenues. Maybe even more important!

Types of Cash Flow Statements

In the same way as reserves were divided into categories in the previous chapters, there are also three types of cash flow mechanisms:

➤ The *basic cash flow* measures the income and outflow of cash. Specific priorities aren't recognized; this is just the activities of the money funnel and includes start-up cash or reserves.

➤ The *operating cash flow* is based entirely on operating revenue and expenses without taking reserves into account. A healthy operating cash flow indicates a healthy company because this is the true measure of financial business.

➤ The *discretionary cash flow* is simply the operating cash flow segmented into specific groups or areas. Subdividing these categories is one of the best ways to measure performance in individual areas, particularly in payment or collections. This also is a good way to measure administrative efficiency or the internal use of funds prior to disbursement.

Of the three, the operating cash flow is probably the most useful because it measures both your cash flow and the financial success of your company. Consider the following simplistic example for a very small business.

XYZ Business Operating Cash Flow Statement, Second Quarter

	April	May	June
A. CASH RECEIVED			
Receivables collected	$19,340	$13,060	$16,188
Dividends	100	100	100
Other	0	476	10
OPERATING CASH INFLOW	$19,440	$13,636	$16,298
B. CASH DISBURSED			
Salaries	$4,512	$4,512	$4,512
Rent	1,100	1,100	1,100
Utilities	670	468	320
Marketing/promotion	300	300	200
Telephone	225	174	186
Supplies	135	60	71
Miscellaneous	200	0	44
Depreciation	175	175	175
OPERATING CASH OUTFLOW	$7,317	$6,789	$6,608
NET OPERATING CASH FLOW	$12,123	$6,847	$9,690
BEGINNING CASH BALANCE	$9,108	$21,231	$28,078
ENDING CASH BALANCE	$21,231	$28,078	$37,768

The Bottom Line

The operating cash flow is a somewhat simplistic version of a more complex and comprehensive cash flow, but it makes a handy point. Charting cash flow is not the same as charting profits or budget. Both can be very positive, but unless funds have been reserved for those times of rough sailing, there could be serious problems.

And even if the sailing isn't rough, just a little uneven, it's better to have all the knowledge you need on hand to better manage your financial forecasting.

The Least You Need to Know

➤ Financial forecasting deals with the future, while accounting deals with the past.

➤ Good projections integrate different aspects of a financial management system.

➤ It's difficult at best to forecast effectively, even with a good working knowledge of the numbers.

➤ An assumptions statement effectively combines the active elements of a sales forecast and a profit and loss statement.

➤ Accurate expense measurement plays an important role in any plan or forecast.

➤ Cash flow management is the most critical factor affecting new companies.

➤ Operating cash flow is one of the clearest indicators of business success or failure.

HUT
HUT
HUT

Chapter 22

Preserving the Bottom Line

In This Chapter

➤ Maintaining income and expenses

➤ Maximizing the value of every dollar

➤ Determining what you need in a money manager

➤ Working with your money manager

➤ Understanding the market as a part of the strategic plan

➤ Using investment terminology

If someone had never seen a bucket and sieve and were shown one next to the other, from the side, chances are that person would see very little difference from the side. They have similar shapes and we put substances, often liquids, into them from the top.

Their purpose, of course, is very different, as can be seen from the bottom, but not from our side view. A bucket gathers and holds its contents; a sieve strains and directs its contents. One can never replace the other in function because the single most important elements in their designs—their bottoms—determine what they do and how well they do it.

Obvious as this example may be, there are many people in businesses, especially in new businesses, who fail to make the distinction when it comes to preserving their assets. Some operate like buckets, gathering and holding assets without reinvesting them in the company. Consequently they end up drowning in a very small puddle. Others operate like sieves: No matter how much revenue comes in through the top, it all ends up going out through the bottom, leaving the companies without reserves at a time when they may need them the most.

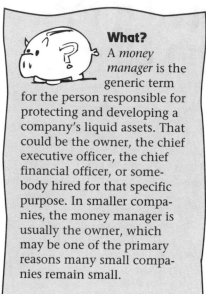

What?
A *money manager* is the generic term for the person responsible for protecting and developing a company's liquid assets. That could be the owner, the chief executive officer, the chief financial officer, or somebody hired for that specific purpose. In smaller companies, the money manager is usually the owner, which may be one of the primary reasons many small companies remain small.

Whether a business is a bucket or a sieve is really a question of the relative strength of its "bottom" line and, more important, how the company protects it as a resource. Strong companies assign that responsibility to someone with enough financial savvy to know that the company assets must be developed and used for the good of the organization and to help it achieve its strategic and economic goals.

Most managers, if they aren't working in accounting or finance, aren't in a position to make such a recommendation—although they may be invited to offer their educated opinions about the sort of money manager a company needs or even about specific candidates for that position.

Even if you're not involved in assessing company needs or candidates, it's good to know something about what the money manager should be doing if your company expects to thrive.

Hiring a Money Manager

Companies can ignore their bottom-line concerns and chances are those concerns will go away. But so will the bottom line. Any company with a concern about its future really needs to hire someone who will be responsible for preserving and growing that bottom line. Hiring a money manager might be in order.

Size matters, of course, here as in other business matters. A large corporation will have a full-time money manager, perhaps called the treasurer or the controller. Smaller companies may not be able to afford a full-time money manager, but they must have somebody who is knowledgeable about finances and experienced in controlling cash. That person serves as the money manager.

What's true for a company may also be true for its individual departments. A manager who doesn't keep a close watch on income and expenses is taking chances. The department may operate comfortably for a while, but its financial well-being is likely to erode. And so will the career of that manager.

> ## Journal Entry
>
> Is there a benchmark against which a company can measure its need for a money manager? Some consultants say a retirement portfolio of $100,000 or more requires a higher level of management. That's as good a stepping-off point as any, but there may be unique situations faced by a company that will define when a money manager is necessary. If the costs of supporting that money manager—whether on staff or outside—are significantly less than the resulting financial growth, then investing in such a relationship may be a very good option.

What Money Managers Do

The primary job of the money manager is generally not to build the bottom line. Making money is the responsibility of the sales staff, the people out in the field bringing in the revenues. (That's why we distinguish between the money makers and the money manager.)

What the money manager contributes to the company is more subtle. He or she should squeeze the maximum value out of every dollar earned. There are two basic ways to do that:

1. They invest.
2. They monitor expenses.

That's very simple—in principle.

The money manager invests excess income in financial vehicles that most closely match the company's goals in their philosophy and performance. To do that properly, he or she needs to know not only about investment possibilities, of course, but also about what's right for the company.

For some firms, that means short-term, high-risk investments with a high-yield return. Fast-growth, high-tech firms with large cash needs operating in a dynamic environment tend to fall into this category.

For other firms, that means long-term stable investments that offer a lower yield but greater security. Older, asset-heavy insurance companies tend to favor this type of conservative approach.

In choosing investment options, the money manager is responsible for acting according to the nature and needs of the company, producing the most income at the least risk, and helping to build the bottom line. That's it in a nutshell.

The money manager also protects existing assets by keeping a close watch on expenses. This is where such individuals really earn their worth, by stopping up money drains and questioning proposed expenditures.

Is a proposed capital purchase really necessary? Will an additional employee generate significant enough revenue over the long haul to make him or her a worthwhile addition to the staff? How will the cost of expansion into new markets affect the cost of internal operations back at headquarters?

The money manager asks these questions and more because:

➤ Expenditures, both new and current, must always be justified, especially for companies operating in dynamic, changing environments.

➤ Chances are no one else will question them. Department heads enthused with their projects are likely to minimize the costs and risks. The money manager must look at such ideas in terms of their overall contribution to the organization's strategies and goals and make recommendations accordingly.

If you're thinking it's tough to be a money manager—an optimistic gambler with investments (yet be so tight you squeak when it comes to expenses) and a pessimistic tightwad when new proposals pop up—yes, it's definitely not a responsibility for just anyone.

Qualifications of a Money Manager

Assuming he or she has the background and desire, the best person to protect the assets of any organization may naturally be the owner, principal shareholder, or chief executive officer (CEO). But then again, he or she may not.

Business leaders have to be positive and strong about their wishes and desires in order to lead their companies. It's not easy to come up with a brilliant idea and immediately begin questioning its validity and worth. People who try raining on their own parades often get rained out. And people who try wearing too many hats often end up losing their heads—or at least not knowing where they're at.

That means a company needs someone who cares about business outcomes enough to run the risk of challenging some sacred cows, someone with the expertise and background to make intelligent recommendations and recognize the long-term implications of actions even before they take place.

What characteristics identify a likely candidate? There are some distinct traits to look for. We outline them here, even though you may never be invited to participate in the search for a money manager. Why? For two basic reasons: So you can better appreciate the talent of a good money manager, and because sometimes a manager who shows knowledge and interest is drawn into important decisions, even if informally.

224

Comparative Performance

You should require credentials and references, as you would of any potential employee, whether on paper or during the interview process. But companies also must be able to compare past performances, especially on the investment side, to market performance. Rating services and financial publications often provide the necessary background against which to measure past performance. Also, as we stressed in terms of choosing a lender (see Chapter 14), it's essential to find a good fit between the candidate and your company.

Companies will want a money manager with past investment activities that have displayed growth. But the value of that growth should be measured in light of both the market environment and vehicles utilized. A 10 percent growth rate may be good if the rest of the market is performing at eight percent. A 15 percent growth rate, although higher, is less impressive if the rest of the market is performing at 20 percent. A big company offering a big salary for managing big amounts of money can set its expectations high. A smaller company might set its sights somewhat lower. It's a question of fit: Who can do the best job with your money at a cost you can afford?

Adjust Expectations Based on Inflation

The financial context, again, is critical to measuring comparative performance. One of the most reliable ways to measure market conditions is simply the standard rate of inflation. Growing the company's bottom line at the rate of inflation means no real growth at all. A 10 percent growth rate, when inflation was rising at eight percent, signals a minimal performer. That same 10 percent growth rate, during a period with an 11 percent inflation rate, is a real red flag.

Watch for Capital Preservation Strategies

This is an area where money managers earn their stripes, both in couching their investments and questioning company expenditures. In both areas of responsibility, the context in which that person has operated reveals as much as the numbers about a money manager's success. A candidate may not have impressive numbers, but if he's

Red Flag

It's not enough just to appoint a qualified money manager. That person must be free to act according to his or her best judgment. That may seem obvious. But in too many companies, the owner or the chief executive officer interferes with the money manager. Such "micromanaging" (meddling) obviously undermines any money manager's ability to do the job.

Shortcut

The quickest measure of a money manager's past performance may be several years' worth of performance statistics measured against Standard & Poor's Index. Such market barometers provide the empirical data necessary to judge how well this person has done within the context of the marketplace.

managed to keep a struggling company from going under, that's a success. Another candidate might also have low numbers, but got them the hard way, with a company mired in very conservative fiscal attitudes.

The secret behind any capital preservation is to maximize growth while minimizing threats to the company's bottom line. Quite simply, in most situations, it's not enough to do just one or the other. It's a matter of juggling company financial interests.

Consider the following two scenarios as examples:

A money manager reduces capital expenditures by 15 percent. Good, huh? Well, not if you know that her reduction has resulted in a downturn in revenues because the company failed to use its available resources to compete.

A money manager invests conservatively in a turbulent economy, so the company runs little risk. Wise? Not if his timid investment strategy has put the company's portfolio behind the average market yield—or significantly behind the return enjoyed by its chief competitor.

In these two cases, we know the money managers didn't make the right decisions. (Ah, the benefits of hindsight!) So their strategies, while motivated by the best intentions, were not very successful. The moral of our two little stories: Know the context before applauding the performance.

Make Money Management Part of Your Company's Overall Strategy

Red Flag

Some companies hire outside consulting help or simply operate through a brokerage firm to manage their investments. That's one way to reduce staff costs, but make sure the consultant or brokerage firm understands your goals and has your company's best interests at heart. You can always fire the firm, but you can't make up for missed opportunities.

Another important point when choosing a money manager: No matter how well he or she may have performed, that performance must fit with the overall strategic goals and expectations of your company. That means two things when you're considering each candidate:

➤ *Check into the nature of the companies where the candidate has worked.* How well did his or her strategies fit with each company's goals and expectations? Was she a poker player in a bridge club environment? Did he invest the money as if it belonged to his grandparents, when the company was trying to score capital funds in a hurry? What's the cost of a money manager out of sync with the company?

➤ *Consider how well the candidate's skills and experience fit with your company's plans.* This just makes good sense, but sometimes the dollars obscure our thinking. Just as the best marketer in the world wouldn't be right if you were looking for a die maker or the most successful sales rep would be wrong if you needed a proofreader, so the money manager with the best record might be a bad fit with your company's goals and expectations.

You're not going to find this information on a candidate's resume or in the business section of the local newspaper. This could be a test of your company's intelligence operations. Managers might be asked to call their contacts at other companies or to nose around discreetly at the health club or country club. But considering the stakes involved, getting the right person to be your money manager is worth a lot of effort.

Now, a Quick Quiz...

Yes, a quiz may be a valuable part of assessing your potential money manager. And even the candidates who don't make the grade can teach you something about your company.

In this section we've emphasized the money manager's role as an investor. But we listed a second role for that person: to monitor expenses. The image of a guardian may be less glamorous than the image of a gambler, but watchful, inquisitive money managers have saved many a company.

How do you find out if your candidate is a good watchdog? After all, the evidence may not be there in black and white, outside of claims on a resume or praise in a letter of reference. That's why we suggest a quiz.

Prepare copies of your company's principal financial documents. (If you're concerned about the confidentiality of the data, you could have your accountant change the figures slightly on the spreadsheets—an easy way to allay any concerns.) Then, when meeting with your candidate, show the documents and ask him or her to consider them. (You might want to suspend the meeting for an hour or so, to allow the candidate to reflect on the figures in peace.) After he or she has had sufficient time to peruse the papers, ask what questions or observations come to mind. The results should reveal a lot about how well this person could monitor expenses for your company.

Journal Entry

What if you find a candidate who's a shrewd investor and seems in tune with your company's thinking and another candidate who's an excellent bloodhound when it comes to sniffing out suspicious expenses? Maybe you should hire them both. After all, minimizing expenses and maximizing assets are not opposites, but two sides of the same financial coin. If your company can afford it (think of the long-term savings and earnings!), hire both. If not, consider the economic climate. If it's bullish, it might be wise to pick the investor. If things are down, however, the bloodhound might be your best bet.

Working with Your Money Manager

Okay, so you've hired a money manager with experience that shows a good fit with your needs and objectives. Now what?

The top-level managers should meet with that person to sketch out some guidelines. The result should be a general agreement about risks and returns—a sort of "financial wish list." Then, those managers should get back to their jobs and just turn that money manager loose.

Money managers must have enough latitude to act professionally on opportunities they see in the marketplace. As we cautioned earlier, their performance shouldn't be micromanaged. Of course, a company should be aware of the results of the money management plan and call for clarifications and explanations as needed.

Finally, if the performance of your money manager either fails to meet your expressed expectations or exceeds those expectations, the managers should meet to better understand why, just as they would meet to discuss differences between budget projections and the actual P & L statement. But it's not an occasion to point fingers or just to applaud and slap backs. It's a time to consider revising the plan so the money manager doesn't miss critical opportunities or engage unnecessarily in greater risks in what is apparently a changing marketplace.

Of course, if the money manager turns out to be incompetent or just not a good fit, then it's necessary to find another, rather than try to force things. As my uncle used to put it, Arabians and Percherons are beautiful animals—but I wouldn't hitch them both together to plow my fields.

Understanding the Market

Trying to provide a comprehensive investment lesson within the remaining pages of this chapter is a little like trying to discuss the origin of the universe in 25 words or less. It can be done, but not well enough to provide the necessary understanding to make it work effectively.

There's also no proven investment formula that works for all companies. Companies in different phases of their existence need different levels of capital liquidity in order to function.

Dynamic start-up companies need maximum liquidity to finance growth and development prior to any significant revenue infusion. On the other hand, mature companies with well-established products can invest significant assets, knowing that revenue flow will continue to support operational costs. The investment profiles of these two companies will differ greatly. For us to attempt to prescribe the right scenarios for each would be difficult and dangerous.

There is one truism to remember: Assets should be invested in ways that will enhance the financial foundation and growth of the company. That may include buying the real estate on which your company operates, investing in upgrades to improve your current production capacities, or increasing research and development. That also may mean siphoning off funds for stock market investments with an eye to establishing assets while creating an additional revenue stream through dividend payments. Regardless of the approach, it must be part of your company's strategic plan.

Keeping Track

There are reliable resources that your company should make available for your money manager to consult when deciding on investments. Actually, it wouldn't be a bad idea for all managers to be familiar with these resources.

There's no foolproof way to predict what the stock market is going to do—no matter what some investment consultants may claim. But keeping track of market fluctuations allows for better guesses about where to put company funds. It's also critical to understand basic business trends as well as activities in the specific industries in which your company has invested or is considering investing. Heavy-duty investors make *The Wall Street Journal* their daily reading.

There are other indicators worth considering. Standard & Poor's 500 Composite Stock Price Index offers one of the more comprehensive measurement tools available. The S&P 500 tracks 500 companies traded on the New York Stock Exchange. The list consists of 400 industrials, 40 financial institutions, 40 public utilities, and 20 transportation firms. S&P measures its chosen companies through computers linked directly to the stock market every two minutes, better enabling licensed brokers to keep close tabs on client stocks and make buying and selling recommendations throughout the business day.

This differs from the Dow Jones Industrial Average, which results from an averaging of some 30 stocks. The Dow Jones average often runs close to the S&P 500 in the short term, but can vary significantly when measured over the long haul.

Shortcut

You don't have to spend long hours at the library or subscribe to a lot of business newspapers and magazines to learn more about investments. Check out the numerous World Wide Web sites. For example, WebScout provides an easy way to link to various business information sources (http://www.webscout.com/links/business). A little time spent on the Web can pay big benefits for any manager.

> ### Journal Entry
>
> One option executives have as personal investors is to pool funds with employees and form an investment group. This is especially useful when it comes to larger investments in tax shelters that require more funds than any of the investors may have individually. By sharing the cost of attendant fees involved in such transactions—attorney's fees, sales commission, and the like—each member of the investing group will wind up with a greater actual investment.

Investment Terminology

If you're not a financial wizard, you can improve your knowledge and communicate better with your company's money manager by understanding a few simple terms. Like all areas of business, investments have a language of their own. Here are some of the more common investment words and phrases:

Asking Price—Also known as the *offering price*, this is the current cost per share of the investment. The price is computed by adding the net asset value per share and the sales fee, if there is one.

Back-End Load—This is the commission charged when redeeming shares of an investment.

Bidding Price—The stock market is based entirely on the activity of buying and selling shares. The bidding price, also known as the *offer price*, is the what a prospective owner of a security, commodity, or other property formally offers to buy. It's also the price at which the company will buy back the stock, usually computed at the net asset value per share.

Capital Gains Distribution—An annual payment of gains resulting from investment sales. The distribution measures the amount of increase (gain) earned on an investment (capital).

Capital Growth—When an investment's security increases in market value, that increase generally is reflected in an increased net value of fund shares. That's known as capital growth.

Diversification—Mutual funds tend to spread their investments among different securities in order to minimize investment risk. This diversification provides greater protection for both the investment and its investors.

Dividend—A distribution of the assets of a corporation to its stockholders, in proportion to the number of shares held by each. The board of directors decides whether to declare dividends and determines the amount.

Net Asset Value per Share—An investment's share value is derived by subtracting liabilities from its aggregate assets, including cash and securities. The NAVPS usually represents the market price, subject to a possible sales or redemption charge.

No-Load Fund—When shares of an investment are made available for purchase at net asset value, without the addition of a sales or service charge, it's called a no-load fund.

Objective—Like any part of the business plan, the investment program should have an objective to help define the investment strategy.

Portfolio—The sum total of a company's investment activity (funds, stocks, bonds, and other investments) constitute its portfolio.

Redeem—To redeem a mutual fund is to sell it.

Redemption Price—The actual amount received when redeeming (selling) the share: the value of the investment at the bidding price minus the redemption charge.

Sales Fee—The seller's commission or charge for facilitating the sales transaction, added to the net value per share and paid by the buyer. The maximum fee is 8.5 percent of the transaction amount.

The definitions by themselves offer a glimpse into the issues a company's money manager faces daily when investing the company assets.

The Least You Need to Know

➤ A money manager helps a company preserve its assets while fostering financial growth through successful investment activity.

➤ All investment activity must be defined in terms of the goals of the company's strategic plan.

➤ Context is critical in measuring a money manager's past performance.

➤ Understanding financial concepts, terminology, and resources is basic for any manager responsible in any way for company liquid assets.

➤ Excess assets should be invested in things that strengthen the financial foundation of the company.

Chapter 23

Developing Growth Strategies

In This Chapter

➤ Knowing and responding to product life cycles

➤ Understanding business life cycles

➤ Considering your company's controlled or explosive growth

➤ Expanding your resources through management

When a company is newly formed, the key objective usually is business growth. Product development growth. Market growth. Sales growth. Growth in the number of employees and branches. Growth in income. Growth in status.

The type of growth doesn't always matter when a company is new and struggling. As long as something is growing—other than debt or those activities that contribute to debt—and showing signs of progress for all the hard work, company executives are generally happy.

But, strange as it sounds, some businesses experience too much growth. Or they grow too fast for the conditions under which they're operating. Finding they've seriously under-estimated market demand, these businesses may be suddenly swamped with orders for products they're ill-prepared to support. The opportunity for increased revenue is great—if they can meet that demand.

When does healthy growth become too much growth? And when does growth become detrimental to the success and even continued life of your business? Planning for growth is as critical as planning to prevent failure and loss. Maybe more so. Companies that don't plan for growth may not be able to control it. And if they can't control it, they may not be able to survive it.

From a department manager's point of view, the dilemma is no different. Different functions within a company may suddenly take off and slip from the grasp of their managers. The company may overall be experiencing mature, controlled growth, while an individual area may be raging out of control. In the worst case, that unfettered activity can actually endanger the financial well-being of the company. In such a case, a manager who's unprepared for the situation cannot hide behind his or her ignorance of growth management strategies.

Examine these lessons closely and decide how you can implement them within your function. They can mean the difference between safe, efficient growth and allowing your department and company to run unnecessary risks of serious damages, both short-term and long-term.

Identifying Product Life Cycles

Businesses have life cycles just like products have life cycles. Knowing those life cycles and responding accordingly is critical to success, both for the products and for the company.

Business life cycles may influence product life cycles, but product life cycles, taken in aggregate, definitely influence the life cycles of the company. Department managers, even those without financial responsibilities, have more impact than they realize on the safe and sound growth of their company. Those who plan for their contribution to the company's growth cycle as well as their own department's cycle are likely to be more valuable to the company—and experience less stress with success.

Journal Entry

Most companies are governed by the 80/20 rule. This is a very general guideline, meaning that 20 percent of customers provide 80 percent of revenue and 80 percent of problems come from 20 percent of staff. Companies measure many product life spans in the same way. Eighty percent of the success ratio will be attributable to 20 percent of the products. Capitalize on that 20 percent as both products and business run through their developmental phases, and success will be greater at the end.

Each product goes through several fairly distinct periods during which it is introduced, attracts a following, becomes a critical need, and then declines in public interest until, ultimately, it is shelved right next to the buggy whip and the Edsel. According to the traditional lore of marketers—those folks responsible for making the most of any product from birth to death—most product cycles follow a similar pattern.

Stage 1: Introduction

Products stem from different sources, but all have to be introduced to the public, the target customers. That introduction can be soft and subtle or it can be an explosion of advertising and publicity. But whatever the product and whatever the strategy, the introduction needs to be staged in some way so that potential buyers can learn about the benefits of the product.

During this period, overhead and marketing expenses are high, while sales of the new product tend to be slight. This is a major period of investment for the company launching the product and may result in an initially higher price tag to help recover research and development costs. Consider the retail price of the first hand-held calculators. Now, they're given away as premiums. Such is the nature of that product in its cycle.

Stage 2: Growth

Once the product has taken flight, it enters a growth stage that can be highly profitable for the producer. The public has come to know, accept, and use the product, and R&D costs from development have been covered, more or less. The company has become confident in its ability to sell the product. The increasing revenue and decreasing costs cross each other on the charts and profits rise.

This is also the point where competitors enter the picture, so there may be a greater need for marketing, at least to build on the importance of product name recognition. The allotment of resources is significantly lower than it was during the introductory phase, as all those earlier efforts have begun to pay off.

Stage 3: Maturity

At some point, the growth arc will begin leveling off and the product will enter its mature phase, a time when competitors, some firmly entrenched, begin to give the product a serious run for its money. Costs will increase as the need grows for more promotion to keep the product competitive.

This is also where discounting begins, in an attempt to keep sales at least on an even keel. The profit margin decreases but, if the product has been successful, the volume of sales will keep the picture fairly profitable.

However, the profit margin may decrease to a point at which the profits are insufficient to cover production costs and marketing expenses. Then the company should decide whether to discontinue discounts and let the product live or die naturally or to kill the product.

For some products, maturity comes slowly and lasts a long time. Some of the items that our parents bought may still be on our shopping lists now, years later. But sometimes maturity comes and goes quickly.

Journal Entry

Consider breakfast cereals, for just one example. The brand of corn flakes or oatmeal that you enjoyed as a kid may be on your shelves today—or at least at the grocery store, competing against newer national brands and generic versions. But then think of how many cereals have come and gone over the same period of time. Many cereals burst onto the market and perhaps enjoy meteoric popularity for a few months, perhaps because of heavy marketing or because they promise something new to awaken taste buds. Then most of those cereals suddenly become old, getting edged aside by other cereals and abandoned by changing tastes. Then, on your next trip to the grocery store, you don't find them on the shelves. In their place, new cereals!

Stage 4: Decline

It's inevitable, in human life and in the products we buy and sell. No matter how successful, sooner or later the product will go into decline and, eventually, be discontinued. Companies may make attempts to breath new life into such products through changes in packaging, pricing, targeting, and distribution strategies. But eventually the products will outlive their use, lose out to competing products, or just become too expensive to continue. So, they get relegated to the back shelf. Then, the company just ceases production.

Business Life Cycles

Like products, businesses—and departments within businesses, for that matter—go through similar phases of growth and development.

During its introductory phase, the business is an entity new to its industry and eager to grow and to succeed. This is a dangerous time for new businesses, just as it is for anything else starting out in the world. Most new businesses fail during this period. Critical to the success of a business in this phase are good resource management and straight-line growth—and, of course, adequate capitalization.

The growth phase, which comes next, is a lot like the growth phase of a product. The public has found out about the enterprise and is knocking on the door. Sales are growing and the public is accepting and using the products and services. Profits tend to be high during this phase—and so does the energy required to keep pace with the market.

Businesses reach a maturity plateau in the same way products do, leveling off as the market for their products and services becomes saturated. Sailing is smooth, but there's a good chance it will continue to slow unless changes are made or external forces change the situation. This is a dangerous time in any business for those not paying attention. If you think, "If it ain't broke, don't fix it," then it's likely to be broke.

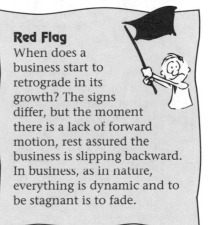

Red Flag
When does a business start to retrograde in its growth? The signs differ, but the moment there is a lack of forward motion, rest assured the business is slipping backward. In business, as in nature, everything is dynamic and to be stagnant is to fade.

Finally, the business begins to decline for any number of reasons. If efforts aren't made to revitalize the concept or operation, chances are the business will eventually dissolve. Unfortunately, for companies as for all of us, getting back into shape is harder as the years pass.

Knowing this, how can a company plan for controlled growth in an orderly way? In other words, how can the managers set up a growth scenario to make the most of each stage of existence?

Controlled Growth vs. Explosive Growth

Controlled growth is more than just an influx of funds from a sudden breakthrough. It's not pennies from heaven. It's a defined expansion that is the result of planned and budgeted activities and goals set against the background of a distinct marketplace.

In other words, good growth is the result of every effort made by a company, its managers, and its employees to raise revenues while keeping expenses in line. Growth is anticipated and welcomed to the degree that the company can manage the expenses and changes resulting from that growth.

Bad growth—yes, growth can sometimes be bad—is generally growth that exceeds expectations. The opportunities and revenues that would mean success for a company that's prepared for growth can ruin a company that's not prepared. It's usually just as simple as that.

The concept of growth being detrimental may sound strange until you realize some of the expenses that come in response to unplanned growth. Consider the following possible effects, for example:

Shortcut

A company will grow more successfully if it has a growth guardian keeping a close eye out for danger signs and making sure executives are following the plan. That may be the chief executive officer, the chief financial officer, or anyone with the financial and strategic acumen to recognize growing pains and take measures to minimize the risks. It depends on the size and nature of the business, but someone needs to serve as watchdog and be held accountable.

Red Flag

Avoid the temptation of "More is better." If your company can manage through its growth phase without a new data processing system or more employees, the system or employees may no longer be necessary when the product or the business starts to plateau. Some managers view expansion as a power game. No matter who wins that game, the company loses—especially when "Grow, grow!" becomes "slow grow" or even "no grow."

➤ The company needs to hire additional workers during a high-activity period—many of whom may lose their value to the company when the flurry of activity ends.

➤ The company's structure and management grow to accommodate numerous initiatives, forming a hierarchy and bureaucracy that end up becoming cumbersome and costly down the road.

➤ The employee turnover rate grows because of bad direction and dissatisfaction with a fragmenting work environment.

➤ Managers are stretched beyond their skill and experience to handle new areas and levels of responsibility.

➤ Costs run out of control as a result of trying to keep pace with runaway demands.

➤ Dissatisfaction, dissension, and dysfunction grow among staff as other problems increase.

Remember: Planned growth can strengthen and grow the company, while unplanned growth can drive a company out of business.

Planning Ahead

Most of us seem to believe you can never have too much money. But a business can't run like that. Careful planning for growth is the only way to manage good fortune in a way that will promote orderly, healthy development. Here are some guidelines that can help not only the company's executive team but also enterprising department heads keep all the elements in line:

➤ Set financial targets that pinpoint realistic goals and then determine the strategies to get there.

➤ Watch resource expenditures carefully and be stingy with additional expenditures.

➤ Develop a growth pattern in stages. Cite goals for each stage and do not embark on the next step until those goals have been achieved.

➤ Reserve for expenses and budget as necessary. The worst thing that can happen during a growth cycle is running out of capital while trying to keep up with growth. Planning ahead for expenses as well as revenues can help prevent that from happening.

➤ Reinvest in the company's own growth and shore up operational needs by putting profits back into operations. It will all pay off in the end.

Evaluating Your Management

Businesses—both new and mature—fail for many reasons, but most of them revolve around poor management. Most companies can survive the challenges of a bad product, economic downturns, tough competition, inadequate financing, or a few problem workers. But they can all fail if the managers are not properly trained and capable of leading the company.

Bad management can be a big problem in a stagnant company—but it can mean death in a growing, dynamic environment. It's like a kid riding a bike that's too big, beyond his abilities. At low speeds, he's likely to just fall, with minimal injury and damage. But if that bike gets going fast, his inability might mean a major crash.

Managers, first and foremost, need to be trained in the skills of management. Specifics about the industry really come later. That rationale flies in the face of the tough old buzzards who have fought their way up through the ranks, starting out in the mail room and rising to become company president. But in most cases those tough old buzzards learned a thing or two along the way about leadership and are nothing like the mail room clerks they started out being.

Red Flag
If hiring new managers is part of the plan, great. But never allow it to be the sum total of the plan. Staff at any level is a resource to help achieve goals. New management is not a goal in itself, but just part of the process.

Cultivating or bringing in an executive to manage growth is a lot like expending any other resource. Paying a lot for someone does not necessarily mean you'll get the best the executive pool has to offer. Moreover, the company may be stuck with that person, like an expensive piece of equipment, long after his or her value to the firm has dropped. There's nothing worse than a mismatched manager who the company doesn't really need.

What to Do?

Like other challenges facing companies, there are guidelines for finding the right management match to guide either a company or an operation. Often the guidelines differ from industry to industry. Here are a few suggestions that are more universal in scope.

➤ Look for individuals, preferably a team, who can provide the required expertise to manage growth successfully. There are executives who specialize in troubleshooting. If they're not adaptable to a more tranquil environment, hire their expertise with the least amount of long-term commitment possible. That may mean a long-term consulting agreement or a short-term contract.

➤ Find a match in management and leadership ability and experience within the industry, to better shorten the learning curve. That may mean paying a little more up front, but will be money well spent.

➤ Empower those people to do the job they need to do. Once the management staff is in place, cut it loose and let it work. That may result in staff changes and organizational reconfigurations. But as long as those changes are in line with the goals of the organization, the new management's way may be a better way to get there.

➤ Take frequent stock in the progress of your growth plan. Remember: Your managers have been hired to support an overall plan developed by the company that will lead to success in an orderly fashion. Evaluate their success and performance and make any adjustments accordingly.

All in the Family

The most difficult management problems may be found in family-owned businesses, large or small. Most such businesses are started by an entrepreneur with vision, guts, pluck, or just some strange quality that allows that person to succeed. However, when it comes time to pass the baton, there may be no clear successor to provide the same level of leadership or the entrepreneur may simply be reluctant to step aside and allow another to take over the business.

If that passing coincides with a strong growth period, suddenly the need for a capable successor is not only necessary but also critical to the future of the business. Maybe the founder himself or herself would be ill-prepared to manage the growth. Certainly the smell of money has torn apart families, friends, and businesses. So, what do you do? Here are some ideas:

➤ Be honest about the management resources at hand and look to fill a need, not satisfy an ego.

➤ Don't let personalities, jealousies, and family squabbles get in the way of business. Keep the business separate from the personal.

➤ If necessary, get an outsider's opinion before taking an important leap. Many lawyers and accountants are retained for just this reason. Their expertise often is an excellent investment.

Shortcut

Sometimes it's wisest to turn the family business over to outsiders, at least temporarily. There are management firms that specialize in family succession matters. They can run the business and serve as arbitrators or even therapists. It's an investment that can keep companies in business and families together.

Rest assured that such problems likely won't crop up if the company is growing in accordance to a well-defined and executed business plan. It's the only way to go.

The Least You Need to Know

➤ Business life cycles, like product life cycles, will require a different level of effort at each stage to support growth.

➤ Good growth is the result of every effort made by staff and its board members to raise the revenues of the organization while keeping the expenses in line.

➤ Significant growth can be worse for companies than slow growth. Companies must plan for success as carefully as they try to prevent failure.

➤ Set financial targets based on realistic goals and the methodology to get there.

➤ New businesses fail for many reasons, but most of them fail because of inadequate management. This is especially true during high-growth scenarios.

➤ Look for individuals, preferably a team, who can provide you with the expertise you need to manage growth successfully.

Chapter 24

Partnering with Vendors

In This Chapter

➤ Cooperating with other businesses

➤ Finding the best vendor partners

➤ Negotiating a partnership plan

➤ Realizing the potential pitfalls of partnering

With apologies to the poet, no business is an island, entirely of itself. All businesses coexist in a cooperative world. They depend on suppliers to bring the required raw materials, market intelligence, delivery services, and the like, or to refine, package, distribute, and sell their products and services.

A company in the glass business, for example, supplies pickle jars to the pickler and wine bottles to the vintner. In many respects, the glass company is a partner in helping bring those pickles and wines to the marketplace. In a similar way, a commercial trucking firm is a partner with the glass company in delivering the jars and bottles to the pickler and vintner. They all work together in what is known as the *supply chain*.

A supply chain is the system of businesses that are linked together in providing a product or service for consumers. In recent years, attention has focused on supply-chain management as a way to improve quality, better meet customers' expectations, decrease costs, and increase profits.

Part of this move toward partnership among businesses stems from the quality movement, which emphasizes improving all business processes, both within a company and upstream and downstream in the supply chain. But in many respects it's just the old-fashioned concept of teamwork. A company should be emphasizing a spirit of partnership and teamwork among its employees if the owners expect to stay in business. From an economic and operational standpoint, it's time to extend that partnership mentality beyond the four walls.

Beyond the Buying/Selling Relationship

The concept of cooperation among businesses isn't new, but it's being newly redefined for numerous industries that are looking for ways to better leverage the supply chain, particularly in terms of the cost and availability of materials, and to maximize their resources.

Today it's no longer enough to find the lowest possible cost. There's also a growing need for value. There's a distinct difference between the two.

A product can be cheap, but if it doesn't serve a company's purpose, it has no value. The raw materials and services a company needs also may be cheap. But if they don't do the necessary job appropriately, they have no value.

Suppliers feel a similar pinch. At a time when margins are being trimmed to their thinnest edge, a customer who demands the lowest price and highest quality may or may not reward the supplier with enough business to make the effort worthwhile. At some point, when it's no longer worth the effort to please the customer, that supplier may just pull in her reins and take her product somewhere where it will make her more money. Suddenly the company is left with the *opportunity* to find a new supplier, one who may or may not be able to do the job.

Enter the concept of partnership.

The buyer and the seller reach an agreement in which each leverages the advantages offered by the other. By working more closely together, as partners, the pair can meet the customers' needs with the highest possible quality at the lowest possible cost. The best part is that each side benefits.

Journal Entry

Partnering between client and vendor can be positioned as an added customer value. MacWarehouse—a leading mail-order supplier of Apple and Macintosh computers, peripherals, and software—offers overnight delivery of all orders under five pounds for just $3 through Airborne Express. The rate is significantly less than the deliverer makes on single shipments of similar weight. But by allowing MacWarehouse to ship at such a low cost, Airborne Express is guaranteed a high volume of business through the computer firm's tireless promotion of what is quickly perceived as a MacWarehouse customer benefit.

Defining Partnering Conditions

Let's consider an example from the association industry. It serves to make the point loud and clear.

An association professional found himself with a rare opportunity. He ran a department of a major trade association dedicated to professional development. The trade association wasn't doing right by his membership, so he seized the first opportunity to take that membership and turn it into an organization of its own. Unfortunately, he found himself without the resources of the mammoth trade association, yet facing the same expectation for high-level professionalism from his membership.

The association professional found a vendor, a sales representative for a local printing company, and formed a partnership. The rep sold a very high-quality product, which the association needed. The rep also was in a position to provide a high level of personal service in a day when good service sometimes meant no more than answering the phone politely. The rep became the unofficial production manager, print counselor, contest organizer, and Dutch uncle for the fledgling association. The situation clearly went beyond the realm of customer and vendor into a much more integrated relationship.

Make no mistake. The rep made his fair share and then some from the association. But the association head also got an ersatz staff member, expert consultant, and a high-quality print product, all by paying about 10 percent more on print charges, instead of trying to knuckle the rep on price. When the association needed extended credit, the rep saw to it that it was granted. When the printers at the rep's shop went on strike and customers stayed away in droves, the association kept sending the rep business. Each looked out for the other.

But each also got what he wanted and needed. And knowing what's needed and wanted from a vendor partner is the first thing a company should identify.

> **Shortcut**
> One of the key benefits of a successful partnership is the partner's ability to understand a company's system and business philosophy, and more closely match services to those criteria. In most cases, that results in higher quality and better service. If the plan is properly negotiated, it also might mean a discount in costs.

Identifying Vendor Partners

The best vendor partners are companies with similar concepts in business that are integral parts of the supply chain. Vendors who want to compete on price alone aren't good candidates for partnership. If their service strategy is simply based on cutting price, then they're also probably going to cut quality in some ways at some point. That would violate a cardinal rule of vendor partnering:

> **There can never be a question of quality of product or services from the vendor partner. The vendor must be as committed as the company to providing the best possible product to *the company's* customer.**

The rep understood the rule and that's what made him a successful vendor partner for the association for nearly 20 years. The quality of print product always was superb. And, most often, so was the service.

There's a second critical rule to successful vendor partnerships:

> **While cost is always a concern, it can't be the driving factor in determining the success of a vendor partnership.**

The partnership must be constructed around the idea that both partners will benefit from the relationship in terms of revenue, quality, and service. That's what a partnership means.

The rep and the executive both knew that. The executive occasionally lamented to his staff about how much he was paying the rep. He knew he could buy printing cheaper and he might even have been able to match the quality he was receiving at a lower price. But he'd never match the service package or relationship he'd built with the rep over the years. That's what haggling about price would have cost him. And there are some things that money can't buy.

Red Flag
When negotiating partnership terms, remember that your partner also will be looking for advantages. Yield on items in which there is some flexibility, but take a hard line on areas where the company requires the most support. The company's end goal should be to capitalize on vendor resources where you need them the most.

Finally, there's a third critical factor governing successful vendor partnerships:

> **There's value to finding vendor partners similar in size to your company, *or at least vendors who manage as if they are.***

A partnership that consists of a huge conglomerate and a small service supplier can, for a short time at least, work very well in allowing partners to function as equals.

In the rep's case, his printing company far outstripped the association in size and expertise. But the rep managed his end of the relationship as if he were the only one on staff. The association head never dealt with anyone else from the printing company, even though he knew he could have at any time. For both parties, the strategy worked.

Establishing a Partnership Plan

A partnership plan, like a contract, needs to be negotiated. And it should be negotiated carefully, for the following reasons:

➤ The agreement likely will govern the working relationship with the vendor partner from now until the relationship ends.

➤ In many cases, the agreement will restrict or eliminate the opportunity to negotiate further over hard-edged practical issues like price reductions or delivery timetables. If the agreement works as it should, the partners will need to agree on that information up front so each side can tailor production to accommodate the other.

➤ The agreement should provide for changes. Partners may schedule regular negotiations, perhaps every season or every year, to assess the business climate and determine prices, quantities, and other matters that reflect economic changes.

➤ The agreement will serve as a model for other such agreements, or at least be another link in a continuing network as the company progresses in building such relationships with all vendors. Since your first agreement will be a model for your next agreement, make sure you've thought out the best possible terms.

A good vendor partnership plan specifically outlines the benefits and expectations for both sides of the relationship—what the company expects from the vendor and what the vendor expects from the company. And both vendor and company should be able to expect its partner to live up to the agreement.

Red Flag
One of the least anticipated pitfalls in vendor partnerships comes when the liaison with whom the company has been working moves on. Companies that haven't laid the proper groundwork or established a solid relationship may find that the partnership dies when the liaison leaves. Make sure he or she is representing the company, not just working as a maverick, when you agree to terms. And get them in writing!

What Should Your Vendor Partner Agreement Include?

Inclusions may vary based on the company and industry, but here are some basics that apply in most cases:

➤ *Identify the expected life of the agreement so there's no mistake in anyone's mind.* This may be a short-term agreement for a special project or initiative, or it may define a long-term relationship between the two firms. Short-term agreements allow both parties to test a potential partnership. How well does it work? How good are the terms? Of course, short-term agreements can work to the company's advantage—or against it.

➤ *Identify performance standards for both partners.* This may mean the vendor must meet a certain level of quality for the product, and certain criteria for reliability and terms for delivery. For the company, that may involve agreeing to certain payment terms, conditions, and guarantees. Vendor partners have a right to expect preferential payment treatment. That might include something less than 30 days net, if that is the industry standard, or payment before other vendors if the company's cash flow becomes tight. Preferred payment treatment likely will be a hard negotiating point for vendors, and should be for the company when it finds itself on that side of the fence.

Shortcut
The key factor in any vendor-client partnership is the ability to build a relationship between the two parties. A solid relationship goes well beyond the daily negotiations of product deals, and trades on trust first, followed by price and convenience second. That trust on both sides can go a long way in getting the type of prices and services you want from your suppliers.

➤ *List any exceptions to terms and conditions, as well as market and industry situations, under which other exceptions might arise.* This is a very sensitive point because, while the company doesn't want to lock itself into situations that may make it difficult to fulfill the agreement, it also doesn't want the vendor partner to treat the terms of the agreement lightly.

Obviously, the company will want maximum flexibility without giving up all to the partner. At the same time, however, the partner shouldn't feel as if the benefits are one-sided. Good negotiators get the terms they want and make the other side think they are getting the advantage. The same rule applies here, too.

Potential Pitfalls of Partnering

No matter how hard the company works to establish a strong vendor partnership, there are pitfalls. Some are obvious, some are not, but be sure to consider as many as possible prior to formalizing any agreement.

Here are a few we've become familiar with:

➤ *The best deal might not look as attractive under new conditions.* Things may change at the company or within the industry that might make the deal negotiated less valuable—not the least of which would be the appearance of a newer, more valuable partner. Unless the company has signed an actual contract, of course, it's free to break its agreement. But do that too often and suddenly it'll be the last company with which vendors want to partner.

➤ *An agreement could be construed as a contract.* In some industries, a handshake is almost as good as a written contract. Hollywood actress Kim Bassinger paid several million dollars in restitution after backing out of the film project *Boxing Helena*. She had made only a verbal commitment to the producers, but the court held that in the film industry, multi-million-dollar deals are often closed with just a handshake. If you renege on an agreement in which a vendor has committed time and money, a court might construe that as lack of good faith. At the very least, the maneuver could cause the firm significant headache and cost. Make partnership agreements meaningfully and purposefully—or prepare to suffer the consequences.

➤ *Partnership agreements reduce flexibility.* A company may need to adjust its production and delivery schedules based on an agreement. This might not be a problem—unless other schedules change and the lack of flexibility results in a loss of business.

➤ *An incomplete agreement may cost more money elsewhere.* If a company strikes an arrangement with the vendor for a product or service, the company must make sure the agreement is as comprehensive as possible for all products and services the vendor provides. Vendors may give up cost benefits in one area and attempt to make it up by charging more in another. When negotiating, cover all bases as much as possible.

➤ *Develop an agreement that provides an incentive for the vendor to do even better.* If a company can build in an additional incentive layer into the agreement with the vendor, it could help improve already preferential performance. For example, a company might agree to pay a slightly higher price for materials if defects in previous shipments have been below a certain level. Not only will the company more likely get the prices and services it seeks, but it also has established a multi-dimensional level that will help strengthen the relationship between the two parties. And that serves everyone better.

Red Flag
Partnerships require faith. After all, we've all been conditioned to believe that competition improves products and services, that vendors will treat us better if they're fighting for our business. So, it makes sense to partner only when there's already a good business relationship—or when you're sure the benefits of partnering will keep both partners satisfied and not allow either to become complacent.

Watch for similar scenarios from customers who consider your company a vendor partner. Once your company has established its own vendor partner protocol, it should be better able to spot those strategies as they develop among customers. Take the lead in developing and fostering such relationships, no matter which side of the equation your company is on, and you'll be further ahead in reaching financial and partnership goals.

The Least You Need to Know

> ➤ Vendor partners can increase the value of services a company receives in terms of both price and quality.

> ➤ Knowing what you should require from a vendor partner is the first step.

> ➤ Vendor partners must be as committed as the company is to providing the highest quality products and services possible to the *company's* customers.

> ➤ Cost can't be the only factor driving vendor partnerships.

> ➤ Vendor partners should be similar to the company in both size and philosophy.

> ➤ Negotiate the partnership plan that best benefits the company, and be aware of the pitfalls in partnering.

Chapter 25

Troubleshooting Your Business System

In This Chapter

➤ Identifying trouble in your business

➤ Building control systems

➤ Deciding to audit the business

➤ Uncovering errors

➤ Determining your effectiveness

The first evidence that someone or something ever deviated from standard operating procedures came the moment Eve suggested that Adam take a bite from the apple. In addition to being an act of direct insubordination to a superior, the bite compromised operating procedures in the Garden of Eden. After all, the rule was to enjoy the garden and all the fruits, but to stay away from the tree of knowledge. So the two managers were cast out and, presumably, replaced by a new regime. But then, like today, the availability of qualified candidates was extremely limited.

That fanciful example shows that, despite the best-laid plans and the clearest instructions, things can and do go wrong with businesses, both operationally and financially. Managers of any company that has been through such problems already know the importance of internal controls.

In Chapter 13, we covered internal financial controls for bookkeeping systems. But that's just part of a business. It's important that a company have the proper controls in place for the entire business, both for those times when the error is intentional as well as when things just sort of happen.

That's as true for individual operations within the company as it is for the entire company itself. So, whether you're in the office at the top or in charge of a department, you should know about troubleshooting the system.

Is Trouble Brewing?

Red Flag
The time to establish internal controls is right now, before problems begin. Once you're facing a major crisis, creating and implementing internal controls is a little like trying to fill the gas tank of a racing car as it speeds around the track. It's something you don't really want to try to do. And nobody's going to drop a yellow flag to slow down your competitors so you can make a pit stop.

Sometimes it's easy to tell when trouble is brewing in the shop. Daily financials don't always balance and cash flow becomes a problem. Production lags and staff productivity begins to suffer. Overall, management decision-making seems off. Market position begins to slip. Morale is declining.

If a company has defined a strategic plan with action steps, the first task is to see if these action steps have been met. If not, that could be the obvious answer to the problem. Businesses are interactive entities, both from a fiscal as well as operational point of view. If one goal is missed, that will impact all others, either directly or indirectly. Rectify that problem and the company may be on the road to healing all wounds.

But business problems tend to be both more subtle and more complex than that, with problems running deeper and in different directions than is obvious at first. Internal controls are generally designed to provide the tools to ferret out these problems.

Is It a Good Control System?

Control systems are critical to the safety of the business, but it's critical to the success of the control system that it doesn't become an end in itself. How do you recognize a good system?

➤ It is flexible and easily managed.

➤ It is not costly to develop and maintain.

➤ It is not highly bureaucratic.

➤ Most important, it is able to measure the cause and effect of various situations, allowing the company to diagnose what's wrong with its operations.

The construction of a good control mechanism is fairly obvious, but bears repeating:

➤ The basis of a good control system requires set standards of performance. Whether it's a manufacturing function, sales effort, or distribution system, each step in the control system must have standards against which performance is measured. Without those standards, executives will have no point of reference to help them know something is wrong—or they may disagree among themselves over a situation.

➤ A company must use those standards to measure actual performance. The annual budget, for example, is the *absolute* against which year-to-date sales figures are measured. Everything else—from manufacturing output to sales performance—trickles down or up from there. That should seem obvious, but companies are basically groups of people...and most people are only human.

➤ When deviations occur, controls should determine if the deviations are excessive. There may be a company-wide policy that deviations of plus or minus five percent cause the sirens to wail and the Red Flags to go up. Or you may determine deviation acceptability on a department-by-department or project-by-project basis. Those deviations should be built into the control mechanisms. Don't wait until you're sliding to determine how much decline is too much.

➤ Once a deviation becomes excessive by the set criteria, be prepared to take corrective actions. Such actions may also be defined in the procedures.

These guidelines for constructing a control mechanism may seem basic. But there are some finer characteristics to help determine the success or failure of any control system. Here's a look at some key characteristics in greater detail.

Applied and Timely

Control mechanisms that exist in theory but not in practice might as well not exist at all. In that same vein, those that exist but are exercised too infrequently also do little good. Create and apply measurement criteria in such a way that the results can be used to better evaluate procedures.

Let's use a retail example for this point, specifically a wine and spirits merchant faced with a good deal on a specialty item. One of the key business failures in any retail setting comes from not anticipating and demanding the proper level of performance, weekly and monthly, from the various products in stock. The retailer in this example failed to apply timely controls in advance, and it cost him dearly.

Consider some expensive cases of Irish whiskey he bought. The wholesaler gave him a price that allowed for an excellent margin, as well as a decorative pub mirror, for buying three cases of the whiskey. Unfortunately, the retailer failed to measure the likelihood of selling all three cases in a timely fashion—six months would have been the outside time limit, even given the margin.

When he ultimately sold the store 18 months later, he still had two-and-one-half cases left. The buyer's price included a flat fee for existing inventory, about 38 cents on the dollar. The retailer lost not only his margin but a considerable investment as well. At that point the attractive pub mirror offered little consolation, although he did a lot of reflecting.

Economical to Create, Maintain, and Operate

The key failure for many control systems is that they command considerable resources, usually in staff time, to execute. With the typical "more is better" thinking, some businesses create a series of checks and balances that cost more to administer than they manage to save.

That's not the right way to go about it. Keep it simple and, if possible, automated. That way, you can make decisions quickly by comparing data against pre-existing criteria, with no need to put a lot of time and energy into long and involved analysis.

Shortcut
When using in-house control systems, remember to measure activity based on core performance requirements. Byproduct activity and processes sometimes cloud the issue and distort the results. Stick to the primary activities and processes at each step, for a truer measurement.

In the retailer's case, that simply might have been a spreadsheet plugged into a laptop computer loaded with acceptable shelf lives for products based on different profit margins. The lower the margin, the shorter the shelf life would have to be, since volume will have to drive profits for that item. That's a simple solution that works wonders for the vast majority of retailers.

The slightly higher margin on the Irish whiskey may have made the product more attractive to the retailer. But had he stopped to measure the amount of Irish whiskey he'd sold in the past few years—two bottles in three years of operation—he quickly would have realized the risk he was taking. Owning a shop devoted primarily to wine, he should have realized the failure in his purchasing logic. The biggest profit margin means little if you can't sell the goods.

As Accurate as Possible

Although the person designated to ensure your controls must ultimately make decisions on performance, he or she will do so based on data. Whoever is involved in gathering that data will have to be accurate. The best decision-maker is only as good as the data behind those decisions. This is true whether the business is a small retail beverage store or a large manufacturing conglomerate.

If the retailer had been foresighted enough to exercise internal controls once the six-month window of acceptability had passed, he might have thought to examine such factors as:

➤ The shelf placement of his Irish whiskey

➤ The cleanliness of a product that hasn't moved, relative to other stock that more frequently turns over

➤ Its history as part of the "featured product" displays in the store

➤ The proximity of purchase and sales relative to appropriate holidays, such as St. Patrick's Day

Keeping track of all the details may seem complicated, but it certainly beats going out of business!

Help Analyze the Cause of the Problem

Failures to perform are obvious when compared with the appropriate standards set. Less obvious are the reasons behind those failures. Part of the purpose of a control system is to identify and rectify those problems so they don't keep happening.

In an episode of the old television sitcom *WKRP in Cincinnati*, ad salesman Herb Tarlick talked about one particularly difficult client from whom he had trouble collecting, and often bemoaned the excuses the client used to avoid payment.

"He did that to me 20 times. Then I got wise," Tarlick said. Obviously Herb and his superiors were failing to analyze and rectify the cause of the problem. It's funny when it happens on TV, but it can be tragic when it happens to your company or your department.

Single Accountability

The person responsible for managing and running your control systems could be the department manager or the business operations manager. It probably shouldn't be the chief executive officer, because the CEO will have to act on the recommendations for making corrections. (Think of it in these terms: you wouldn't expect a judge to also serve as a police officer.) But it's essential that responsibility for the control systems rests with one person. Otherwise the task will not get done. We know what they say about committees: The responsibility of everybody is the responsibility of nobody.

Red Flag

No matter how a company chooses to go about it, remember that all good control systems demand quantifiable results. Knowing that there is a problem is not enough. A company must understand the level of damage in order to make a decision on corrective action. Every boat rocks from time to time; what matters is the amount of rocking. Are you riding with the waves on a comfortable cruise? Or are you dancing to the orchestra on the *Titanic*?

Auditing the Business

When control systems fail or just plain aren't in place when trouble hits, an audit of the business may be necessary. That can be just as comprehensive and difficult as it sounds.

In business, the audit is most familiar as a financial procedure that results in a full and complete examination of a business, often by an outside source, independent of the company. Many businesses undertake this initiative on their own every year, to make sure their financial methodologies, accounts, and amounts are on track. It's expensive, but it may be a worthwhile investment. An audit not only helps the accounting department balance its books for the new year, but provides evidence to other parties—boards of directors and the IRS being two of the more important ones—that the numbers are in their places and all is right with the world.

But any procedure can be audited within a business, in any area from manufacturing to sales to service. Think of an audit as a thorough inspection to ensure that a process is working properly and that procedures are being followed correctly.

Audits differ from control systems in that they are the ultimate control procedure. Most controls are isolated analyses of specific aspects of businesses. Consider our example of the retailer who was unable to sell three cases of Irish whiskey in six months. In an audit, examiners not only would have considered performance failure of that particular item, but also more global conditions, including:

➤ When and why the whiskey was purchased

➤ What wholesaler sold the whiskey and what the history of that wholesaler had been with the store

➤ The financial impact the purchase had on the store's overall financial period for that week, that month, that quarter, and that year

➤ The rationale and relative decision-making ability of the purchaser in light of other business decisions made

Of course, the audit would cover a variety of business activities and procedures. Was the whiskey fiasco an anomaly? Maybe it was just the worst of several bad buying decisions. Maybe the whiskey might have sold better under different circumstances, so that it could become a solidly profitable item. An audit can detect problems, explore causes and conditions, and perhaps reveal hidden strengths and potential opportunities.

Businesses tend to fear audits for what they may uncover, just like most of us are afraid of getting an annual physical exam. But, for that very reason, an audit should be welcomed as the best way to verify the performance of a department or detect errors and omissions that keep that department from doing its best.

Contrary to popular belief and fears, few careers have been wrecked over the results of an audit. In fact, generally the results are quite the opposite. Operational inefficiencies have been uncovered and corrected, resulting in greater economies and earnings. Staff training needs have been identified and employees have developed. A lot depends on the attitude brought to an audit and what you do with the resulting information.

Journal Entry

The most recent development in audits is in conjunction with quality management and ISO 9000, a series of quality standards initiated in 1987 by the International Organization for Standardization, a federation of national standards bodies from more than 100 countries. The basic goal is to facilitate the international exchange of goods and services. A company wishing to be certified as being in compliance with ISO 9000 undergoes a series of audits.

Reviewing Decision-Making Systems

One of the things that comprehensive audits (as opposed to financial audits) often uncover are errors in the ways managers in the company arrive at their decisions. In many cases, particularly family-owned business that have grown more or less spontaneously, decision-making is the result of a patchwork approach to personal procedures that Uncle Marv and Aunt Gertie may have used when they founded the business. As you can imagine, that can only lead to problems—even if science finds a way to clone every Marv and Gertie.

Good business is the result of good decision-making. It's just that simple—to understand, yes, but not that easy to achieve. Here are guidelines to help you make good business decisions:

➤ *Restate the issue in light of the company's objectives.* Decisions must be made in a variety of contexts, not the least of which are the marketplace and the company's goals and objectives. If there is a problem, restate it in terms of how it supports objectives in order to gain the right perspective for the decision.

➤ *Define your objectives and approach to the problem.* Once you've defined the problem, identify the goal in addressing the issue and the methodology by which to proceed. Define the time frame, budget expenditure, and anything else necessary to identify in order to reach that goal. We all know what happens when managers skip this step: they simply stomp on flames wildly, reacting to whatever hot spots develop, being controlled by crises instead of working to command the situation.

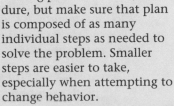

Shortcut
Define an action plan as part of the decision-making procedure, but make sure that plan is composed of as many individual steps as needed to solve the problem. Smaller steps are easier to take, especially when attempting to change behavior.

➤ *Collect all the necessary data.* In identifying the problem, you've probably considered some evidence. That evidence may be enough to compel you to react, but it may not be enough to help you decide how. Before proceeding, collect all the necessary data and analyze it according to your initial goal and your operational methodology. Responses can be easily skewed when all the information isn't at hand. The more information available, even if it's repetitive, the better response a company will be able to make.

Red Flag

In any company of any complexity, follow-up is crucial. If a manager solves a problem in her department, but her solution creates a problem for another department, the company may not gain anything at all as "the torch" is passed. In fact, the situation is likely to get worse, if only because territorial attitudes may evolve that breed dissension and power struggles.

➤ *Decide on an implementation plan—and use it.* After you've examined the evidence in light of the situation, goals, and operating philosophy, decide on a course of action to rectify the situation. Then implement it. Make sure this course of action is comprehensive in its scope and complete in its thrust. British statesman David Lloyd George once said that the hardest thing to do was leap a chasm in two jumps. The same philosophy applies here.

➤ *Review the results and follow up.* The first question to ask yourself is: Has the problem been solved? The second question: What are the implications in other areas? Review the impact of the decision in rectifying the problem. Determine the value of the approach in other areas—whether they're problem areas or not—of the overall operation. But most important, go back in six, nine, and twelve months to make sure that the fix that has been implemented has had the desired results.

Ten Measurements of Effectiveness

In order to thrive, any business needs to have systems in place to anticipate and address problems as they develop. It also needs a decision-making structure that makes operations more effective. All of that will go a long way in helping guide the company's success.

Systems and structures are essential, of course. But individuals also play an important role—perhaps the most important role—in the success of the operation.

Do you operate in the most effective way possible to ensure that your company can and will succeed? Consider the items on the following list and see if you and those around you are making all the right moves on behalf of the company:

1. *Are there written goals and procedures that govern both your time and company time?* If plans aren't on paper, they don't really exist. And if they don't govern the way managers think and operate on behalf of the company, then they may be worse than no plans at all.

2. *Do you operate at the highest level possible all the time?* Although the classic definition of management is accomplishing tasks through other people, most managers do more than simply supervise. But beware of doing things yourself that you should delegate to others. The company is paying you to make your department run as effectively and efficiently as possible.

3. *Do you know your company's financials inside and out?* Some dentists have this sign in their office: "Ignore your teeth and they will go away." The same holds true for your financial assets. Sure, there's someone responsible for the finances—bookkeepers and accountants—but do you leave the entire responsibility for the health of your teeth to your dentist? Do your part for your company's fiscal fitness.

Red Flag
Beware the "us-them" mentality that undermines most companies. Many managers feel that, in managing their department, they must focus on managing the people who report to them. Too often, they neglect to manage themselves. Managers should always serve as models of proper employee conduct and the company work ethic, because that's how the people they supervise view them.

4. *Do you hold yourself responsible for the tasks you've assigned yourself?* If you're above the rules, then the rules don't really exist. And those are rules you need to guide your operation. Remember: managers are role models for other workers, for better or for worse. Would you like to manage employees who treat their job responsibilities as you treat yours?

5. *Do you perform a reality check on your goals and initiatives?* Things change. We all know that, but generally we still just keep moving along toward the same goals, pursuing the same initiatives. Unless you're omnipotent, those changes around you are likely to affect what you're trying to do. If you're fighting against a current of changes, it might be wise to change horses in midstream or to aim for another spot across the river. That's why a friend claims that sailboats are the best place for training managers. Those who are sensitive to the winds and set their tack accordingly make great progress. On the other hand, those who doggedly insist on maintaining certain bearings regardless of conditions end up out of the race...and maybe in over their heads.

6. *Do you perform periodic self-evaluations and solicit input from others?* It may be lonely at the top, and even at every rung going up the ladder, but smart managers know how to minimize that loneliness. They know they can't afford to operate without the input of people who understand their goals.

Another important point to make here: if you've empowered your employees to help you make decisions, trust their judgment. After all, the less responsibility and authority you allow people working under you, the more they're likely to expect you to supervise them closely. We live up to expectations—or down to them.

Journal Entry

When it comes to looking at what's closest to us—ourselves and our performance—we're all myopic. If you don't solicit input from others in good position to measure your performance—superiors, peers, and even subordinates—you're cheating both yourself and your company.

You don't need to emulate Ed Koch, former mayor of New York, who would regularly greet residents of that city with the question, "How'm I doin'?" But you should encourage your colleagues and subordinates to be candid and honest with you. Then, show you appreciate their help. Remember: Employees who question and express concerns provide more real support for a manager than employees who simply smile and go along with everything.

7. *Are policies and procedures reviewed periodically?* Regular evaluation of all steps your company goes through to address the marketplace is critical to its continued ability to do so. Some managers even like to "zero base" everything. Just imagine if you were starting the company or the department from scratch. What policies would you set? What procedures would you establish? Now, how do your current policies and procedures compare with those you imagine? A company with outdated policies and procedures is a museum.

8. *Have you protected your company by protecting yourself and your role in it?* If you're the only one with the secret recipe for success, then you better plan on living forever. If you can't, then share the knowledge and protect yourself so your business can operate in your absence. Sure, it's inconvenient to document what you do and to train others to do it. And you certainly may feel like you're undermining your job security. But it's a form of insurance.

9. *Do you seek the appropriate internal and external advice when your company needs it?* Smart executives know they don't know it all, but they do know where to go to find out what they need. Sometimes that may mean an expensive consultant, but sometimes you can find out a lot just by talking with those around you.

10. *Do you truly communicate with your staff, your board, your suppliers, and your customers?* The vast majority of management problems come from poor communications. But remember: In the word "communicate," "u" comes before "i"—it's more important to listen than to talk.

If you can answer all of these questions positively, you're probably not causing problems for your company. (Great! Keep up the good work!) If you've missed one or two, however, it's time to go back to the start of this chapter and begin by closely examining yourself.

The poet Goethe says to know oneself is genius. At the very least, it's the key to your business success.

The Least You Need to Know

➤ Control systems are critical to the safety of a business, but it's critical to the success of the control system that it doesn't become an end in itself.

➤ Control systems are built around setting and maintaining standards.

➤ When control systems fail or just plain aren't in place when trouble hits, a general business audit may be necessary.

➤ Some of the things that general business audits often uncover are errors in the ways decisions are made in the company.

➤ Good business is the result of good decision-making—and that's not something easily achieved.

➤ People play the most important role in the success of any operation.

➤ Knowing yourself is the key to your business success.

What's My Data?

One of the secrets to financial management for the nonfinancial manager is access to the proper tools. In the world of accounting, that boils down to data and documents. Knowing which ones you need in order to answer the questions you're asked is half the battle.

Unfortunately, accountants live in a world of numbers far more complex than your own. Knowing which document to consult for the proper financial application is second nature to them, and sometimes they fail to explain it to the financial neophytes with whom they do business. Then everyone becomes frustrated.

The following scenarios are designed to help you identify which sources of information you'll need to consult to answer certain questions. It will help you look bright and be right the first time you're called upon for a financial report in those dreaded management meetings.

Scenario 1: Your Department on the Line

Question: Phyllis, the company's chief financial officer (CFO), is giving a mid-year update on the company's financial position. As is the case for any company, her financial report has highs and lows. Unfortunately, one of those lows is about to hit your area. Mr. Bigg, the company chief executive officer (CEO), wants to know what to expect from your department for the rest of the year. What data do you consult?

Answer: Your first thought may be to produce sales reports and cash flow statements. Those are useful in knowing where you are financially, but they measure only activity that already has passed. What Mr. Bigg wants to see is your budget, which by its nature charts the course that lies ahead.

In order to answer his question correctly given the situation, you'll need to consult your department's operational budget rather than the overall strategic budget. Why? Because the operational budget predicts and measures potential operational expenses and their resulting revenue.

In a nutshell, it shows you were thinking about the balance between revenue and expense last year when you created the financial scenario for this year. If you've been on target to this point, your budget should roughly parallel your actual revenue and expense line items to date.

If there have been variations between budget figures and actual figures, the document will allow you to measure those variables and discover patterns of discrepancies. You can then apply those patterns to the remaining months measured by the operational budget and devise an intelligent answer to Mr. Bigg's question.

Scenario 2: Expansion...or Else

Question: As the brand new director of marketing, you walk out of your first executive meeting with a critical assignment: Expand the western territory and increase sales 30 percent. Hobbs, your predecessor, failed to do that. Hobbs is no longer with the company. Mr. Bigg, it would seem, is serious in his assignment—and his expectations.

You meet with Marcus, your information systems employee, and ask for market data segmented by state, locality, population, and past competitive buying patterns. You'll need 15 different data sorts for 30 different regions by end of the day tomorrow.

Marcus smiles and notes that Hobbs had requested the same information for six months running, but that the current 10-year-old hardware/software configuration wouldn't support such a complex request. The only way to answer these questions and open up the western territory would be to purchase a new configuration package for $20K and change. Where do you go to see if you can afford that investment?

Answer: You may first think to check the company's strategic budget to see whether or not it says anything about market development and allows for any expenses to support that development. And you may find some information about such growth patterns company-wide, but that won't give you all you need to answer your question.

The first place you'll want to check is your capital budget. That's the document that charts funds set aside for major capital purchases, such as computer systems, real estate, and other expenses that have residual value for the company and represent capital that can be liquidated or expensed as necessary. Chances are Hobbs hasn't set aside any funds to purchase the necessary computer system. But if he did, it would be reflected in the department's capital budget. If you don't find it, you'll have to rely on your wits—and your sense of company politics and culture. (Sometimes the machine works differently when the CEO is behind a request.) Unfortunately, the answers to business questions are not always in the figures!

Scenario 3: So Many Figures, So Little Time

Question: As director of sales, you need a full and accurate sense of your financial picture as of the close of the last quarter. Miller and Martin, two regional sales managers, have been liberally recording revenues and expenses at such a rapid rate that you can't mentally manage the impact both are having on your bottom line. What's more, you'll need a firm handle on this information for the upcoming executive retreat. What document will you request from Phyllis, the CFO?

Answer: Your budget won't do you much good here. It may provide you with a useful benchmark, but the budget reflects the goals, not the reality, of the department's financial situation.

The first document you should check is the income statement, a summary of business revenue and expenses for a specific period of time. If Miller's and Martin's activities have been accurately documented, then both revenue and expenses should show up on the income statement for the quarter in question. If they haven't been handled correctly, chances are the income statement will show it.

If you think the question is one of an accounting error rather than carelessness on the part of sales staff, check the balance sheet, also known as the T diagram, which balances both income and expenses according to an algebraic equation. If your balance sheet doesn't balance, either expenses or revenues have been improperly recorded. Then you need to confront your sales staff and maybe explain the discrepancies to the boss. How you deal with that fact is a matter of tact—something nobody can learn from a guide to finance and accounting.

Scenario 4: The Check Is in the Mail

Question: Not all your clients are as capable or as honest as they could be. That's the sad situation for one of your clients in the southeast region. Your billing department's 120-day past-due notice brought an irate call from the client's accountant, who said her company paid the bill "long ago." How do you check out her story?

Answer: This is a job for the general ledger, which reports all financial activity through the balance sheet and income statement, two components of this integrated system.

But if you stop here, you've done only half the job. The general ledger is a comprehensive document made up of many components, including documentation of all transactions. In order to verify whether your client's accountant is telling the truth, you'll need to move from the general ledger to the subledger in which payments for sales are recorded. If there are a lot of such payments, chances are they have their own batch groups, which allows your accountant to post this activity to the subledger periodically, rather than every day.

Ask your client's accountant—tactfully, of course—for the date of the supposed payment and check it against the appropriate batch. Once you've found the batch, go through the files and look for the appropriate supporting documentation—like an invoice that has been date-stamped PAID or even a copy of the check—to verify the claim. If you can't come up with such documentation, it's time to call your collections department. Of course, this difference may be the result of a simple error by your client's accountant and you don't want to lose the client over this matter. But you should definitely takes steps to get what is yours.

Scenario 5: The Devil Is into Details

Question: As head of production, you're faced with maintaining a revenue stream for your company that offsets and explains the expenses you incur in producing that revenue stream. (The old "you have to spend money to make money" scenario.) Mr. Bigg, the CEO, asks you to provide a detailed report on sales in the Cleveland-Toledo market during the second quarter. Where do you go for this information?

Answer: You could check the income statement, which will give you a complete record of net revenues after the expenses have been subtracted from gross income. Unfortunately, that will tell you nothing about the geographic earning patterns that Mr. Bigg wants to know.

Your best bet is to request a report of your accounts receivable, particularly cash receipts, sorted for the Cleveland-Toledo market. In addition to providing information on your revenue stream, accounts receivable also will show sales and income patterns and how they relate to your department's overall financial activity.

And, if you really want to impress Mr. Bigg, find out from his secretary why he wants the data on the Cleveland-Toledo market in the first place. By digging down through accounts receivable subledgers and the supporting documentation, you may be able to provide interpretive information without being asked. Then you've got answers before he even asks the questions.

Scenario 6: No Need to Worry About Good Buys

Question: Your department has made some purchases to support its operation. Phyllis, the CFO, has asked all department heads to review their purchase patterns over the last 90 days and provide the appropriate rationale. The combined reports of all departments will be synthesized for the board of directors to review. Since all your purchases were legitimate, you're not worried. But you've still got to put together your report, just like all the department managers. What document do you request from Phyllis so you can fulfill her request?

Answer: Both the capital and operating budgets will tell you what you budgeted to spend, but will not give you an actual figure of what you have spent. You need to request a report of your accounts payable. The report will list not only your current payment record, but also amounts that your department still owes suppliers.

This last part is important because it will help Phyllis, the board of directors, or anybody else who needs the information, not only to see where your department is, but also to know about all of the real financial obligations the department has incurred. Because that's the next information the board will need, you'll be ahead of the game if you provide the answer before the question is asked. You will impress them as a manager who knows what's going on—and isn't afraid of a little scrutiny.

Scenario 7: Better Than a Crystal Ball

Question: You've asked Phyllis, the CFO, for a report on how much money your department has to run its operation over the next 120 days. She says that all depends on your spending patterns and asks you what type of document you need for your evaluations. What answer do you give her?

Answer: The budget will do you no good here. Nor will reports from your accounts receivable or accounts payable. All of these documents will provide useful information, but you really want to know your current financial position in terms of operating capital. You need a cash flow report.

Cash flow is neither profit nor loss, just the way money moves through your company and department. By monitoring your cash flow through the various months as chronicled on your cash flow report, you may be able to detect patterns that will help you determine if your projected cash flow will adequately match what has come before and whether or not you'll have the necessary liquidity to meet your expenses.

Scenario 8: Rounding Up Stray Cattle

Question: Milbourne, head of collections, has asked for your assistance in tracking late payments in several areas. Some impact your department, others do not. But as a manager committed to the overall good of the company beyond your area of responsibility, you're happy to help. What type of documentation will help you and Milbourne chase down these errant funds?

Answer: Accounts payable is the first place you stop. Once you've identified specifics about when the amount due was posted to the general ledger, you can track down the batch to the appropriate subledger to come up with the information you'll need to pursue the debt.

Central to this pursuit will be finding the appropriate aging bucket—the record of how far the account is past due. Account aging is shown in 30, 60, 90, and 120-day increments. The age of the past due account—as well as the amount, of course—will determine how hard you and Milbourne want to pursue the debtor. If the account is only 30 days past due, it's might not be a major concern. But once an account is 120 days past due, the likelihood of collecting the debt is minimal. Using these two documents—accounts payable and the aging bucket—to carefully monitor account aging will help you save you from the financial mess of having too many accounts that wind up as uncollected. That's bad for the company, of course, and for Milbourne, but it can also be bad for you.

Scenario 9: Beating the Salary Stalk

Question: Mr. Bigg, the company CEO, is alarmed about the growing cost of payroll. Even though he realizes labor is the company's greatest operational expense, he's seeing more expense growth in your area than anywhere else in the company. He wants an explanation. What do you do?

Answer: Forget any thoughts about arguing based on budget, even if your departmental increases fall within the labor cost parameters you've set. Clearly, Mr. Bigg is past that point and looking for hard data. You need to consult your payroll records.

Payroll records report actual amounts paid to staff for work performed, including all types of pay rendered in all kinds of ways. Since the amount is growing at a rate faster than expected, something is wrong with the original budget, the way time is accounted for, or the way the system displays the data. That's means you'll have to dig down past the biweekly and monthly payroll roundup into support documentation.

It will be necessary to check time cards. Accounting should have that support data in its files for your department. These would include piecework reports as well.

You'll also have to check salaries. That task will be simpler, since salaries are based on an established and expected annual amount. Make sure those salary percentages awarded every two weeks are proper divisions, based on the total annual figure for the salaried employees in your department. Finally, if some of your staff are paid on commission, make sure there are corresponding gross sales figures and that percentages have been computed properly. This is an especially vulnerable area.

Even if you can't gather the figures to justify for Mr. Bigg all the payroll expenses in your department, your diligence and knowledge about financial matters should show him that *your* pay, at least, is well-justified.

Scenario 10: Deep in the Art of Taxes

Question: The Internal Revenue Service has called Mr. Bigg to say that it will be auditing his payroll taxes next week. The CEO has asked all department heads, including you, to work with accounting to verify that the proper records have been kept. How can you help?

Answer: Your first step is to request all federal withholding W-2 forms for your staff and 1099 forms for contract and consulting labor. Verify that all those people for whom you are financially responsible are represented and have completed the appropriate documentation. Flag any duplicates, omissions, or incomplete forms.

If there are errors in this process, they likely will be accounting mistakes and errors of omission. Your assistance in verifying the human side of the equation will save time, allowing the accountants to concentrate their efforts and cross-check the computation. They will appreciate your effort in helping dispatch the IRS request cleanly and effectively. Uncle Sam can be a tough relative when he comes to visit.

Well, how did you do in these ten scenarios? If you had any problems, that's normal: Accounting and finance can be difficult for nonfinancial managers. You may want to refer to specific chapters in this guide to review areas where you feel weak—and remember to keep this guide handy, for when scenario 11 occurs in your company.

Flexing Your Financial Muscles

Like any good manager or department head, you have to learn to think on your feet and respond with the right answer when that pivotal question is asked. You probably have few problems coming up with answers in your areas of expertise and experience. But when it comes to financial management, do you even know what the numbers jockeys are talking about?

The next set of exercises is designed to help you respond intelligently to financial questions asked in a public forum. You may not have the depth and breadth of knowledge your accounting counterparts have, but understanding key terms and how they're used can go a long way in showing your value as a manager when it comes to knowing the numbers.

Take a few minutes now to consider the following scenarios. (We urge you not to peek at the analysis before you've done your best to come up with answers.) Of course, not all of the scenarios will apply to your current position. It's a good idea to try them anyway, to test your knowledge of the concepts—and to better appreciate what your fellow managers need to do.

Scenario A: What's It to You?

Situation: At the management retreat called by Mr. Bigg, the chief financial officer, Phyllis, gives a presentation in which she mentions that within six months the entire company will move to a cost accounting basis. Mr. Bigg wants the managers to discuss how that change will affect each of their departments. Unfortunately, the first manager he calls on is you. So, when he asks what differences the shift in accounting basis will mean to your department, how do you answer?

Analysis: Cost accounting is the method by which all direct and indirect costs to produce products or provide services are taken into account in determining the cost of operations. Direct costs are anything directly attributable to production. The amount of time an assembly line worker spends screwing a nut to a bolt and the cost of those nuts and bolts are direct costs. The percentage of time attributable to hiring and training that worker by the company's human resource department, along with your supervision time, are indirect costs. When determining the value of a product or service, it's important to take into account both types of costs.

If your company and department hasn't been running under a cost accounting scenario, chances are the costs attributable to production and distribution aren't the actual costs of the products. Companies that measure only direct costs often leave the overhead and administrative charges to be accounted for somewhere else. The move to cost accounting will put those costs against each individual product or service and can be a slap in the face for firms and for departments that may think they're operating profitably.

Your answer to Mr. Bigg is that your cost of operations will increase, possibly dramatically, depending on how the accounting had been handled before. (Don't worry: the situation is likely to be the same in any department in your company.) The proper procedure would be to apply a true and accurate measure of both direct and indirect costs to all product lines and measure their profitability against the goals set in the company's strategic plan. (You can promise Mr. Bigg you'll make that evaluation a top priority.) Those lines that don't measure up—that cost the company money rather than generate a profit—will be examined. You may be able to adjust production for some items so they can make a profit. Others you'll probably decide to discontinue. Operating expenses also will be adjusted accordingly, until the budget once again balances under the new cost accounting scenario.

Scenario B: Banking on Your Inventory

Situation: As head of production, you know the value attributed to your inventory is critical, especially when it's used to leverage loans from the company's favorite lender. You've heard recently (through the company grapevine) about plans to borrow some money for a new project. This morning, the lender is sitting in Mr. Bigg's office. After they talk for a few minutes, Mr. Biggs calls you in. He asks you to explain the valuations within your inventory control systems and how you arrive at the cost of goods sold. The purpose in this, he tells you, is to give the lender an approximate running tally of the value of your inventory, at any given time, against which loans may be written. What do you tell the lender?

Analysis: Inventory control systems monitor the costs of the processes through which raw materials become finished products. For example, if your company mastered (and patented) the process from which the carbon in coal could be pressurized into diamonds, you'd easily see, once direct and indirect costs are applied, that the value of raw materials, plus the cost of both process and labor to convert that material, result in a different cost of goods sold. (See scenario A.)

Most likely your company has several valuation steps in its inventory control process. The first is the cost of the raw materials, which must be considered, from an accounting standpoint, as the purchase price paid. If those materials go through three distinct subassemblies, then the cost of each subassembly step can be added to the value of the product. That means, to arrive at the individual amounts you will add at each subassembly stage, you'll first have to know the direct and indirect costs for each subassembly before you can divide the total cost by the number of units.

The final step in the determining your unit cost is to calculate the sum total of all raw material costs and subassembly steps to determine your final cost of goods sold. Manufacturers also include the cost of average warehousing time and delivery costs to bring the product to market.

Obviously, nobody would expect you to come up with all the figures right on the spot. But since you understand what's involved in calculating the cost of goods in inventory at every stage in the production process, you can explain your procedure—and offer to put the figures together in a full report, if needed. Do all this right and the lender will likely understand the full value of your inventory and trust you with a loan. And that will make Mr. Bigg very happy.

Scenario C: Opportunities Lost, Figure the Cost

Situation: At the management retreat, Chumley, the head of a department parallel to yours, is forced to defend a favorite product line his group is responsible for producing. Chumley is very eloquent in defining the rationale and purpose behind introducing the product line. He also notes that, at a minimum, the operation not only covers its costs but makes a small profit, besides helping maintain the company's historic position in that particular market. Phyllis, the chief financial officer (CFO), looks Chumley in the eye and tells him to forget about the market share of the product line and concentrate on what the line means in terms of opportunity costs. What does she mean? What would you do if you were in Chumley's shoes? (After all, it could be your turn next.)

Analysis: Opportunity costs are a part of cost accounting and refer to the money that could be made (potential), as opposed to the money currently being made (actual). The cost of missing an income opportunity is calculated as the additional revenue lost.

If Chumley's staff is earning the company a six percent margin producing a line of goods, that may be less than the 12 percent margin they could be earning if they produced a different line of goods. The six percent difference between the two lines is the cost of missing the opportunity to produce that more profitable line.

In some companies, there's value to maintaining an image or historic market presence, which may make it worthwhile to sacrifice some opportunity costs. In Chumley's case, however, that may not be the situation. Chumley should evaluate the production steps used to produce the current line and see if he can increase the profitability margin by decreasing production costs. (In many companies, products become sacred cows as they age. If a widget was introduced in 1973 and is still being produced "the same old-fashioned way" a quarter-century later, there's definitely a benefit in considering changes in production.) In addition, Chumley should outline steps to phase in new, more highly profitable lines. If he dearly loves producing that favorite product line that's being challenged, he may be able to keep it by boosting his profitability in other areas.

Chumley may still wind up sacrificing the opportunity costs of the initial product line, but the increased income in other areas may make his strategy more acceptable. (Of course, not every business decision is dollars and cents. It would certainly help his cause if Mr. Biggs felt strongly about the line.)

Scenario D: Cash and Collateral

Situation: You've been appointed by Mr. Bigg himself to be part of the new corporate acquisition team. Your task is to find a company for your firm to acquire that will not only present a good investment opportunity but also provide you with a good resource against which loans can be leveraged. "Remember, you're looking for a company with positive cash flow, good collateral, and a strong management team," Mr. Bigg admonishes the group. You understand what he means by a strong management team, but what do the other two terms mean?

Analysis: Companies come up for sale for two reasons: either they were created to be sold once they reached a certain performance or revenue level, or they're in trouble and need to be bailed out. That's the purpose behind the instructions for the corporate acquisition team.

One of the key factors when considering acquiring any company is determining positive cash flow, which means a steady income without undue debt loads. Every company carries some amount of debt. (If not, then it was probably sacrificing some growth opportunities.) But if the costs of basic operations exceed revenues, that means the company is in trouble, now or soon, and that's not the company you want.

The other factor mentioned by Mr. Bigg, good collateral, means items of value against which loans can be leveraged. This includes real estate, inventory, durable goods such as equipment, and even accounts receivable. Good collateral can shore up a company that's currently listing, providing a solid foundation for growing revenues.

As for strong management, the prospective management team should be complete, contain a comprehensive knowledge of all the skills necessary, have maturity in its tenure, and be appropriate to the industry it serves.

You should be able to get most of the information Mr. Bigg wants from the managers of the companies you're considering acquiring—if it's not a hostile takeover and if your intentions are not secret. You may also need the services of a financial analyst...and maybe do some intelligence work with your colleagues around town.

Scenario E: Riding Cycles

Situation: During the management retreat, a strategic planning consultant hired by your company begins to talk about market maturity and, in particular, product life cycles. Each department head is given an hour to determine the life cycles of each of the products in his or her product line. What does that mean? How will you accomplish that task?

Analysis: Each business and each product within that business has a measurable life cycle that can be used to determine not only its profitability but also its very existence and viability in the future. In these highly competitive times, that determination is critical.

All products go through four distinct phases in their life cycle: (1) the introductory phase, in which time and resources are spent familiarizing the market with the new product; (2) the growth phase, in which public acceptance grows and sales build; (3) the mature phase, in which little more than a maintenance effort is needed to keep public acceptance up and sales strong; and (4) the declining phase, in which the product begins to lose favor with the public and descends toward discontinuation.

If you know anything about the history of your product line, you'll be able to easily determine what phase any of the products is in. (Of course, your task is even easier if a product was introduced with the understanding it would have a certain "shelf life.") Looking at resource expenditures and revenue losses or gains can help you identify the current phase of a product. Introductory and growth phases require significantly more resource expenditure, while the maturity phase often sees the product on automatic pilot, with no significant increase in resource expenditure. In the declining phase revenue and cost are decreasing.

While you determine the life cycle of your individual products, remember that businesses also have life cycles. What phase is your company in? Realizing that may determine how far you want to go with the exercise conducted by this strategic planning consultant. In other words, it may be time to focus on growing your product lines or time to revitalize the company, possibly through a spin-off.

Scenario F: Go with the Flow

Situation: As the newest department head, you've taken over an area that has a spotty performance history. It's been highly profitable from time to time and it's also run deeply in the red. As you settle into your office and the other department heads file out after welcoming you, one slaps you on the back and says, "Remember: watch your cash flow!" What does she mean by that? And why would she offer that advice?

Analysis: Cash flow is not a measure of profit and loss for your department, as some people seem inclined to believe. It's simply the way cash flows in and out of your department. There's positive cash flow—that's when revenue exceeds expenses and you're bringing in more money than you're spending. There's also negative cash flow, which is just the opposite.

If the department you've inherited has bled red ink on a regular basis in the past, chances are there are cash flow issues you will need to face. This sometimes comes about in seasonal business, when revenues and expenses don't balance and reserves must be accrued to cover operating costs. This is easily done through monitoring past cash flow activity and adjusting expectations accordingly. Seasonal business can be very profitable—or it can ruin a company. It all depends on how well it's handled.

If your business is not seasonal or up and down according to other cycles, there may be market elements at work that are causing the department problems. That may have to do with the availability of certain products at certain times or even production capacity compared with demand. Assume nothing and examine everything. That's the best way to keep an eye on cash flow. (And remember to thank your colleague for her good advice!)

Scenario G: Welcome to Accrual World

Situation: Phyllis, the CFO, is giving a presentation at the company's management retreat. She mentions that the company is large enough and its accounting system complex enough that the firm needs to move from cash-based to accrual accounting methods. You've heard the word "accrual" before, but you're not sure what it means. When she asks if you think such a method would help your department, how do you respond?

Analysis: Companies that are flush with cash have the luxury to choose between two types of accounting practices: accrual accounting or cash-basis accounting. For firms of any size, accrual accounting is likely the method of choice. But knowing a little bit about both will help you interact more intelligently with those who practice it on a daily basis.

The difference focuses to some degree on the question of cash flow. Accrual accounting, popular with large businesses, records transactions when they are made, regardless of whether any money has changed hands. The company is accruing sales revenue that will be deposited at a future date. Under accrual accounting, the actual cash is incidental to the accounting procedure. The transaction is immediately posted to the general ledger. This is what's known as a generally accepted accounting principle.

In the case of your department, accrual accounting allows for greater opportunity to incur expenses as you need to make them. Under cash-based accounting, you've needed to have corresponding sales posted before you could spend them. In the case of accrual accounting, you can accrue both revenues and expenses through your accounting operation, make purchases when you need them, and post revenues when you receive them. An accrual system greatly increases operational flexibility while better balancing revenue and expenses over a period of time, usually one year of your operational budget cycle.

Tell Phyllis you think it's a great idea for your department and for the company. You can also tell her you're looking forward to working with her during the changeover. As CFO she probably won't believe that last part—but she'll appreciate the respect.

Scenario H: Variables on the Rise

Situation: During the revenue and expense portion of the financial discussions at the management retreat, Phyllis, the CFO, focuses on the cost side of doing business, particularly the operational expenses that are driving overall costs in several departments, including yours. She mentions with pride the stability in the fixed costs of your operation, but is alarmed by the growing variable costs as they pass budgeted expectations. Mr. Bigg, she says, would like an explanation. What do you say?

Analysis: Operational expenses are composed of both fixed and variable costs. The most important costs to manage are fixed costs, those that remain constant throughout the budget year and are impervious to the cycles of business. The rent your company pays from month to month is a fixed cost, because it doesn't vary regardless of what your sales pattern might be. To a large degree, salaries also are fixed costs, although they may have variable components in terms of performance bonuses. Utility costs are the same way. Any expense that remains constant, no matter what the cycle of business, is a fixed cost.

Variable costs fluctuate directly with the amount of business you support. A retail outlet can count as fixed costs its rent, electricity, heat, and management salaries. Variable costs—costs that depend on business ups and downs—include the supplies of goods and materials and, to some degree, part-time labor necessary to make the business operate. These costs allow (or impose) some budgeting flexibility.

Phyllis may be justifiably proud of the company's fixed costs because, as CFO, she no doubt has had a hand in negotiating things like rent, salaries, and utilities and can expect them to grow at a pre-determined rate. She also can feel safe in attacking growing variable costs, because those are costs you as department head likely control and for which she will not be held primarily responsible.

But the figures themselves mean little. What's behind them? Your variable costs may well be growing, but they may be growing to accommodate the needs of increased sales and production which, in turn, reflect increased revenue. If that's the case, you can point with pride to what your department is investing to grow the company—particularly if variable cost increases are lower than the revenues generated.

However, if expenses are growing without corresponding revenue increases, Phyllis may be right in her fears. Check it out thoroughly before getting back to Mr. Bigg with an explanation.

Scenario I: Joining the Bucket Brigade

Situation: Milbourne, head of collections, has joined the group at the executive retreat because he has some concerns to share about the rapidly increasing workload facing his department. Milbourne's staff isn't lazy but, as collections people, they know that not enough care is being taken to qualify and monitor accounts before they turn delinquent. Once an account reaches Milbourne's desk, it's a crisis situation. Milbourne announces that after lunch he will distribute both the accounts receivable and the aging bucket for each department for review and analysis. What is he talking about?

Analysis: Accounts receivable (A/R) is one of several subledgers of the general ledger. This list reflects money owed by customers and other sources to the company. From an asset standpoint, it can be considered as good as money in the bank—provided the accounts receivable list pays off at a high rate. From the sound of Milbourne's analysis, this particular A/R isn't doing very well.

An aging bucket is the total of receivables aging in a certain category. The 30-day aging bucket is a the sum of all accounts past due by 30 days. So, too, with the 60-day aging bucket, the 90-day aging bucket, and so on. The rule of thumb is that, as past due accounts age, the ability to collect them decreases proportionately. If your department has too many accounts beyond the standard 30-day aging cycle, you may be headed for trouble.

Review your aging buckets and see where the majority of past due accounts lie. Identify those accounts and have the appropriate account representatives work with the collections people to clean them up. If an account is too old, write off the amount against funds reserved for just such a purpose, and move on.

And, once you get back to the office, make sure that the collections procedure starts from the very beginning—with pre-qualification steps made at the time of the sale. Are there any patterns behind the problem accounts? Should debt limits be set for certain accounts? You may even consider adjusting how you pay sales commissions, so they are paid only when the sale amount has been collected. You may be surprised how quickly your sales reps start improving the future of your A/R.

Scenario J: Do You Know How to Have Funds?

Situation: Although you've been managing your department for only six months, Mr. Bigg is impressed with your performance and ability to manage the financial side of your operation. (No doubt that's because you've read this book!) He would like you to start up an ancillary operation that expands the product line into a new area. Unfortunately, the company does not have the cash reserves necessary to get rolling. He asks whether you think a commercial loan or a venture capital investment would be the better way to go to fund this new initiative. What do you tell him?

Analysis: The difference between commercial loans and venture capital investments is significant in a variety of ways, including the sources, amount, and purpose of that funding. When it comes right down to it, a loan is a loan is a loan: You borrow some money, you use it to make more money, and you pay back the money borrowed plus a little extra for the service. A venture investment is something else entirely.

Unlike a lending institution, a venture capitalist does not make loans. A venture capitalist makes investments. And as an investor, the venture capitalist is part owner of your firm.

Your company's interests are his or her interests and your company's successes are shared with him or her.

Venture capitalists tend to be individuals or consortiums of individuals who have succeeded admirably in their own businesses and now are looking for a place to invest excess capital. They will take greater risks than commercial lenders, but they will require greater rewards in return. They're also likely to ask more difficult questions and be harder to satisfy. They're interested in your company's financial plans, goals and demonstrated skills, as a lender would be, but they also will more closely consider your product, the market, and the likelihood for corporate growth.

In the end, the venture capital firm will be interested in a company's success because it also is their success. The lender, on the other hand, will be interested mostly in how and when the borrower is going to repay the loan.

If your venture is risky and requires an inordinate amount of money beyond your loan limits, then a venture investment might be the ticket. It will cost you more at the time of payout and you may sacrifice some management control to your new temporary "partners." But the greater amount of money may enable you to do things you couldn't otherwise do and take advantage of important opportunities.

Ask Mr. Bigg for more details before you make your decision. Explain your understanding of the differences to him—and the potential effects of those difference on the company and the new ancillary operation. He'll appreciate your thought and consideration and likely will follow your recommendation. And that can be a great position in which to be.

So, ten situations to allow you to flex your financial muscles. How well did you meet the challenges? Are there areas in which you found some weaknesses in your muscles, where an exercise left you a little sore? You may want to work out a little more with this guide. As you do, think about how all of this stuff applies to your situation and about the ways in which you can use what you're learning about accounting and finance. Remember: It's hard to make good decisions without knowledge—but it's impossible for knowledge alone to make decisions.

Glossary

Accounts payable (A/P) A subledger of the general ledger that lists monies owed by the company to outside sources. (Also known as payables.) A well-designed and well-managed A/P system will reliably track the amount owed each vendor and when to pay based on agreements with that vendor. A/P shows up as a liability on the balance sheet.

Accounts receivable (A/R) A subledger of the general ledger that lists money owed to the company by customers and other sources. (Also known as receivables.) A/R lists items of value to the company, monies owed in the future by clients and customers against which the value of the company is measured, and other financial activities that can be leveraged, such as loans. A/R shows up as an asset on the balance sheet and as revenue on the income statement.

Accrual accounting One of two types of accounting practices. Popular with large businesses, accrual accounting records transactions when they are made—regardless of whether any money has changed hands. Accrual accounting allows for better cash management and a more accurate fiscal picture.

Accrual rates Easy to calculate: the number of hours (or days) of benefit time (sick or vacation) divided by the number of hours (or days) in a work year.

Accrued payroll taxes Monies reserved for the government, but not yet sent. On the balance sheet, these are included among the liabilities.

Active partner In a partnership, someone involved in the business operations of the partnership.

Aging bucket The total of receivables aging in a certain category. The 30-day aging bucket is the sum of all accounts past due by 30 days, the 60-day aging bucket is all accounts past 60 days, and so on.

Amortization   The allocation of the cost of an intangible asset—patent rights, copyrights, trademarks, franchises, loan origination fees, and goodwill—over the period during which benefits are derived from that asset.

Articles of incorporation   If approved by the state, become a sort of contract (known as the company charter) between the principals (or incorporators) and the state.

ARTS   A basic accounting guideline meaning that the accounting function should be Accurate, Relevant, Timely, and Simple in reporting financial data.

Asking price   Also known as the *offering price*, the current cost per share of the investment. The price is computed by adding the net asset value per share and the sales fee, if there is one.

Assumption statement   Weaves together elements of both the sales projection and profit and loss statement, resulting in a comprehensive financial forecast based specifically on a demonstrated—or at least budgeted—expense statement.

Back-end load   The commission charged when redeeming shares of an investment.

Bad debts   Can result from many things, but they all boil down to one simple definition from an accounting point of view: uncollectible amounts that are too small to be worth pursuing through legal channels. In the end they are written off the books to keep the accounts in balance.

Balance sheet   One of the primary accounting statements for any company—a summary of the assets, liabilities, and net worth of the business as of a specific date, usually the end of the financial month or fiscal year. The balance sheet is divided into debits and credits that reflect financial activity. Its ultimate goal is to keep all accounts in balance. A typical balance sheet could include current assets, inventory, accounts receivable, accounts payable, expenses, miscellaneous debts, long-term liabilities, accrued payroll taxes, and the company's capital.

Balancing out   The process by which accountants periodically compare the amounts in the general ledger against the amounts in the subledgers. They may do so in order to prepare financial reports or just to ensure accuracy.

Batching   A way of streamlining the process of posting from the subledgers to the general ledger. Subledger's items are batched for entry, combining several entries into one posted entry. Accountants prefer to keep batches small, say 15 to 20 entries per batch, since that makes it easier to track down problems if a batch doesn't balance properly. Automated accounting systems often allow for easy entry of individual items, making the batching process obsolete.

Bidding price   Also known as the *offer price*, the amount at which the company will buy back the stock. It is usually computed at the net asset value per share.

Business plan   The where, when, how, and why of what a company must do to implement its business strategy. It offers general and specific guidance on reaching company goals and it outlines actions. Business plans are usually annual, based on the fiscal year.

But there also are multiple-year plans, the most common of which is the five-year plan. An annual plan is operational and necessary to manage the company's economic needs for the coming year. A five-year plan is more strategic and designed to chart the firm's direction. In addition, five-year plans should be rolling plans.

Capital   The net worth of a company, computed as assets in excess of liabilities. For a sole proprietorship or a partnership, this might be called owners' or partners' equity. For corporations, outstanding capital stock value would be listed at its original price of issue.

Capital gains distribution   An annual payment of long-term gains resulting from investment sales. Measures the amount of increase (gain) earned on an investment (capital).

Capital growth   The increase in market value of an investment.

Cash   Your most valuable asset, one you need to protect with all your might.

Cash basis accounting   One of two types of accounting practices. A simpler method of recording business transactions, nothing is recorded until cash has traded hands.

Cash flow   The movement of money in and out of the business. It's as simple as that, in terms of accounting. But there are a lot more challenges related to cash flow than accounting for it. A company that doesn't protect its cash flow can find itself without adequate capital to buy raw materials or pay employees. Profit margins could be wonderful, and demand for products could be high, but cash flow problems could keep a company from making the most of a good situation.

Cash flow statements   Three types of statements that show the three types of cash flows: the basic cash flow statement measures the income and outflow of cash to the company; the operating cash flow statement measures operating revenue and expenses, without taking reserves into account; and the discretionary cash flow statement simply segments the operating cash flow into specific groups or areas.

CEO (chief executive officer)   Generic term for the person with the highest authority in a company, often having a title such as "president."

CFO (chief financial officer)   Generic term for the person with the highest responsibilities for financial matters in a company, often having a title such as "controller" or "vice president of finance," depending on the nature, structure, and size of the company.

Chart of accounts   An organized list of all usual sources of revenue and expenses for the company's business activities, arranged and numbered in a logical order for easy and consistent use in keeping track of funds flow.

Charter   A sort of "corporation contract" established between the principals who are incorporating and the state, when the state approves the articles of incorporation.

Collateral   Real estate, equipment, inventory, and even accounts receivable pledged as security when a company borrows money from a lending institution. (The resulting loan is known as a secured loan.)

Commercial loan   Traditionally defined as a loan to a company with more than $5 million in annual sales. Loans to smaller companies are usually called small business loans.

Company charter   A sort of contract between the principals (or incorporators) and the state, formed by the articles of incorporation as approved by the state.

Control system   A system of internal controls for identifying problems within a company unit. Standards are set by which performance will be measured. Those standards are applied systematically. The control system determines if any deviations from the standards are excessive; if so, the company takes action, preferably according to defined corrective procedures.

Corporation   A legal body formed by one or more people, to do business as an entity separate from any and all of them.

Cost accounting   The process of measuring all the costs associated with doing business, both direct costs—materials, labor, marketing, and sometimes distribution—and indirect costs (or overhead)—facilities, rent, utilities, cleaning, maintenance, depreciation, property taxes and insurance, and administration.

Costing (inventory)   There are four common methods to calculate the cost of inventory: average costing (assumes that the cost of inventory is the sum of the average costs of goods on hand when the accounting period began and goods purchased since that moment), lower of cost or market cost (measures ending inventory valued as the lower of the purchase cost of the materials or the present market value), first-in, first-out (assumes that the older goods are sold first), and last-in, first-out (assumes that you're selling the goods most recently purchased).

Credit memo   Documentation required by the accounting system for any credit to be recorded in accounts receivable.

Credits   Represent an increase in items such as business liability, owners' equity, and revenue accounts. Credits always appear on the right-hand side of the general ledger.

Debits   Represent an increase in asset and expense accounts. Debits are always listed on the left-hand side of the general ledger.

Depreciation   The allocation of the cost of a tangible asset over the period during which benefits are derived from that asset, which gradually converts the cost of the asset into an expense.

Direct costs   Include production materials, labor, marketing, and sometimes distribution.

Diversification   The spread of mutual fund investments among different securities, to minimize risks for the fund and the investors.

Dividend   The distribution of a corporation's to its stockholders, in proportion to the number of shares held by each, with the amount determined by the board of directors.

80/20 rule   A general business guideline with several applications: 20 percent of the customers provide 80 percent of revenue, 80 percent of problems come from 20 percent of the staff, 80 percent of the profit comes from 20 percent of the products.

Enterprise zone   A district established by a government to promote business growth and opportunities in an economically distressed area, through tax benefits and other incentives.

Equity, owners' or partners'   The net worth of a sole proprietorship or a partnership, computed as assets in excess of liabilities, on the balance sheet.

General ledger (G/L)   A centralized listing of all financial transactions of the business. It includes all the transactions that have also been listed in more specialized subledgers devoted to particular types of transactions.

Income statement   Projects earnings over time, usually a year at a time, balanced by relevant expenses. It ties to the sales forecast, but provides more detail.

Indirect costs   Expenses associated with facilities—rent, utilities, cleaning, maintenance, depreciation, property taxes, and insurance—and administration—back office operations such as accounting, human resources, and managerial salaries. Indirect costs are sometimes called overhead.

Inventory   Any supply of goods. Inventory may include items held for sale as finished goods, goods in production, or raw materials and supplies to be used in the production process.

Invoice   The documentation required by the accounting system before any sale can be recorded in accounts receivable. Any good receivables system will provide proof that all invoices have been correctly posted to the customer accounts, usually through a daily comparison of invoices and the A/R postings.

ISO 9000   A series of quality standards initiated in 1987 by the International Organization for Standardization, a federation of national standards bodies from more than 100 countries, to facilitate the international exchange of goods and services.

Journal entry form   Includes account numbers, date of transaction, what accounts were debited and credited as a result of the transaction, who the transaction was with, the date, and who prepared it. This permanent record of a specific transaction is then entered into the G/L and appropriate subledgers.

Labor (costs)   Includes two types: direct and indirect. In cost accounting, it may be beneficial to distinguish between the two. Direct labor costs are: work responsible for helping produce, market, or distribute the product in question and perhaps also commissions from selling the product. Indirect labor costs are: work that supports production at a distance, including managerial expenses. Direct labor costs should be allocated to the cost of the product. Indirect labor costs should be allocated based on the amount of contributions made. In the case of managers, the cost of their work should be allocated by percentage to all appropriate cost centers.

Life cycle   According to marketers, a pattern of four fairly distinct periods in the life of a product: introduction, growth, maturity, and decline. Businesses go through similar phases.

Limited liability company (LLC)   A business structure with some advantages of both partnerships and corporations. It offers the tax benefits of a partnership, and the pass-through advantages and limited liability of a corporation.

Limited partner   In a partnership, someone who is passive in terms of any involvement in business operations and liable only to the extent of his or her investment in the partnership.

Liquidity   Refers to how much cash the company has access to and can use in its business operations.

Money manager   The generic term for the person responsible for protecting and developing a company's liquid assets. He or she could be the owner, the CEO, the CFO, or somebody hired for that specific purpose. In smaller companies, the money manager is usually the owner.

Net asset value per share   An investment's share value, derived by subtracting liabilities from its aggregate assets, including cash and securities, less any sales cost that might be added on. The NAVPS usually represents the market price, subject to a possible sales or redemption charge.

Niche   A particular segment of a specific economy—the slice of the dollar pie a business hopes to claim, that piece of the public consciousness it wants to capture and hold.

No-load fund   Shares of an investment made available for purchase at net asset value, without the addition of a sales or service charge.

Overhead   The indirect, general costs of doing business, to be shared by every unit of the company, according to some system of allocation.

Partner   Someone involved in a partnership, in one of several legal capacities, including active, silent, secret, and limited. The term "partners" is also used to describe a buyer and a seller who have formed a special relationship, each agreeing to leverage the advantages offered by the other and to work more closely together.

Partnership   Defined by law as "the association of two or more persons to carry on as co-owners of a business for profit." The partners may be equal or unequal, silent or active, and the structure may follow any one of dozens of variations that bring together their assets, ideas, and expertise. The term is also used to refer to a special relationship between buyers and sellers who agree to work more closely together in a business symbiosis.

"Pass-through" tax entities   Business structures for which no tax returns are filed, as profits and losses are reported on the individual tax returns of the owners. Sole proprietorships, partnerships, most LLCs, and S corporations are "pass-through" tax entities.

Playing the float   Also known as predicting cash outflow. It allows companies to predict the time it will take vendors to receive and process payments as a way to capitalize on company cash.

Portfolio   The sum total of a company's investment activity—funds, stocks, bonds, and other investments.

Post   Means to enter a transaction in a subledger and the general ledger, to provide a permanent record that anyone, including auditors, can use later to understand the transaction.

Profit and loss statement (P & L)   Prepared annually, quarterly, or monthly. Provides a very basic measurement of the success of a business. What a company chooses to include in its P & L depends largely on the type of business. The P & L typically shows figures for the following categories: gross monthly sales, net sales, cost of goods sold, gross profit, operating expenses (including salaries, rent, utilities, telephone, supplies, and depreciation), operating profit, and net income.

Redeem   To sell a mutual fund.

Redemption price   The actual amount received when redeeming (selling) shares of a mutual fund: the value of the shares at the bidding price minus the redemption charge.

Rolling plan   A perpetual motion engine for your business vehicle. This may be a five-year business plan, an annual budget, or other schedules. When a period (year or month) ends, the same period is planned at the end of the calendar, so that the five-year plan always looks five years ahead and the annual budget always prepares for the next 12 months.

Rollup, subaccount   A way to simplify a detailed chart of accounts. Accountants sometimes create a series of subaccounts that roll up into one category of the balance sheet. That saves some time and space, yet provides managers with the business details they need.

S corporation   As defined by the IRS (Subchapter S), a certain type of small corporation that is taxed as a pass-through entity, like a proprietorship or a partnership.

Sales fee   The seller's commission or charge for facilitating the sale of an investment, added to the net value per share and paid by the buyer (also known as a load).

Sales forecast   A prediction of sales performance, based on empirical data and a knowledge of sales history—and often shaped by an optimistic or pessimistic attitude.

Secret partner   In a partnership, someone who is actively involved in business operations but unknown to the public.

Secured loan   Means that the borrower pledges collateral to offset the loss to the lender in case of default.

Silent partner   In a partnership, someone who provides capital for the partnership, but does not participate in the management of business operations.

287

Small business loan   Traditionally defined as a loan to a company with less than $5 million in annual sales. Often such loans can be handled by the lender's small business loan department. Loans to larger companies are usually called commercial loans.

Sole proprietorship   The simplest type of business structure, it is a company owned and operated by a single person. The proprietorship is the same legal and economic unit as the individual who forms it. That person receives all profits, pays for all losses, and is liable for all the obligations incurred by the proprietorship.

Strategy   An approach designed to help the business reach its goal through a prescribed series of steps.

Subledger   A subaccount for categorizing and sorting revenue and expense items. Transactions are recorded in the subledgers and journals, then posted to the general ledger, with a reference number. Later, summaries from the subledgers and journals are posted to the G/L, again with a reference number. Subledgers typically include accounts receivable and accounts payable. Journals typically include cash disbursements, cash receipts, sales, and purchases.

Supply chain   The system of businesses that are linked together in providing a product or service for consumers.

Taxes   The price of success, including income taxes, employment taxes, estimated taxes, sales taxes (paying and collecting), usage taxes, property taxes, and any specialized taxes the company might owe to local, state, and federal authorities.

Trade discount   A price reduction offered for prompt payments, generally from a discount of 1 percent to 3 percent if the invoice is paid within ten days, as opposed to the usual net 30 days and beyond.

Unsecured loan   Means that the borrower is not pledging any collateral to offset the loss to the lender in case of default. Unsecured loans tend to cost more in terms of higher interest rates because of the greater risk to the lender.

Venture capital   Financial support in the form of an investment, as an alternative to loans from commercial lenders, such as banks or credit unions. The venture capitalist, as an investor, becomes part owner of the company receiving the venture capital.

Weighted average invoice aging   The principle behind a policy that many companies have for paying invoices, so payment terms and trade discounts make little difference. The system dictates how old the invoice must be before it will be paid. In some industries, that time is regulated.

Withholding taxes   The percentages withheld from each employee's paycheck for federal and state taxes. The company accountants determine the percentages, and then send the amounts to the taxing authority within the statutory time limits—or risk being fined. Some companies submit withholding taxes on the same day they distribute paychecks. On the other hand, some companies and many commercial tax preparers keep the funds invested as long as possible, earning the maximum interest.

Index

Q-R